Welcome to the sixth volume of **The Mac Book**. Whether you've just bought a Mac or have been using one for years, there are always new things to learn. This book has been compiled to give every Mac user some serious food for thought. Whether you are keen to improve your knowledge of OS X so that your Mac use is streamlined and always productive, or if you want to get a handle on things, like setting up networks or getting to the bottom of System Preferences, the answer is here. If your creative streak needs a gentle nudge into action, you'll find tons of tutorials on all the iLife applications. Not only will these teach you valuable, practical techniques, but they'll also give you some great ideas for creative projects. Taking things beyond the realm of iLife we delve into iTunes and the goodness that lies therein. After that, we take a look at Apple's very own productivity suite, iWork. Here we examine how these applications can offer incredible scope for creativity. You may just add extra polish to a CV or move on to complete complex layouts in Pages. In Numbers you can master the basics of spreadsheets and work your way up to adding graphics and charts to enhance your work. In Keynote we'll take you through the basics and send you sailing towards the more complex. The final element of this book introduces you to third-party applications (those not made by Apple). The scope and remit of these are far too broad to mention here, but rest assured they will not only inspire but invigorate your Mac usage. This book is the perfect companion for every Mac user and a great way to get more from your Mac.

Welcome to the Mac Book

Imagine Publishing Ltd
Richmond House
33 Richmond Hill
Bournemouth
Dorset BH2 6EZ
☎ +44 (0) 1202 586200
Website: www.imagine-publishing.co.uk

Compiled by
Jimmy Hayes

Art Editor
Danielle Dixon

Editor in Chief
Dave Harfield

Head of Design
Ross Andrews

Printed by
William Gibbons, 26 Planetary Road, Willenhall, West Midlands, WV13 3XT

Distributed in the UK & Eire by
Imagine Publishing Ltd, www.imagineshop.co.uk. Tel 01202 586200

Distributed in Australia by
Gordon & Gotch, Equinox Centre, 18 Rodborough Road, Frenchs Forest,
NSW 2086. Tel + 61 2 9972 8800

Distributed in the Rest of the World by
Marketforce, Blue Fin Building, 110 Southwark Street, London, SE1 0SU.

The Mac Book 06 © 2010 Imagine Publishing Ltd

ISBN 978 1 906078 72 0

IMAGINE
PUBLISHING

The Mac Book
Contents...

Features...

Ultimate backup 008
Keeping the contents of your Mac safely backed up is one of the most important things you can do. With this in-depth guide you can make the most of keeping your files safe and sound

Master Airport 016
Apple's wireless solution has far more features than you ever knew. This feature will take you through every single one of its impressive features

20 Mac tips 062
Everyone needs a bit of a helping hand from time to time, and this feature is designed to help you get through some of those sticky situations and get more from your Mac

iLife journal 068
Whether you're new to iLife or a seasoned pro, a great way to get more from each app is to use third-party plug-ins. This guide will point you in the right direction

Create your own website 077
One of the coolest things you can do with a Mac is to create your own website using iWeb. Learn how to get started and get yourself online here

Are you an artist? 176
We give you a complete run-down of every single app you need to become an iLife artist. All you need is a creative spark, this guide and one or more of these excellent applications

Tutorials & advice...

Mac OS X

OS X Snow Leopard 024
Get to know your operating system – not only will it make your everyday computing much easier, but you can use it to bring your own sense of style to your Mac

iLife

iPhoto 084
Make the most of your digital photographs with this amazing application. Use it for storage and viewing, as well as creating amazing projects

iMovie 106
Create stunning, professional quality home movies from clips. Our guides will give you the pro tips you need

iWeb 142
One of the simplest and most effective of all the iLife applications, iWeb is an essential tool for every Mac user

GarageBand 154
Whether you're musical or not, you can have great fun using GarageBand. It's easy to use and has the engine of an advanced audio-editing suite

iTunes 196
Apple's digital jukebox has gone from strength to strength in recent years. Get more from it here

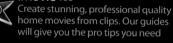

iWork 204
The productivity suite created by Apple was designed to rival Microsoft's Office suite. Well, it does more than rival it, offering the option for incredible creativity in a word processor, spreadsheet application and presentation tool

We're Excited 236
A selection of third-party applications that we think are well worth getting excited about

Check out the contents of your free CD on page 258

The missing iLife apps 186
Despite our love for all of the iLife apps, there are just some things they can't do. So, we've compiled a feature detailing the apps that Apple should have included in the suite

"Keeping the contents of your Mac safely backed up is one of the most important things you can do"

OS X is at the core of every Mac. Not only does it take control of making sure everything runs well, but it also gives you the power to make your Mac your own. Our guides will help you get the most from your OS

Contents . . .

Feature: Ultimate backup 008
Keeping the contents of your Mac safely backed up is one of the most important things you can do

Feature: Master Airport 016
Apple's wireless solution has far more aspects than you ever knew. This will take you through its impressive features

Feature: 20 Mac tips 062
Everyone needs a helping hand from time to time and this feature is designed to help you get through some of those sticky situations

Tutorial: MobileMe syncing 024
Quickly check that your Mac is in sync with Apple's cloud services

Tutorial: Set your Mac to restart 026
Use this vital safety feature to check your computer after power failure

Tutorial: System Preferences 028
We take a look at the Sharing settings within the System Preferences application

Tutorial: Add drives to the Dock 030
Keep regularly used hard drives and servers in the dock on your desktop

Tutorial: Add apps to spaces 032
Keep your Mac use as efficient as possible by assigning apps to different spaces

Tutorial: System Preferences 034
We take a look at the Settings element of the System Preferences application

Tutorial: Track flights in Mail 036
Amazingly, Mail can detect flight numbers and help you track arrivals and departures

Tutorial: QuickTime X 038
Use the new features in QuickTime X to rapidly trim audio files

Tutorial: Using Activity Monitor 040
This useful application will give you an insight into the running of your Mac

Tutorial: Stream video 042
Use your Mac to stream video to a wireless device like an iPad

Tutorial: Use Growl 044
Keep tabs on what the applications on your Mac are doing with Growl

Tutorial: Automator for iCal 046
Use the awesome Automator application to create iCal events quickly and simply

Tutorial: Locations in Finder 048
Create simple shortcuts to locations that will appear in every Finder window

Tutorial: Update TomTom 050
You can use your Mac to keep your satnav device loaded with updates

Tutorial: Search in Spotlight 053
The search tool in OS X can be customised to make it more efficient for your daily tasks

Tutorial: Magic Mouse 054
Set up your Magic Mouse using the System Preferences application in OS X

Tutorial: Add URLs to the Dock 056
A great way to save time on the web is to add a favourite or important page to your dock

Tutorial: Portable Wi-Fi 058
Use a third-party product to take a wireless network with you…

d with OS X

Check out the contents of your free CD on page **258**

"Everyone needs a helping hand from time to time and this feature is designed to help you get through some of those sticky situations."

Macs are very reliable when you consider how much they are used. Many are switched on all day every day, and some aren't even turned off at night, and yet they run for years and never experience a problem. However, no device is immune from failure, and that is a tiny but very real risk that we have to live with. And of course, there's human error. Have you ever overwritten a file you discovered later that you really needed? One of the ways in which you can minimise the effects of a fault or human error and guarantee your files are safe is by making backups of the hard disk drive's contents.

Faulty motherboards can be replaced, keyboards and mice can be replaced, screens can be replaced – but what about the hard disk drive? Well, that can be replaced too, but the problem is that it contains so much valuable information that it would be disastrous if it failed. Just think of all the files you have on there, such as iTunes Music Store purchases, photos downloaded from digital cameras, videos imported from camcorders, personal and work documents, website bookmarks, and more. Although the drive can be replaced, its contents cannot. You could not gather everyone together again to reshoot some wedding photos or videos because they were lost. Birthday parties, holidays and children growing up are all one-off never-to-be-repeated events that you might have captured and stored on your Mac. Could you cope in the event of a disaster?

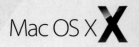

THE ULTIMATE BACK-UP GUIDE

A backup is an insurance policy. You hope you'll never need it, but you'll be glad you've got it if there's ever a problem…

Sudden movement sensors in the Mac do a great job of preventing the disk crashes that used to plague us years ago, but this isn't the only type of error that can occur; bugs in Mac OS X or software you have installed could easily corrupt the data on the disk drive.

The valuable information and files on the disk must be protected from disasters. There is an old saying, "Plan for the worst, but hope for the best." In other words, you should put together a plan to cope with the worst possible situation, which in this case would be a complete hard disk drive failure. However, we hope that it will never happen to us, and it probably won't. In fact, the chances are that the worst will never ever happen, but we all need to have that insurance policy of a backup just in case it does.

So, what can be done about securing valuable files? The obvious solution is to make a backup, which is a copy of your hard disk. Of course, everyone knows they should make a backup, but people rarely do. One reason for this is that, because Macs are so reliable, we think they will never fail. This is true for most people, but it is also because backups are time consuming to perform and require some effort to carry out. When the computer is running smoothly it just seems a waste of time and effort for no benefit. But you must remember that it is effectively an insurance policy – one that you could be extremely thankful for one day – and you will sleep better if you know you are protected. Over the next five pages we'll show you exactly what you need to do.

Time Machine

Everyone knows you should regularly make copies of important files on the disk drive, but few people actually do it. So when Apple introduced Time Machine it was a stroke of genius, meaning that backups were automatic and required no actions to be taken by the user. It works silently and invisibly in the background and copies all of your important files. If disaster should strike, you can enter Time Machine and copy lost files or previous versions of changed files very easily.

Time Machine is brilliant, but it's not the complete solution to your back-up needs because it has some limitations. For instance, it requires a second disk drive. It works by copying the files on the Mac's internal disk drive to an external one that is connected via a USB or FireWire port.

An external USB disk drive is an essential component of any computer setup these days though, and if you don't already have one then you should seriously consider it. Some Macs have quite small hard disk drives and it is easy to fill them, so apart from being a back-up device, the extra disk space is handy for everyday use too. You will find the USB drives in PC stores cheaper than Apple stores and they work perfectly with Macs. Just plug them in and format them with Disk Utility so they can be used with Time Machine.

Another limitation of Time Machine is that it doesn't store everything forever. If you saved some files – such as documents, photos or videos to a DVD-R, for example – then you have a permanent copy of them that can be accessed next week, next year or in ten years' time. Time Machine, however, stores a copy of every file that is changed every time it is changed. It only has a certain amount of space in which to store copies of files (the size of the USB disk), and eventually all the space will be used up. In order to continue working, it deletes the oldest copies of files to create free space for new ones. So eventually old files are lost. For this reason, you should not use Time Machine as your only back-up strategy. It's great at what it does but you might want to store some files forever, so you'll need to consider the alternatives.

> "When Apple introduced Time Machine it was a stroke of genius, meaning backups were automatic"

Partition a USB disk

Dedicating a 1TB USB disk to Time Machine or some other back-up software is a waste of space, so you should partition the drive, which divides it into smaller sections that appear to be separate disks. Create one partition the same size as the Mac's internal disk and use it with Carbon Copy Cloner or SuperDuper!, then create another partition twice the size for Time Machine.

To partition and format a USB disk drive, run Disk Utility in the Applications/Utilities folder and select the drive in the left panel. Click the Partition tab and select a Volume Scheme from the pop-up menu. You can manually define partitions too; select the partition and click the plus button below to split it into two. Select and resize partitions by typing in the Size box. Use the GUID partitioning scheme and the Mac OS Extended (Journaled) format to make the USB drive bootable.

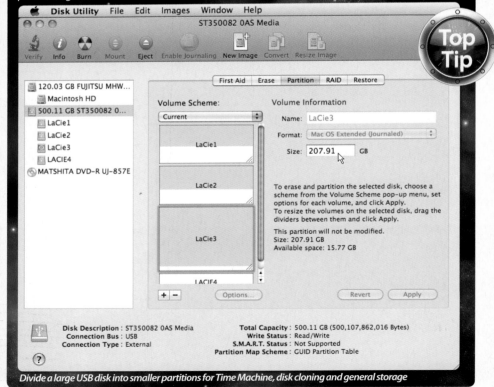

Divide a large USB disk into smaller partitions for Time Machine, disk cloning and general storage

What needs backing up?

There are two broad categories of backup, and you can either make a complete copy of everything on the disk drive or you can just copy the files that are important, such as photos, videos, music, documents and so on. A complete copy or clone of the Mac's disk drive stored on another disk drive can take a long time to carry out, but it means that everything, including Mac OS X system files, are copied. In a worst case scenario you could replace a faulty drive with a new one, or reformat the existing disk to clear the fault and then copy everything back from the clone.

The alternative method of backing up is to copy only the files that are irreplaceable. For example, you could back up just the Home folders of everyone that has an account on your Mac. This includes almost everything that is important, such as documents, photos, videos and so on. However, if you have stored files elsewhere you should include these too. Although you don't have a copy of every file on the disk, if disaster strikes then you can reinstall Mac OS X from the DVD and either

install applications from discs or download them. Then you just need to copy the backed-up Home folder files to be up and running again. Copying only your personal files is quicker than creating an image of the whole disk, but recovering from a problem is not as straightforward. You don't have to choose between these methods of backup as both can be implemented.

Schedule Time Machine backups

Time Machine runs automatically every hour to copy files that have changed. Not everyone needs it to run so frequently or to make so many backups, but the schedule cannot be changed. TimeMachineEditor (**http://timesoftware.free.fr/timemachineeditor**) and TimeMachineScheduler (**www.klieme.com/TimeMachineScheduler**) can add this facility. You can choose hourly, daily, weekly or monthly, only to back up between certain hours or at a specific

Check your Mac's specs by selecting About This Mac from the Apple menu

Enable Time Machine

Set up and customise Time Machine to work exactly as you want it to

Choose a disk

Go to Time Machine in System Preferences and click 'Select a Disk'. All the USB and FireWire disk drives are listed and you can choose a disk or partition to store the backups. (There's also an option to set up an Apple Time Capsule too).

Set the options

Click the Options button and you can exclude items from the backup. Why would you want to? Well, some files aren't important – like recorded television programs, virtual machines running Windows, iDisk, and similar files.

Turn it on

Tick Show Time Machine in the Menu bar so you can see whether it is working. Turn it on to automatically back up your files every hour, or turn it off and click the icon in the Menu bar to manually back up when it suits you best.

Network backup

The fastest and most reliable way to secure your files is to copy them to a USB or FireWire disk drive connected directly to the Mac, but what if you have more than one computer? Do you need multiple drives? No – the solution is to make one drive available on a network. An Apple Time Capsule (**www.apple.com/timecapsule**) is the simplest method and it's an AirPort Extreme wireless router with a built-in disk. The base model has a 1TB disk (£234), but 2TB (£388) is available too. You may think you'll never need 2TB, but it is possible for several Macs to simultaneously back up to the device using Time Machine, and then the extra space really would be needed.

There is a cheaper alternative if Time Capsule is beyond your budget, and you could even consider an AirPort Extreme instead (£142). This wireless router has a USB port, and a cheap USB drive plugged into it can be accessed by all your Macs for backups.

Whether you use Time Capsule or AirPort Extreme with a USB drive, you'll find that it can easily be selected for backups in Time Machine Preferences and other back-up software as though it was directly attached to the Mac. (A USB drive attached to AirPort Extreme appears in Finder windows in the Shared category. Access it in Finder if you don't see it in Time Machine Preferences.)

A networked disk drive, such as Time Capsule, can be used by Time Machine for backups

Clone the disk

An important type of backup to make is an exact copy of the Mac's internal disk on an external USB drive. Clone it and, no matter what happens, you will be able to put everything back exactly as it was when the backup was made. This will protect you from a total loss of the drive, but there are drawbacks. For instance, you can only restore to the last backup, which may be last week or even last month, whereas Time Machine can recover files lost or changed as little as an hour ago.

One of the things you can do with a cloned disk is to boot from it. If you switch on the Mac and hold down the Option key, a list of bootable devices are displayed. You can select the external drive with the arrow keys and boot from it by pressing Return. Your Mac will then be in the exact state it was in when the backup was made.

The most popular programs for disk copying are Carbon Copy Cloner (**www.bombich.com**) and SuperDuper! (**www.shirt-pocket.com**). With Carbon Copy Cloner you select the Mac's disk as the Source and the USB drive as the Target. Choose

> ## "An important backup to make is an exact copy of the Mac's internal disk... this will protect you from a total loss of the drive"

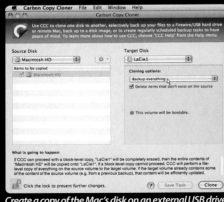

Create a copy of the Mac's disk on an external USB drive. You can then boot from it and restore it

'Back up everything' in the Cloning options and tick 'Delete items that don't exist on the source'. To restore the backup, boot from the USB disk and set the Source as the USB and Target as the Mac.

Disk Utility in the Applications/Utilities folder can also copy the hard drive. Start the Mac using the Mac OS X DVD and holding down 'C'. Choose to run Disk Utility, select the Mac's disk as the Source, click the New Image button, then enter a name for the backup. Now set the Save destination as the USB drive. To restore the disk repeat the process, but Disk Image on the USB drive is the Source and the Mac's drive is the destination.

Another utility you could use is SilverKeeper (**www.lacie.com/silverkeeper**). It's bundled with LaCie USB drives, but it can be used with any drive.

Beware of encryption

If you use any form of encryption to secure the files on the Mac's hard disk you must be careful when backing up. For example, it's possible to encrypt the contents of the Home folder by going to System Preferences>Security and selecting the FileVault tab. Back-up software has been known to corrupt FileVault backups, or to store the files unencrypted on the back-up disk. Create another user account that doesn't use FileVault and back up from there.

"Back-up software has been known to corrupt FileVault backups, or to store the files unencrypted on the back-up disk"

Folder and file sync tools

Carbon Copy Cloner, SuperDuper!, and SilverKeeper don't just clone whole disks – they can copy individual folders too. You could, for example, just back up the /Users folder to copy everyone's Home folder, and this would include all the documents, music, videos and other files that are important.

To do this in Carbon Copy Cloner, for example, you select 'Incremental backup of selected items' in the Cloning options pop-up menu. A list of the disk's contents is then displayed on the left, and tick boxes enable you to select the items to be backed up. SuperDuper! has a handy pop-up menu that enables you to back up just the user files and you don't even need to know

where they are stored. There is also a Smart Update option that is a real time saver once the initial backup has been made, because it copies only new or updated files. There are many other utilities for backing up files and folders, such as Backuplist+ (**http://bit.ly/6gUkks**) and iBackup (**www.grapefruit. ch/iBackup**). Backuplist+ enables you to select a disk and folder to store the backup and then select the items to copy. Multiple back-up sets (scripts) can be created to back up specific folders or files. These tools have restore facilities that copy everything back, but if you lose just one or two files you can simply browse the backup location using Finder and copy files back to the hard disk.

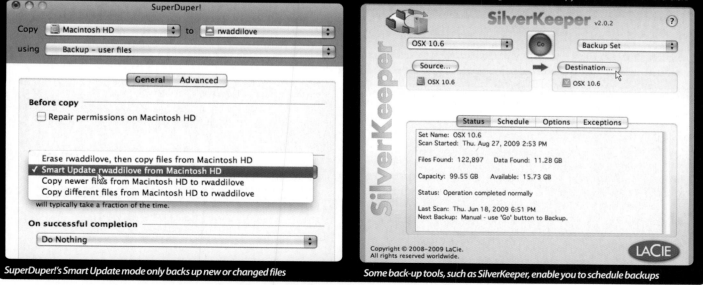

SuperDuper!'s Smart Update mode only backs up new or changed files

Some back-up tools, such as SilverKeeper, enable you to schedule backups

DVD burning

Time Machine is a fantastic tool but it doesn't keep files forever, and if you delete or change a file on the Mac then sooner or later Time Machine will delete it or change it in the backup. To protect valuable files you need a storage medium that stores files permanently, such as DVD-Rs. Backing up to DVD isn't as convenient as backing up to USB disks or online services, and it can be a bit of a pain, but you can store the DVDs and you'll still be able to access your files ten years from now. That's not true of Time Machine.

You can right-click (Ctrl-click) any file or folder in a Finder window and select the Burn option to write it to a DVD-R. If you run Disk Utility you can turn any folder into a disk image and this can be stored on a DVD-R too. Using the compressed option enables even more files to be stored on a disc. Of course, programs like Roxio Toast 10 Titanium (www.roxio.com, £79.99) provide many more features, and backing up is just one of its many functions. ArchiveMac (www.archivemac.com, $24.99) is a simpler and cheaper program that's more than capable of backing up to DVD.

Roxio Toast can be used to back up valuable files to CDs and DVDs for safekeeping

Online backup

You can back up to an online service, but the space, speed and cost cannot compete with a USB drive. Recurring monthly fees add up over time, so you need to weigh up the pros and cons. One advantage to backing up to an online service is that your files are available on any computer with internet access, or even from an iPhone or iPod touch. There are many online file storage services and they can be accessed using a web browser or software installed in the Mac. MobileMe (www.me.com) membership provides 20GB of online storage space for £59 per year, but 40GB or 60GB is available for an extra fee. MobileMe adds an iDisk icon to the desktop and any file you put in it is copied to your online storage space. If the Mac's disk had to be replaced or formatted, when you set up MobileMe again everything in the online iDisk will be automatically downloaded.

There are several similar services, and Dropbox (www.dropbox.com) provides 2GB of online space for free, with anything you put in the Dropbox folder being backed up online. In the event of a disk disaster you just re-install Dropbox and all your files are automatically restored. Wuala (www.wuala.com) provides 1GB of space for free, and you can trade disk space on your Mac for free

online storage space. For each gigabyte of your Mac's disk you allocate to Wuala, you get 1GB of online storage space for free. You can also specify back-up folders that enable you to automatically copy files on the disk drive to the internet. ADrive

(www.adrive.com) provides 50GB of online storage space for free, but you need a Signature account ($6.95 per month) to use the Adobe AIR-based back-up software that is provided. It's worth considering, though.

Files placed in the iDisk on your Mac are automatically uploaded, and it can be used to safely store important files

You can back up your files to Wuala for free and then access them from any computer, even Windows or Linux PCs

iCandy
iMac

iMac The machining on the iMac is incredibly precise, every hole in the speaker grill has been milled to perfection.

Master the AirPort
Extreme

Underneath the AirPort's plain and simple exterior is a powerful networking device that has a wealth of features. We show you how to use them...

The AirPort Extreme is a device that enables you to connect multiple computers and devices to each other and to the internet. Although it is sold by Apple and Apple Stores to Apple users, it's not just for Macs – Windows and Linux computers can also benefit from its advanced features and functions. It's not just for computers either, as the iPhone and other smartphones, the iPod touch and the iPad can use it too. It's a fantastic device with a

cool white exterior and a feature-packed interior. All of your computers and devices can connect to the AirPort Extreme wirelessly, and up to 50 users are supported. But there are also LAN sockets on the back of the box to enable connection using standard network cables too. That's enough connectivity for a small business, never mind the home! What's more, when the AirPort Extreme is connected to the internet, all of the users that connect to it can simultaneously access the web, their email and other online services. AirPort

Extreme is a great device for internet-connection sharing in the home or a small office.

One of the ways in which the AirPort Extreme goes further than other devices of this type (they are routers with built in Wi-Fi access points) is the addition of a USB socket, which enables you to attach an external USB disk drive or a printer. This means that any computer or device in your home or office can print or access shared files and storage. NAS is a buzzword you may have heard of, standing for 'Network Attached Storage', and

the AirPort Extreme provides a similar service. Just imagine adding a 1TB external hard drive to the back of one and being able to access all of your your media files from any Mac connected to the network! can even be used for backups with Time Machine, just like a Time Capsule.

The AirPort Extreme has a very friendly setup utility that guides you step by step when setting it up. It's brilliantly simple, but the software can appear to be quite complicated if you need to access any of the advanced features – and there

are plenty of them. If you don't mind getting a bit technical occasionally, you can unlock lots of powerful features in the device. Let's take a look at some of the advanced facilities that are on offer…

"The iPhone and other smartphones, the iPod touch, and the iPad can use AirPort Extreme too"

Share a public IP address

You can talk to anyone anywhere in the world using the telephone system; you just dial their unique number to connect to them. It doesn't matter which country they are in or how many wires and cables the electrical signal has to traverse, somehow your call finds the right person. And the internet works in a similar way, with computers able to communicate with each other no matter where they are because each one has a unique number. It's called an IP address, and your ISP provides it when you connect to the internet.

It doesn't take a second to realise that one isn't enough. You have a Mac, possibly two, an iPhone, an iPod touch, and so on. They all need IP addresses. The one from your ISP is your public IP address and, to enable more than one device in your home or office to access the internet, the AirPort Extreme can give private IP addresses to everything that connects to it. Run AirPort Utility and, in Manual Setup, click the Internet button in the toolbar then select the Internet Connection tab. Set Connection Sharing to 'Share a public IP address'.

This process is called DHCP and NAT (you'll see tabs appear). It doesn't really matter what these terms stand for, they simply ensure devices on your network with private IP addresses can communicate with computers on the internet through your public IP address. There is a snag though; an AirPort Extreme cannot connect to the internet using broadband through the telephone system, and you need a router/ADSL modem. The router plugs into the phone socket and a cable connects the AirPort's WAN socket to a LAN socket on the router/modem. Only one device must have DHCP and NAT enabled and all others must be turned off or they clash.

If you already have a router/ADSL modem that provides DHCP and NAT, the AirPort Extreme's must be turned off. Run AirPort Utility and choose Manual Setup. Click the Internet button in the toolbar and then select the Internet Connection tab. Set Connection Sharing to 'Off (Bridge Mode). (Alternatively, you could put the router/ADSL modem into Bridge Mode instead and details should be in the device's manual.)

DHCP and NAT are available if you share an IP address, but use Bridge Mode if your router/ADSL modem does it

Check for updates

The software used to access the AirPort Extreme and the software built into the device itself may be updated from time to time. It is always a good idea to check for updates and to install the latest software. It may cure problems, and it could even add new features or make it easier to use. To check for updates, open the AirPort Utility in the Applications/Utilities folder and select AirPort Utility,

Check For Updates. The software in the AirPort Extreme is called firmware and you can check for updates by going into Manual Setup in AirPort Utility, selecting the AirPort button in the toolbar and then the Base Station tab. Click the Options button and tick the 'Check for firmware updates' option. You can select from either daily, weekly or monthly updates.

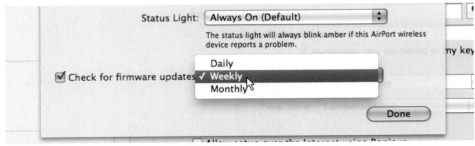

Keep a look-out for firmware updates that enhance features or fix problems using this option

The AirPort Extreme's WAN port

A feature of the AirPort Extreme that may confuse potential purchasers and new users is that it does not provide any means of connecting to the internet. It cannot be plugged into a telephone socket to provide dial-up access and it cannot be plugged into a microfilter designed for broadband connections. You must already have a device that connects to the internet, and that device must have an Ethernet socket.

"To enable the AirPort Extreme to access the internet you must use an Ethernet network cable to connect its WAN port to the ADSL router or cable modem"

When you sign up with a cable TV company for TV and internet access, or sign up with an internet service provider for broadband access through the telephone system, you will probably receive a box that connects to the internet and provides an Ethernet socket. For example, ISPs often provide a router with a built-in ADSL modem. (It might even have wireless capabilities, but the AirPort Extreme is much better for this.)

To enable the AirPort Extreme to access the internet you must use an Ethernet network cable to connect its WAN port to the Ethernet port on the ADSL router or cable modem. All internet traffic from the AirPort Extreme is channelled through the WAN port, which then goes to the router or modem and then on to the internet.

Interpreting the status light

On the front panel of the AirPort Extreme you'll notice an LED light that is used to indicate the status of the device. It can either be amber, green or blue (steady or flashing) and it is important that you know what is normal and what isn't. When something is wrong and you cannot access the device or the internet, the status light can help you to track down the problem.

When you switch on the power the light will initially be green, but then it will change to amber while the device is starting up. The amber light flashes and finally changes to a steady green colour. This means that everything is working correctly. If you run AirPort Utility in the Applications/Utilities folder and open the Preferences window you'll see an option to 'Monitor AirPort wireless devices

for problems'. When this it ticked, if the AirPort Extreme's status light flashes amber, then AirPort Utility will automatically open so that you can

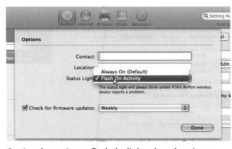

Setting the option to flash the light when there's any network activity is a visual indication that it is working

investigate the problem. That's a useful option to tick, as you won't necessarily know what's wrong with your device.

When you are having problems with the wireless network or the internet, it can be difficult to know what is happening. In fact, is anything happening at all? Instead of a steady green light indicating that everything is okay, it is possible to make the light flash green whenever there is activity. It's useful to see that the device is actually doing something and not just sitting there ignoring your Mac.

To enable this, run AirPort Utility and click Manual Setup. Select AirPort in the toolbar and then the Base Station tab. Click the Options button and choose the Status Light pop-up menu. Now select the Flash On Activity option.

LIGHT	STATUS
FLASHING GREEN	ONLY OCCURS FOR ONE SECOND WHILE STARTING UP
SOLID GREEN	EVERYTHING IS WORKING NORMALLY
FLASHING AMBER	A CONNECTION TO THE INTERNET CANNOT BE MADE. CHECK THE ROUTER OR MODEM THAT PROVIDES INTERNET ACCESS FOR THE AIRPORT EXTREME ON THE WAN PORT
SOLID AMBER	THE DEVICE IS STARTING UP. IT TAKES A FEW SECONDS TO GET GOING, SO WAIT A BIT BEFORE YOU TRY TO ACCESS IT
FLASHING AMBER/GREEN	THERE WAS A PROBLEM STARTING UP. AIRPORT EXTREME WILL RESTART AND TRY AGAIN
SOLID BLUE	APPEARS WHEN YOU ALLOW A WIRELESS CLIENT TO ACCESS THE NETWORK WITHOUT REQUIRING A PASSWORD IN THE ADVANCED SETTINGS

Share a disk

The AirPort Extreme has a USB port at the back for a single device, but it's possible to add a hub to provide additional sockets and then use these to plug in multiple devices. What sort of devices? Printers and disks. The advantage of plugging these into an AirPort Extreme is that any computer in the home or office can access them. Of course, you

can share a Mac's disks and printers, but an AirPort is designed to be permanently on, which means it is always available and it doesn't depend on what the Mac is doing. Adding a disk drive that anyone can access is a simple matter of connecting the USB cable and setting the sharing options in AirPort Utility in the Applications/Utilities folder.

Once sharing is enabled, accessing a disk from a Mac couldn't be easier. Just open a Finder window and in the Shared category (in the left panel) is the AirPort Extreme. Select it and the disk (or disks) will be listed. You can double-click a disk to open it and access the contents – provided you have permission to do so, of course.

View the disks
Start AirPort Utility, enter Manual Setup and then select the Disks icon in the toolbar. The Disks tab lists the drives that are attached and if the disks have been partitioned. Partitions appear as separate disks. You can see the amount of disk space used and what's free, along with the number of users.

Set the security
The File Sharing tab looks complicated but it's not – it is simply concerned with security. The Secure Shared Disks pop-up menu enables you to choose whether to use the AirPort Extreme's password, a disk password of your choosing, or with accounts. The Disk Password option is the simplest.

Create accounts
If you want more security (it's not always needed), choose the Accounts option and an Accounts tab will appear. Select it and click the plus button below the empty list. You can enter a username and password that will enable someone to access the disk, whether they have full or just read access.

Who's on my network?

Do you know who is using your network? Has someone hacked into it? Is your neighbour using some of your bandwidth by accidentally connecting to your wireless network instead of their own? To discover who is connected to your network you should run AirPort Utility and enter Manual Setup. Click the AirPort toolbar button and select the Summary tab. Among the information displayed is Wireless Clients, which shows the number of devices connected (these aren't necessarily computers, as an iPod touch is classed as a client). Click the Wireless Clients tab and you will see a list of devices – well, actually, it's a list of MAC addresses, which are unique codes that identify each network device. You can see the connection speed in the Rate column and the type, such as 802.11b/g/n, in the Type column. If any of these don't match the devices you're using, you know that someone else is accessing your wireless network.

> "Among the information displayed is Wireless Clients, which shows the number of devices connected (these aren't necessarily computers, as an iPod touch is classed as a client)"

Forgotten your password?

When you set up the AirPort Extreme you should set a password so that other people can't come along and change any of the settings. If you haven't already done so, you can do this by running AirPort Utility, selecting AirPort in the toolbar, then the Base Station tab. Enter the password. What if you set a password and forget it? That shouldn't be a problem because it's stored in your keychain, but if you have re-installed Mac OS X at some point then you won't have it stored. If you have forgotten the password you'll have to reset the device by pushing a pen tip into the reset hole at the back.

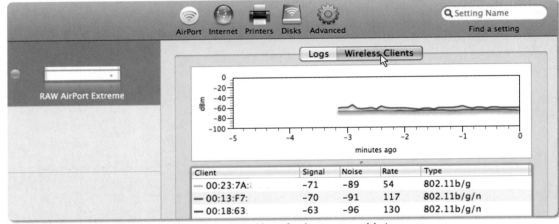

Items in the Wireless Clients column should match the MAC address of each computer and device you use

Select a channel

Wi-Fi networks use channels that are a bit like the channels you might get on walkie talkie-type handheld radios. You can set the AirPort Extreme to use a particular channel, such as 1, 2, 3 and so on. The reason for the different channels is so that different networks can use different channels, to avoid interfering with each other. Wi-Fi signals stray beyond your property neighbouring ones, and if the same channel is used there can be problems – including poor connection and slow speed. Ideally, your channel should be as far from your neighbour's as possible to avoid interference.

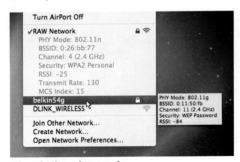

Check the channels
Hold down the Option key and click the AirPort icon in the Menu bar in Snow Leopard. Among the information displayed is the channel you are using. When the mouse hovers over any the other networks on the list, you will see their channels in a pop-up box too.

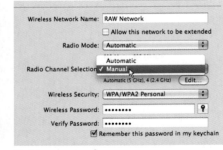

Set to manual
If you need to change the wireless channel number to avoid a clash with a neighbouring network, run AirPort Utility and enter the Manual Setup. Click the AirPort icon in the toolbar and then select the Wireless tab. Now change the Radio Channel Selection to Manual.

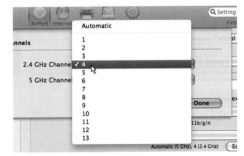

Set the channel
Click the Edit button below Radio Channel Selection and you can set the 2.4GHz Channel, which is the one that causes most problems, to one far away from your neighbour's. It goes up to channel 13, but some Wi-Fi devices only go up to channel 11, so check each device.

The wireless home
You can connect much more than just computers…

Go big screen
With a device like AppleTV you can easily watch your iTunes content on your TV. Perfect if you love to download films and TV shows

Stereo
By using an AirPort Express in your home you can stream music from your Mac to your stereo. You can then use the iPhone Remote app to control what is being played

Remote mobile devices
Whether it's an iPhone, iPod touch or iPad, there are plenty of mobile devices that can connect to your home network and control other elements of the home

Laptop
Having a laptop on the wireless network gives you the freedom to work anywhere

Get connected

Once your home network is up and running you can connect all manner of devices to it. There are the obvious candidates – MacBook, iPhone, iPad and iPod touch – but there are also a whole raft of other products that can benefit from a wireless connection. With the addition of an AirPort Express, you can connect your home stereo and stream music to it from your Mac. You can also connect a remote hard drive or printer. This is ideal if you want to keep all of your devices tucked away and you're not a fan of trailing cables. AppleTV is also a very cool device that can transform the way you

use iTunes content. Apple still considers it a hobby product, but if you're a fan of downloading films and TV shows from iTunes, AppleTV can seamlessly store and play them on your TV.

Once you actually commit to living a wireless lifestyle, the computers and devices you use will take on a brand new role. The integration and constant connectivity it provides means that they are only limited by your imagination. There's nothing like streaming music to a bedroom from the Mac downstairs while lying on the bed, changing playlists with your iPhone.

Having problems? Reset the base station…

If there is a problem with the AirPort Extreme you might find it useful to reset the device. There isn't a power switch so unplug it at the wall, wait a few seconds, and then plug it back in. If it's communicating with the Mac, you can select Reset on the AirPort Utility Base Station menu. If all else fails, push a pen tip into the tiny reset hole in the back of the device and hold it in for five seconds until the status light flashes quickly. The factory settings are applied, so you should immediately log on and change the password from its default 'public'.

Port forwarding - for experts!

Certain applications, such as an FTP server, games, chat programs or another utility that works via the internet might need port forwarding to be set up before it will work. It can be confusing, but once you understand how it works it isn't so difficult. Suppose you want to call Bob who works in the sales department of a company. You call the telephone number of the company and ask the receptionist to put you through to Bob. The receptionist forwards your call to extension 53, which is Bob's phone. Computers work in exactly the same way, and it's called port forwarding.

Each computer on your network is given a private IP address, which is like a telephone extension in a company. The public IP address assigned by your ISP is like the company phone number. When a computer or application on the internet wants to communicate, it sends data to the AirPort Extreme, which then forwards it to the Mac or device that is expecting it. It's like saying "Put me through to Bob," when you call his company switchboard.

In Manual mode, select the Internet icon in the toolbar and the Internet Connection tab. Connection Sharing should be set to 'Share a public IP address'. This is so that several computers and devices can access the internet through the public IP address. In this mode you'll see a DHCP tab. You must ensure the Mac that requires port forwarding always has the same IP address (just as Bob is always

on extension 53). Click the plus button below DHCP Reservations and enter any name you like in the Description box. Click Continue and then enter the MAC address. A MAC address is a unique code that all network equipment has, and you can find it by going to System Preferences on the Apple menu and clicking the Network option. Select AirPort (or Ethernet if you connect via a network cable) and click Advanced. You'll see the AirPort ID, which is the MAC address you need. Now enter this address into the box in AirPort Utility.

After reserving the IP address, click the NAT tab and make sure Enable NAT Port Mapping Protocol is ticked. Now click Configure Port Mappings. Click Plus and enter the public and private UDP or TCP port number (both numbers are usually the same). The Private IP Address is the one you just reserved. Selecting an item on the Service pop-up menu is a quick way to configure common ports like FTP and web servers, and they provide useful examples too. The application you want to run on your Mac will tell you which port it communicates through; web servers always use port 80 and FTP servers always use port 21, for example.

If the AirPort Extreme is in Bridge Mode, then DHCP and NAT will be performed by the router/ADSL modem it is connected to. In this case, port forwarding is set up on that device and not the AirPort Extreme.

Port forwarding directs communications from the internet to the computer that is expecting it

 ## Use a network cable for faster and more reliable access

If you are having a problem connecting to the AirPort Extreme, in order to check it, change the configuration or settings, you will find it easier if you use a network (Ethernet) cable. Plug one end into the Mac and the other end into the base station at the back. This isn't just a good idea for sorting out wireless connection problems, as a direct network connection offers faster and more reliable internet and network access. If your Mac is near enough to the base station to use a network cable, then do so.

Devices that will rock your wireless world

AirPort Express

Making use of incredibly fast 802.11n, the AirPort Express is powerful enough to run a home Wi-Fi network, yet small enough to take on the road. It can boost Wi-Fi signal, connect via USB and stream music.

AppleTV

Apple touts the device as a DVD player for the 21st Century, and the Cupertino company is pretty much bang on. Download content from iTunes and play it on your TV.

iPad

It's the must-have device of the decade and may end up replacing your Mac. Connect it to your wireless network and you can browse the web, play multiplayer games and much more.

iPod touch

The funnest iPod ever released is a great asset to a wireless home – not only can you use it as a universal remote, but you can play games and use the web.

iPhone

A revolutionary product that thrives on a wireless connection, whether it's streaming content from YouTube or just checking the news online.

iCandy
MacBook Pro

MacBook Pro
Apple's finest desktop replacement is a smooth chunk of aluminium carved from one solid 'brick'

Tutorial: Quickly check MobileMe syncing

There's a hidden feature in Mac OS X Snow Leopard that lets you stay up-to-date with all your MobileMe syncs. Here's how to access and make use of it to save time…

Task: Check MobileMe synchronisation

Difficulty: Beginner

Time needed: 5 minutes

X MobileMe syncing is a great feature in Apple's online service that works seamlessly with Mac OS X. Once set up, it works quietly in the background making sure all of your contacts are in sync between multiple computers and your iPhone. Sometimes, however, it's handy to know a little bit more about what's going on with your information – especially if you suspect things aren't running as smoothly as they should. You could, of course, head to the MobileMe System Preferences pane to check things out, but in order to save time this handy tip allows you to find out some basic information, as well as open up System Preferences or diagnose a fault, right from the desktop Menu bar. It's a quick tip, but one that's easily overlooked and could help you fix errors, or at least give you some peace of mind that your information is as up-to-date as possible.

Step-by-step | Mac OS X | Stay updated with MobileMe

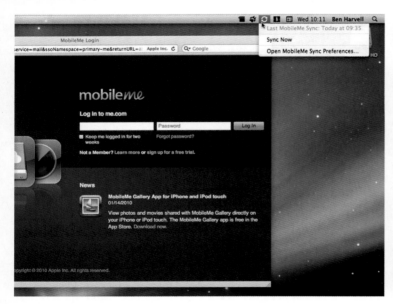

1: Standard view
This Menu bar symbol lets you know how syncing of your MobileMe contacts and calendars is going. When clicked it shows you the last sync, and provides a quick way to initiate a sync of all your info.

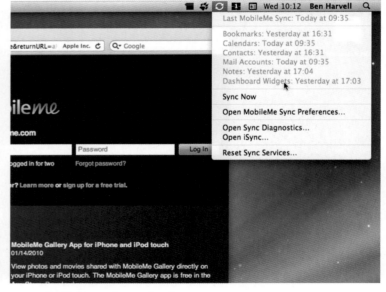

2: Take a closer look
However, if you hold down the Alt key and click the symbol again, you get a much more detailed view that will show you when each MobileMe element was last synced.

Stay on top of your syncs

Keep an eye on MobileMe and its synchronisation

Sync info
Click on this button to access basic updates about your MobileMe syncs. If you hold Alt and click on the same button you'll receive even more detailed stats, as well as more options to make changes to MobileMe

Knowledge base

Keep pushing
To make sure all of your information remains as up-to-date as possible, turn on Push in System Preferences on both your Mac and iPhone (if you are using one) so that any changes are automatically pushed straight to your individual accounts as soon as they are made.

MobileMe online
You can access all of your contacts, calendars and emails online through me.com, and also adjust your account settings if need be. You can do this from any web-connected computer

Options
When Alt-clicking on the MobileMe Sync button you can also access iSync and Sync Diagnostics from your desktop, rather than having to locate and launch them

Basic preferences
System Preferences offers the best way to adjust your sync settings. This pane can be launched from the MobileMe Sync button

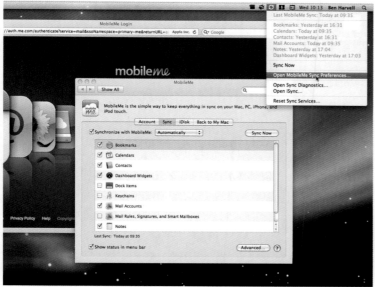

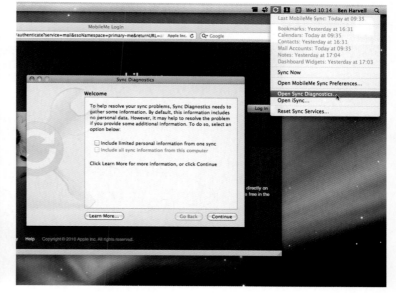

3: Quick preferences
This menu provides a quick way to make changes to your MobileMe syncs – by clicking on the Open MobileMe Sync Preferences option you will immediately be taken to the correct preference pane.

4: Got a problem?
If your adjustments to the sync preferences don't help, you can troubleshoot your syncs by launching Sync Diagnostics from the same menu to help highlight any problems.

Tutorial: Set your Mac to automatically restart

In the case of a power failure or a serious fault, it's always good to set your Mac to automatically restart

Energy Saver

Task: Set your Mac to automatically restart

Difficulty: Beginner

Time needed: 10 minutes

X From time to time we all experience a power cut in our home or office. It's always a little disconcerting to come back to your computer only to find that it's sitting there as if it was never turned on. In the case of a system fault that causes your computer to switch itself off, automatic restarts can be a handy way to let you know something is up – with the start-up chime letting you know each time the error has occurred if you're not in front of your Mac at the time. In this tutorial we'll show you how to set your Mac to turn itself on should it lose power at any given time. The process involves a quick trip to System Preferences, but will help you out should problems strike. Combine this tip with automatically launched applications on startup, and make sure a powercut never ruins your day again.

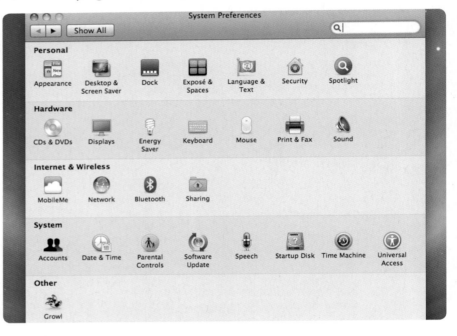

Step-by-step   Mac OS X   Set your Mac to auto-restart

1: System Preferences

Head to the Apple menu and select System Preferences, or launch it from your Dock, and click on the Energy Saver option in the middle of the System Preferences pane.

2: Checkbox

From the checkboxes listed below the sliders for sleep and display sleep, click on the 'Start up automatically after a power failure' box to set your Mac for auto-restart.

Tutorial: Change the size of desktop icons

Can't see what's on your desktop? Changing the size of the icons is a simple and effective way of making your Mac OS X life easier

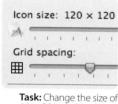

Task: Change the size of Mac OS X desktop icons

Difficulty: Beginner

Time needed: 5 minutes

X Mac OS X is full of handy little things that are designed to make your life a little easier; unlike some operating systems out there, Apple wants people to enjoy using its computers. To this send Apple has built Mac OS X to be as user-friendly as possible. This does mean that in some cases there is more than one way to complete a task, but this never affects the simplicity involved in carrying it out and, in most cases, it means that you can pick and choose the way that is most efficient at the time for you.

A very cool and simple process to improve the look of your desktop is to resize the icons on it. You can make them larger so they are easier to see, or make them smaller so they take up less space. As you can imagine, the process is very straightforward. Follow the two steps below to find out how it's done…

Step-by-step | Mac OS X Resize desktop icons

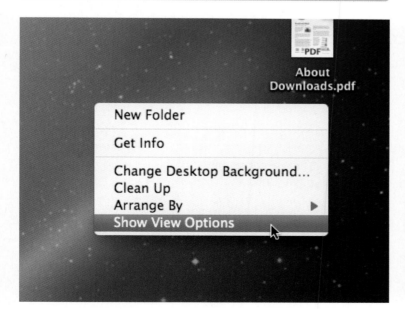

1: Context it
Begin by using a right or Command-click on your desktop to bring up a contextual menu. Now navigate to the bottom of this menu and click Show View Options.

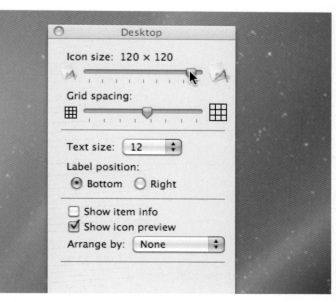

2: Slide away
Use the Icon Size slider to increase or decrease the size of the icons. If you are a new MacBook owner, ignore the previous step and just use a pinch or reverse-pinch on the desktop to change icon sizes.

Inside System Preferences: Sharing

Get to grips with the technology inside your Mac by following this simple guide to the System Preferences. Here we focus on the Sharing aspect of Preferences...

There's one aspect that sets the computers of today far apart from those we were using just ten years ago: networks. Back in 2000 the internet was only just starting to become commonplace, and if you did have it you probably only had it on one computer in the house (which wasn't really a problem, as most houses only had one computer). Now, with the advent of easy Wi-Fi and cheaper computers (plus iPods and iPhones), many houses have a handful of connected devices sharing the airwaves and, with a little setup, sharing their connections, files and data too. The Internet & Wireless row of icons in System Preferences is all about your Networks – local and worldwide – how you interact with them and how you choose to share across them; be it sharing your files, screen, printer or even disc drive.

Network

For most users this should hopefully be one of those 'set it and forget it' preference panes, if you ever need to set it at all. With most modern networks you should find your Mac just connects and configures itself. Bliss.

Bluetooth

Check out the status of the Bluetooth peripherals you have connected to your Mac. To add a new Bluetooth device, like a mouse, keyboard or phone, click the '+' button.

"With most modern networks you should find your Mac just connects and configures itself. Bliss"

Sharing

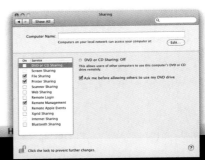

DVD or CD Sharing

Share your DVD drive with a Mac that either has a broken drive or doesn't have one at all, like the MacBook Air or new Mac mini server.

Screen Sharing

Allow another computer (or iPhone) on your network to see your screen, and even control your Mac remotely.

File Sharing

Make files in certain folders available to other computers on your network. You can control who sees what.

Printer Sharing

With a tick of a box you can share any printer connected to your Mac with any other local computer.

Scanner Sharing

Save yourself the hassle of unplugging and swapping one scanner between Macs by sharing it over the network.

Web Sharing

Mac OS X has its own pretty serious web server built right in, which can be enabled by ticking this box.

Remote Login

For those users happy typing commands in Terminal, this setting allows remote login to the Mac.

MobileMe

Account

Get an overview of your account status, including how long you have until your account needs renewing.

Sync

Syncing across MobileMe allows multiple Macs and iPhones, even those in different locations, to share the same bookmarks, address books, calendars and more.

iDisk

The MobileMe iDisk is your virtual hard drive on the internet. You can use it to store photos, movies and files, or to host your iWeb pages and iPhoto galleries. This preference pane lets you check your space and control the security settings.

Back to My Mac

With Back to My Mac turned on you can access your files, folders and applications from another Mac over the internet anywhere in the world. You can even use Screen Sharing to control the Mac as if you were sitting right in front of it.

Remote Management

A step-up from Screen Sharing, Remote Management allows system-level control of your Mac from afar.

Remote Apple Events

For the real power users, Remote Apple Events allows your Mac to be automated by other computers.

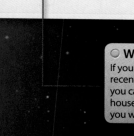

○ Wake it up when you go, go

If your Mac is connected to the internet through a recent Apple AirPort Base station or Time Capsule, you can set your Mac sleeping when you leave the house and it will automatically wake up should you want to access it using Back to My Mac

○ Stay safe

You don't want to let just anyone send your files over Bluetooth, especially if you use a laptop in crowded areas like airports. To be safe, tick both 'Require pairing' boxes and leave the 'When' options as 'Ask What to Do'.

Xgrid Sharing

Share extremely intensive tasks, like video rendering, across multiple macs using Xgrid – for power users only!

Internet Sharing

Share your internet connection with another computer by ticking the box and selecting the correct ports.

Bluetooth Sharing

Share photos, ringtones and more with a mobile phone using Bluetooth Sharing to create a short-range network to pass files across.

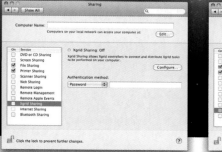

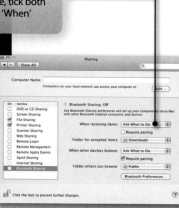

Tutorial: Add drives & servers to your Dock

If you have a drive permanently attached to your Mac, then why not save yourself time accessing its files by adding it to your Dock?

Task: Drag a drive to add it to your Dock

Difficulty: Beginner

Time needed: 10 minutes

X Despite the ever-increasing storage available in new Macs, it's still possible to run out of space. The need to keep your Mac snappy will also prevent you from filling it to the brim with all your movies and music; so it's no wonder that many of us have a hard drive (or two) permanently attached to our Macs. We know that accessing them is pretty simple when they're sat on the desktop, but there is a way to make getting at often-used files even simpler.

The Dock is a great place to keep drives because the Stacks system means easy access. There's no need to open a Finder window or do any double-clicking. And this technique is especially useful if you have more than one drive or a server attached to your Mac. It's even possible to dictate the behaviour of the drive while it resides in the Dock, and you can even change the view options.

Step-by-step | Mac OS X | Add a drive to your Dock

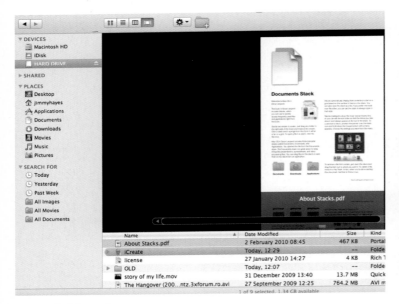

1: Mount up
Begin by making sure that your drives are mounted and visible on the desktop. They normally sit under your Macintosh HD icon in the Devices section of the left-hand panel of the finder.

2: Drag and drop
You can now drag the drive icon onto the Dock on the right-hand side where your Downloads folder sits. Use a slow movement and wait for the other folders there to part, giving you room to place the drive.

Quickly access files from the Dock
Now your files and folders can be reached in an instant

Fans, grids and lists
As well as the cool stack that springs from the Dock it's also possible to see grids or lists. Grids are great if you want to drill down through folders as it can be done from the Dock

Forget Finder
Opening a Finder window is great if you've got time and space on your desktop, but when you want fast access and no extra windows on screen then this is the best way to do it

If you still need the Finder
If you still need to access the Finder after you've opened a stack you can use the top button to reveal that directory in a Finder window

Knowledge base

Disconnection
One of the cool things about this technique is that the icon will remain when the drive unmounts, so when you plug it back in you don't need to repeat the manoeuvre in order to gain quick access to your files and folders.

Quick close
Once a stack or grid is open you can quickly close it by clicking on the arrow at the bottom of the stack

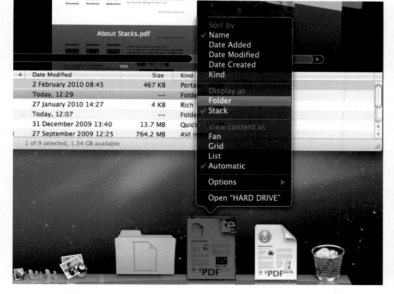

3: View options
The default view once a folder is dropped down is for it to display the first item on the device. To change this, right-click the icon and then select Folder in the Display section.

4: Click and hold
You can now access stacks and grids of the files within the drive straight from the Dock, which is a great way to get to regularly accessed files on a mounted drive.

Tutorial: Add applications to Spaces

Is your desktop often cluttered with running programs? If so discover how to add applications to Spaces…

We all know the troubles of a cluttered desktop; windows and applications begin to overlap, and before you know it the desktop background has vanished under a sea of Finder windows. It's especially a problem for those of us with smaller screens, such as those found on the 13-inch MacBooks. There are a few easy solutions, such as using Exposé or hiding applications as you go. But with the introduction of Leopard came Spaces – a set of easily accessible virtual environments for you to use. It sounds complicated, but as with everything Apple introduces it's a doddle to use. Follow the tutorial as we find out how to add applications to Spaces.

Task: Add individual applications to Spaces

Difficulty: Beginner

Time needed: 15 minutes

Step-by-step | Spaces Add applications to Spaces with this easy guide

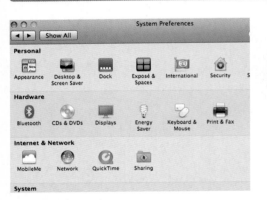

1: Load up Spaces
Open System Preferences, click on the Exposé & Spaces button, and select the Spaces tab to load its Control Panel. If Spaces isn't turned on, enable it.

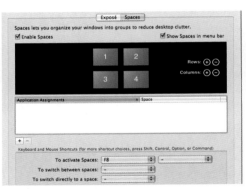

2: Assign a program
Click the plus icon below Application Assignments to see a pop-up window displaying all the running applications. Choose one to add it to Spaces.

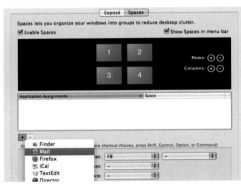

3: Choose a space
The application you choose will automatically be assigned to Space 1. You can choose a different Space using the drop-down menu to the right.

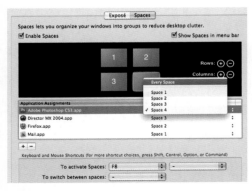

4: Add even more spaces
Add as many programs as you wish via this Control Panel. By using the drop-down menu you can also choose to make an application appear in every Space.

5: Find a program
To add programs from your Applications folder, click the plus icon and select Other. You'll need to manually browse the Applications folder.

6: Drag-and-drop
It's also possible to drag-and-drop applications from one Space to another. Start by activating all Spaces (F8+mouse button 2 by default).

Use Spaces to its fullest

Every element of Spaces can be controlled from one window

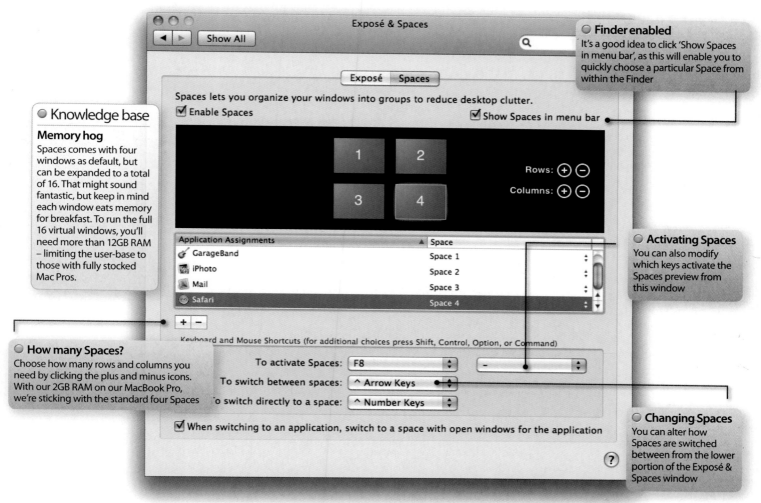

○ Finder enabled
It's a good idea to click 'Show Spaces in menu bar', as this will enable you to quickly choose a particular Space from within the Finder

○ Knowledge base

Memory hog
Spaces comes with four windows as default, but can be expanded to a total of 16. That might sound fantastic, but keep in mind each window eats memory for breakfast. To run the full 16 virtual windows, you'll need more than 12GB RAM – limiting the user-base to those with fully stocked Mac Pros.

○ Activating Spaces
You can also modify which keys activate the Spaces preview from this window

○ How many Spaces?
Choose how many rows and columns you need by clicking the plus and minus icons. With our 2GB RAM on our MacBook Pro, we're sticking with the standard four Spaces

○ Changing Spaces
You can alter how Spaces are switched between from the lower portion of the Exposé & Spaces window

7: It saves time
Next, simply drag an application window from one Space to another. This is a great time saver for organising your programs.

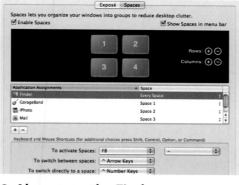

8: Always see the Finder
It's a good idea to set the Finder to appear in all Spaces, enabling you to easily access your files while keeping an application on the screen.

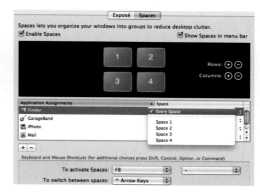

9: Every Space
To do this simply add the Finder to Spaces, and then choose Every Space under the drop-down menu. You'll now see the Finder in every Space.

Inside System Preferences: Settings

Get to grips with the technology inside your Mac by following this simple guide to the System Preferences. Here we look at the System settings

The System settings, like the Network row above them, get deep down and dirty into the depths of Mac OS X. Many of the changes affect all users of the Mac, and it's here where you'll discover the tools you need to control which users can do what. It's also where you'll find Universal Access, the first place you should go if you have physical difficulties that make it hard for you to enjoy your Mac.

Startup Disk

For power users, with different versions of Mac OS X installed across multiple hard drives, this pane enables you to pick the drive you'd like to start from.

Date & time

Date & Time

Always be sure that your Mac's clock is bang on time by setting it to automatically stay synchronised with Apple's time servers over the internet.

Time Zone

Let your Mac know where you are in the world by clicking the map near where you are, then choosing the closest city to you from the pop-up menu at the bottom of the screen.

Clock

Set how your Menu bar displays the date and time. If Menu bar space is at a premium you can choose to see a tiny analog clock, or even get rid of it completely and have your Mac announce the time on the hour, every hour.

Accounts

Password

The left panel of the Accounts screen allows you to create new user accounts, or select the account you wish to edit (only if you're an Admin user though). The settings on the right enable you to change your password and name (but not your short name that's used elsewhere on the system).

Login Items

Adding an application, by clicking the '+' button, sets it to automatically launch when you log in to your Mac. You're not limited to just applications though, as you can also set your regularly used documents to automatically open by adding them in the same way.

Speech

Speech Recognition

Chances are you may not have realised that it's possible to control your Mac using your voice. Okay, so it's not perfect – in fact, it's likely to turn into one of the most frustrating experiences you've had on a Mac, but it's still cool. And for the rare few that have it working perfectly, invaluable.

Text to speech

Not only can you talk to your Mac, it can talk straight back at you. Text to Speech can give you valuable audio feedback when your Mac requires your attention, speaking alert boxes and more. You can also choose your Mac's voice from a wide range of styles and speeds.

Time Machine

Mac OS X comes with what is arguably the best 'set it and forget it' back-up utility: Time Machine. Turn it on, select a disk and rest assured that your data is safe.

Parental Controls

Kids spending too much time on the Mac? Heading to unsuitable websites or playing too many games? Parental Controls give you the power to manage their Mac use.

Universal Access

Seeing

For those of us with less than perfect sight, Universal Access aims improve how you interact with your Mac – you can even have every element on screen read out to you using VoiceOver.

Hearing

If you have trouble with your hearing, Universal Access has two very simple settings to help you out. The first will flash the screen every time an alert sound is played, while the second checkbox plays stereo sound equally between left and right speakers – great if you suffer from deafness in one ear only.

Keyboard

If you have difficulty operating your Mac's keyboard, then this Universal Access pane could make your life a great deal easier. You can use Sticky Keys to help with key combinations and turn on Slow Keys to turn down your keyboard's sensitivity and avoid any unwanted key presses.

Mouse

Turning Mouse Keys on enables you to use your keyboard to move the mouse cursor, which many people with limited mobility will find easier than the arm and hand movements that are required to move the mouse itself. You can also make the on-screen cursor larger if you have difficulty seeing it.

> "Control your Mac using your voice. Okay, so it's not perfect – in fact, it's likely to turn into one of the most frustrating experiences you've had"

Software Update

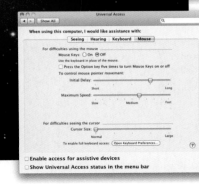

Scheduled Check

Software Update runs automatically to ensure your Mac is always running the most up-to-date version of any Apple software you have installed, including Mac OS X, iLife and the Apple Pro applications. You can choose how often you'd like it to check for updates or run a manual check yourself.

Installed Software

By using this pane you can quickly check the version numbers of any Apple software you have installed and when it was last updated. This can come in handy if you're trying to troubleshoot a problem and think it might be down to a recent update or software install.

Detect and track flights from within Mail

Mail is getting smarter all the time, and now it can even recognise flight details…

X When Mail was first able to recognise dates, phone numbers and other contact details, we were pretty impressed. We've lost track of the amount of times we'd think to ourselves 'I must add that person to my address book' or 'I must remember to add that as an iCal event' and then completely forgotten to do it. Now, we can simply hover our mouse over the pertinent data, click a link and – in the words of Steve Jobs – boom! Not only can Mail detect contact details and dates, but it can go in another very interesting direction and track flight numbers. The integration involved is very cool and, as you would expect, it works flawlessly. So, if you receive details of a flight from someone in an email you can instantly check the details of that flight on your Mac. Sadly it does mean you want to get away with leaving your mother-in-law stranded at the arrivals lounge…

Task: Use Mail to detect flight details

Difficulty: Beginner

Time needed: 10 minutes

Step-by-step | Mac OS X Track flight details with Mail

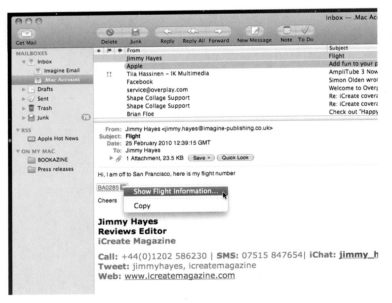

1: Get flight number
When you get an email with flight details in it, all you need to do is hover your mouse over the details for a dotted line and menu arrow to appear over them.

2: Click it
Click the menu arrow and a contextual menu will appear with two options: Show Flight Information and Copy. Select Show Flight Information – this is where the magic happens.

Get flight information in Mail

Mail and Dashboard work together to detect and track flights

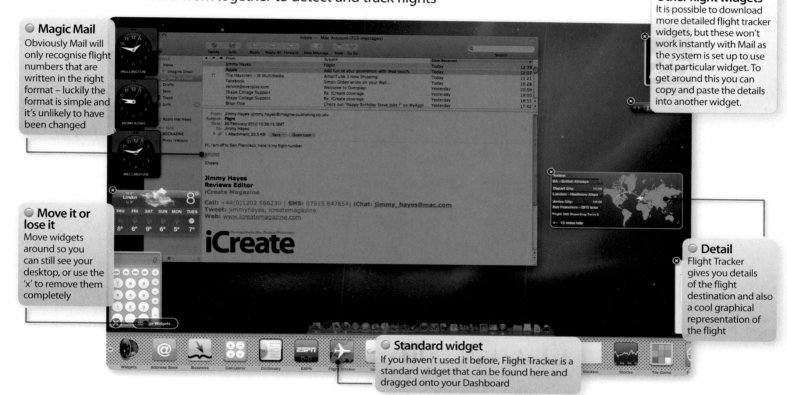

Magic Mail
Obviously Mail will only recognise flight numbers that are written in the right format – luckily the format is simple and it's unlikely to have been changed

Move it or lose it
Move widgets around so you can still see your desktop, or use the 'x' to remove them completely

Detail
Flight Tracker gives you details of the flight destination and also a cool graphical representation of the flight

Standard widget
If you haven't used it before, Flight Tracker is a standard widget that can be found here and dragged onto your Dashboard

3: Dash it
As if by magic, Dashboard will open and the Flight Tracker widget will launch showing you details of the flight in question. You even get a cool graphic of the flight.

4: More options
You can now check different details from within the widget, like the flight progress or its status. The information is very easy to access and laid out clearly for you to understand.

Tutorial: Trim your audio with QuickTime X

Use QuickTime X to quickly perform a basic audio trim

Task: Trim an audio clip with QuickTime X

Difficulty: Beginner

Time needed: 10 minutes

X We wouldn't blame you if you thought that QuickTime X was only good for video; a lot of people don't know it can process and play audio. QuickTime is a very cool way to play audio when you don't want to have it imported and played through iTunes. On top of this, thanks to QuickTime's new 'X' status, you can now do some limited editing. This is perfect for when you're about to use audio in one of the iLife apps and you want to check it out first, and maybe trim it down before firing up a processor-intensive application.

It's even more useful if you have more than one piece of audio to edit and you want them all open in their own cool little windows. Trimming with QuickTime X is incredibly simple and there is even a sweet little automatic function that could save you even more time in the long run. Just follow the four steps below…

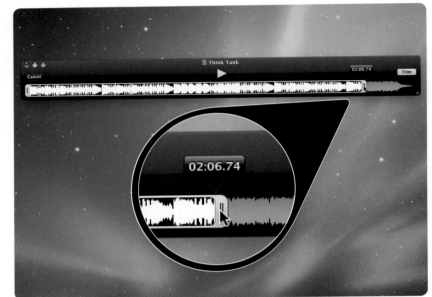

Step-by-step | Mac OS X | Trim your audio footage in QuickTime

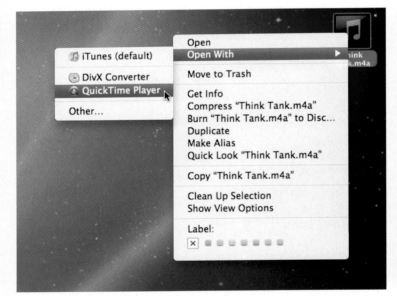

1: Open on the QT
Most audio files will open in iTunes if you double-click them, so use an Option-click or right-click to see the contextual menu. Now select Open With and choose QuickTime Player.

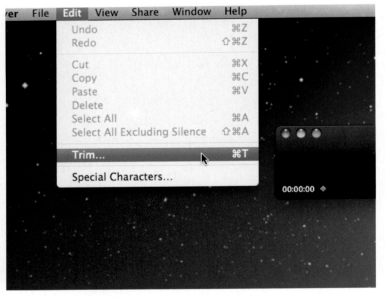

2: Edit the hit
Once the file has loaded, go to the top menu and select Edit>Trim. The trimming bar will now appear around the audio, and you will see an analysis of the waveform as it's presented.

Having a trim couldn't be simpler

Get to grips with audio in QuickTime

● **iPhone interface**
QuickTime X uses the same trimming interface as is used on the iPhone 3GS. It's simplicity personified; just drag the sliders left or right

● Knowledge base

Apple+Z
As always, if you make a mistake in haste you can quickly revert back to the uncut version by pressing Cmd+Z. This will only work while the file is open and you haven't saved it; once a save takes place you won't be able to action an undo.

● **Menu or shortcut**
Like most Mac OS X apps, the menu system is simple to navigate and the keyboard shortcut is also offered next to the command

● **Wave form**
When the trimming mode is activated, the audio is analysed and the wave form can be seen in the viewer. This is to help you detect the places you want to trim

"QuickTime is a very cool way to play audio when you don't want to have it imported and played through iTunes"

● **Button it**
Once you've done a bit of dragging and decided what you're going to chop away, just hit the Trim button and QuickTime will resize the track, getting rid of what's not wanted

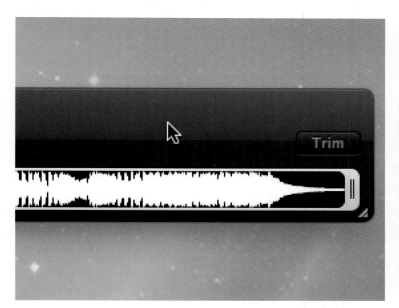

3: Manual moves
You can now drag the trimming bar left or right to cut out the ends of the track. You won't be able to cut bits out of the middle of the track, just the ends of it.

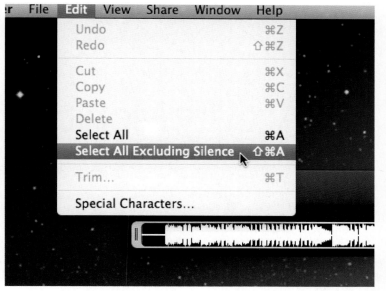

4: Automatic trim
Head back to the Menu bar to use an automatic trim that will remove any silence from the front and back of the track. The menu option you want is Select All Excluding Silence. Hit Trim to action the command.

Quit apps
If an errant program is using all of your CPU, click the Quit button in the top-left corner. It's quite the time saver

Search for apps
The Filter window enables you to type an application or process name and find it immediately – handy if you have hundreds of processes running at once

Activity Monitor

My Processes ⊟ | Q▾ Filter

Quit Process   Inspect   Sample Process

Show   Filter

Process ID	Process Name	User	▼ CPU	# Threads	Real Memory	Virtual Memory	Kind
199	Firefox	Tom	37.3	31	209.46 MB	486.28 MB	Intel
3174	Director	Tom	4.5	7	127.72 MB	1.40 GB	PowerPC
3865	Activity Monitor	Tom	2.3	6	23.52 MB	879.72 MB	Intel
4767	screencapture	Tom	1.9	1	2.51 MB	756.98 MB	Intel
302	Photoshop	Tom	0.7	20	638.20 MB	2.09 GB	Intel
130	ATSServer	Tom	0.3	2	8.48 MB	652.20 MB	Intel
135	Finder	Tom	0.1	1			
134	SystemUIServer	Tom	0.0				
107	launchd	Tom	0.0				
198	Mail	Tom	0.0	1			
	TextEdit	Tom	0.0				
	Image Capture Extension	Tom	0.0				
	MassStorage	Tom	0.0				
	MagicMenu	Tom	0.0				
	al	Tom	0.0				
	board	Tom	0.0				
	dworker	Tom	0.0				
	MagicMenuHotKeyDaemon	Tom	0.0				
	AppleVNCServer	Tom	0.0				
	AppleSpell.service	Tom	0.0				
	Spotlight	Tom	0.0				
	Dock	Tom	0.0				
	ARDAgent	Tom	0.0				
	Quick Look Server	Tom	0.0				

Knowledge base

Inspector
Click the Inspect button when an app is chosen to see detailed statistics about it. You'll be able to see how much RAM it's using, how many threads and ports are in use, and what percentage of the CPU it is eating up.

Firefox (199)

Parent Process: launchd (107)   User: Tom (502)
Process Group: Firefox (199)
% CPU: 37.28   Recent hangs: 0

Memory | Statistics | Open Files and Ports

Threads:	31	Page Ins:	14532
Ports:	342	Mach Messages In:	5418850
CPU Time:	47:30.99	Mach Messages Out:	7934423
Context Switches:	6836996	Mach System Calls:	50303314
Faults:	4856219	Unix System Calls:	9267843

Sample ●   Quit

CPU | System Memory | Disk Activity | Disk Usage | Network

CPU Usage

% User: 36.54
% System: 26.92
% Nice: 0.00
% Idle: 36.54

Threads: 346
Processes: 71

Information display
The lower section of the screen is filled with detailed information. From here you can see exactly what processes are running

Test samples
Click the Sample Process button to see exactly what a program is up to. Be aware, however, that the information displayed will only make sense to a programmer

Use Activity Monitor to speed up your Mac

Is your Mac running slow? Chances are a background task or program is using up any available resources. Learn how to use Activity Monitor to track down the culprit…

Free:	118.13 MB ☐
Wired:	179.46 MB ☐
Active:	1.11 GB ☐
Inactive:	610.98 MB ☐
Used :	1.88 GB

Task: Discover what resources are in use with Activity Monitor

Difficulty: Intermediate

Time needed: 10 minutes

X Found within the Applications folder on every Mac is a suite of utilities designed by Apple. These come pre-installed with the operating system and offer a wealth of tools that enable you to truly take advantage of your Mac. One of the most useful utilities – certainly when it comes to running your Mac at its most efficient – is Activity Monitor. Open it up and you'll discover windows for monitoring the CPU usage, hard drive activity, system memory, disk usage and network statistics. It's especially useful if your Mac has suddenly slowed to a crawl. Open Activity Monitor, and whichever errant program with the highest CPU cycles will be the culprit. You'll find options to inspect the program, quit it and sample the current processes it's using. On first appearance this is a simple monitor of the hardware within your Mac but, as we'll explain in this tutorial, this is a powerful yet easy-to-use app…

Step-by-step | Mac OS X Use Activity Monitor to optimise your Mac

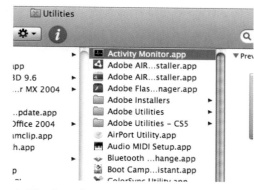

1: Find and open
Open Activity Monitor, which can be found in Utilities. Once opened you'll see a list of running processes with various stats displayed.

2: Check out the processes
Processes will be displayed in alphabetical order. Programs that are open will have an icon displayed, the other listings are background processes.

3: The running stats
The tabs detail usage in visual form. The CPU tab displays user processes in green, system processes in red and spare processor power in black.

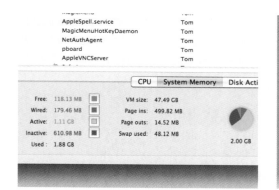

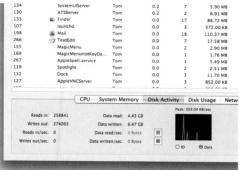

4: System Memory tab
Click on System Memory to see how much RAM is being used. Our test system has 2GB of RAM, most of which is in use (we clearly need more RAM!).

5: Internet data
The Disk Activity and Disk Usage tabs display info about the hard disk. The Network tab shows data being sent and received via Ethernet and Wi-Fi.

6: Organise those apps
You can organise every running process by the amount of resources it is using by clicking on the header of choice, as seen in this image.

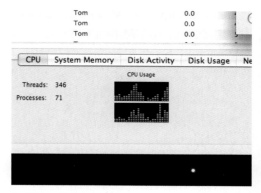

7: The top buttons
The three buttons at the top of the screen enable you to quit programs, inspect them and see what processes they are currently using.

8: Detailed stats
Click the Inspect button to see a detailed overview of the chosen program. If you have multiple users then you can see who launched each app.

9: Timeline graph
The small coloured graph at the bottom of the screen is a timeline of the process chosen. Here we can see the CPU usage over several minutes.

Tutorial: Stream video directly to your iPad

Discover how to stream video from your Mac to your iPad. It's incredibly easy, free, and will save you considerable time

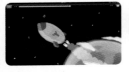

Task: Learn how to stream video over a network

Difficulty: Beginner

Time needed: 10 minutes

With it's large 9.7-inch Multi-Touch display, the iPad is perfect for watching video content away from your Mac and TV. Getting video onto it is another matter, however. iTunes is great at converting QuickTime videos or syncing content from iTunes, but if you have any video content that's not in a native Mac format (such as .avi/.wmv/.mkv) then you're looking at a time-consuming and expensive endeavour to convert it. Thankfully, Air Video is here to help, as it can stream any video to your iPad from your Mac. Whatever video content you have, Air Video will play it – even native Windows video files. It's incredibly easy to set up and use, and costs only £1.79.

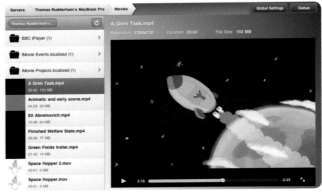

Step-by-step | Air Video Stream video wirelessly

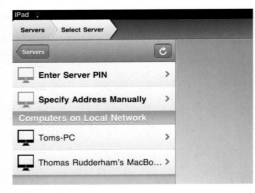

1: Get downloading
Download Air Video to your iPad from the App Store, plus Air Video Server for your Mac from **www. inmethod.com**. Now open the Air Video Server.

2: Choose a location
Click the Add Disk Folder button at the bottom of the screen, and choose whichever folder contains the videos you wish to watch on your iPad.

3: Load up your iPad
Your Mac is now running a video server that your iPad can connect to. Open Air Video on your iPad and click the plus icon in the top-left corner.

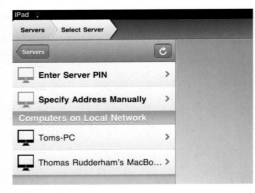

4: Local network
You'll see your Mac listed in the field to the left of the screen. Simply tap it to add it to your Server list. Now tap on your Mac again to access your videos.

5: Videos listed
You'll see every video listed on your Mac, each with a preview thumbnail. When you tap a video, the main window will display a number of options.

6: Playing video
Tap on the 'Play With Live Conversion' button to immediately play the video. Depending on the speed of your Mac this may take a few seconds.

Use Air Video to stream your videos

Stream directly from your Mac to your iPad

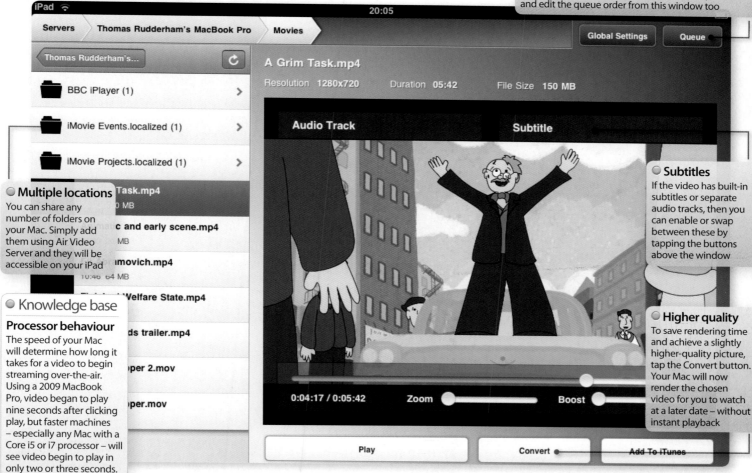

Queue content
The Queue button in the top-right corner of the screen will display any videos that are currently rendering on your Mac for later playback. You can stop any videos and edit the queue order from this window too

iPad · 20:05

Servers · Thomas Rudderham's MacBook Pro · Movies

Global Settings · Queue

Thomas Rudderham's...

BBC iPlayer (1)

iMovie Events.localized (1)

iMovie Projects.localized (1)

A Grim Task.mp4
Resolution 1280x720 · Duration 05:42 · File Size 150 MB

Audio Track · Subtitle

0:04:17 / 0:05:42 · Zoom · Boost

Play · Convert · Add To iTunes

Multiple locations
You can share any number of folders on your Mac. Simply add them using Air Video Server and they will be accessible on your iPad

Subtitles
If the video has built-in subtitles or separate audio tracks, then you can enable or swap between these by tapping the buttons above the window

Higher quality
To save rendering time and achieve a slightly higher-quality picture, tap the Convert button. Your Mac will now render the chosen video for you to watch at a later date – without instant playback

Knowledge base

Processor behaviour

The speed of your Mac will determine how long it takes for a video to begin streaming over-the-air. Using a 2009 MacBook Pro, video began to play nine seconds after clicking play, but faster machines – especially any Mac with a Core i5 or i7 processor – will see video begin to play in only two or three seconds.

7: Controls

Air Video plays content exactly the same as any movie on your iPad, so you can scrub through the video and play it full-screen using standard controls.

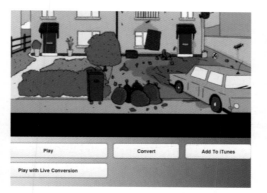

8: Other options

To convert a video for later playback, simply tap the Convert button and Air Video will render the video in the background. You can also send it to iTunes.

9: Video resolution

Tap the Global Setting button to change the resolution. You can max the settings for crystal clear video, but your Mac will take longer to stream video.

Individual application settings
The Applications tab has a surprising amount of options. Click on the Applications Settings sub-tab to change Display Style, inform Growl when a notification is clicked and the custom starting position

Unique notifications
By clicking the Notifications sub-tab you can tell Growl when to notify you when a specific event (such as new mail) happens. You can also choose from a wide range of Display Styles

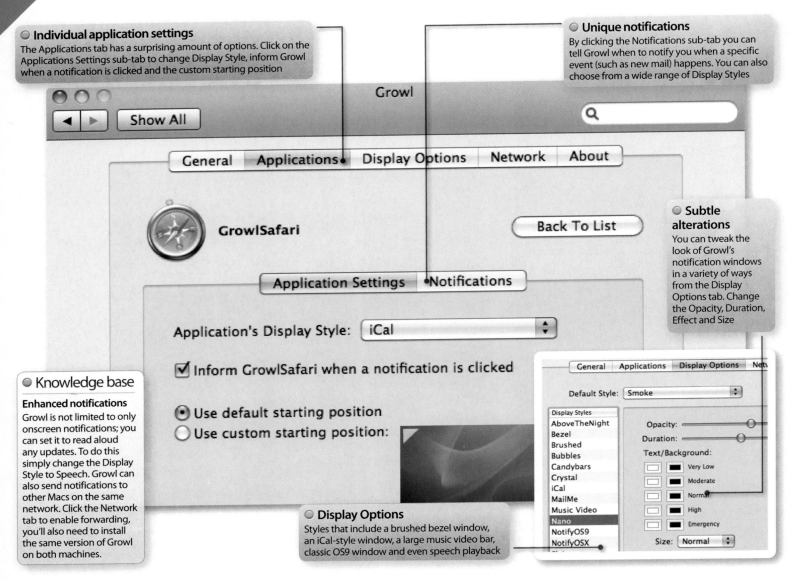

Subtle alterations
You can tweak the look of Growl's notification windows in a variety of ways from the Display Options tab. Change the Opacity, Duration, Effect and Size

Knowledge base

Enhanced notifications
Growl is not limited to only onscreen notifications; you can set it to read aloud any updates. To do this simply change the Display Style to Speech. Growl can also send notifications to other Macs on the same network. Click the Network tab to enable forwarding, you'll also need to install the same version of Growl on both machines.

Display Options
Styles that include a brushed bezel window, an iCal-style window, a large music video bar, classic OS9 window and even speech playback

Enhance Mac apps with Growl notifications

Want to increase your productivity? Be alerted to new mail messages, hardware changes, completed downloads and more…

Task: Learn how to use Growl to enhance application notifications

Difficulty: Intermediate

Time needed: 15 minutes

X Mac OS X includes many features to notify you of new messages, changes to an application, updates and hardware alterations. These can include bouncing icons in the Dock and red badges. But what if you prefer to hide the Dock or have located it on a secondary screen? You might miss an important email or system update, only to spot it when you're about to turn off your machine.

That's where Growl comes to the rescue. Growl is a useful add-on that enhances notifications for a handful of Apple applications and the Finder, and it will enable you to both see and hear prompts when applications want to alert you to something. So follow us over the next two pages as we explain how to install and use Growl notifications…

Step-by-step | Growl Use Growl to enhance application notifications

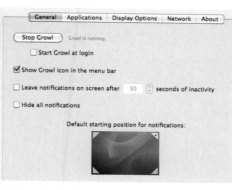

1: Download for free
Download Growl from www.growl.info – it's totally free and only 5.4MB in size. You'll also find a copy on this issue's CD.

2: The Growl icon
Once installed, System Preferences will pop up. It's useful to have the Growl icon in the Finder menu, so click the 'Show Growl icon in the menu bar' button.

3: Increase the Growl
By default, Growl only supports notifications from itself – which isn't much help. Open the Growl disk image on your desktop and you'll see an Extras folder.

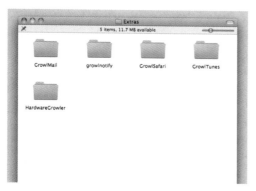

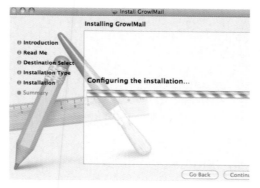

4: Add more apps
Inside are add-ons that add Growl support for Apple's Mail, Safari, iTunes and third-party hardware, such as portable hard drives and USB sticks.

5: Mail notifications
We suggest installing GrowlMail and GrowlSafari, which both notify you of completed downloads, new mail, junk mail and more.

6: Restart Growl
In the System Preferences Growl panel click the Applications tab. If nothing appears, click the Growl icon in the Finder menu, then Restart Growl.

7: Configure apps
You should now see all of the supported running apps in the Growl Applications window. You can customise any programs by clicking the Configure button.

8: Display styles
The Display Style drop-down menu enables you to change how Growl notifies you of new events. Choose one and you'll see a preview of it on the desktop.

9: Customise the look
You can further change the appearance of notifications using the Display Options tab. You'll find options to alter the Opacity, Duration, Size and more here.

Tutorial: Add iCal events using Automator

Tired of opening iCal and manually adding Events? Use Automator to simplify and speed up the process…

Task: Use Automator's iCal Events action

Difficulty: Beginner

Time needed: 5 minutes

iCal is a fantastic app for managing your events, birthdays and to-dos. With only a few clicks you can add a custom event to any date, with location details, from-and-to dates, repeats, attendees, attachments and alarms.

But what if you're busy working in an application and quickly want to add an event to iCal without closing the current window and switching programs? There's an easy solution using Automator – Apple's clever scripting program that takes time-consuming processes and simplifies them into one click. Follow us over the next two pages as we explain how to create an Automator script that enables you to add an event to iCal.

Step-by-step | Automator Quickly update iCal with new events via Automator

1: Launch Automator
Open Automator. If you're running Mac OS X 10.5 choose Custom from the drop-down window. Mac OS X 10.6 users should click the Application button.

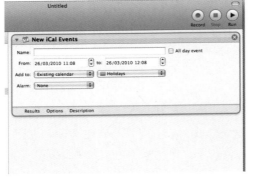

2: New iCal Events
Click on the Calendar listing in the left-hand column, and double-click the New iCal Events action. The action details will appear in the main window.

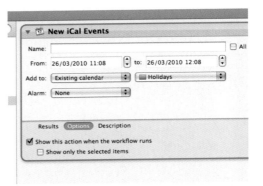

3: Detailed options
Click the Options button at the bottom of the action window, and enable the button that says 'Show this action when the workflow runs'.

4: Customising details
By clicking this button you're telling Automator to make this action interactive, enabling you to customise the details of each new iCal Event.

5: No need to name
Don't worry about adding a name right now, as it's likely each new iCal Event will be unique. This is how our new iCal Events box looks.

6: Saving…
Click the File button in the Finder and choose Save. Give your new action a name, such as "Create iCal Event". Under File Format, choose Application.

The Automator iCal Events action

Discover how easy it is to use Automator

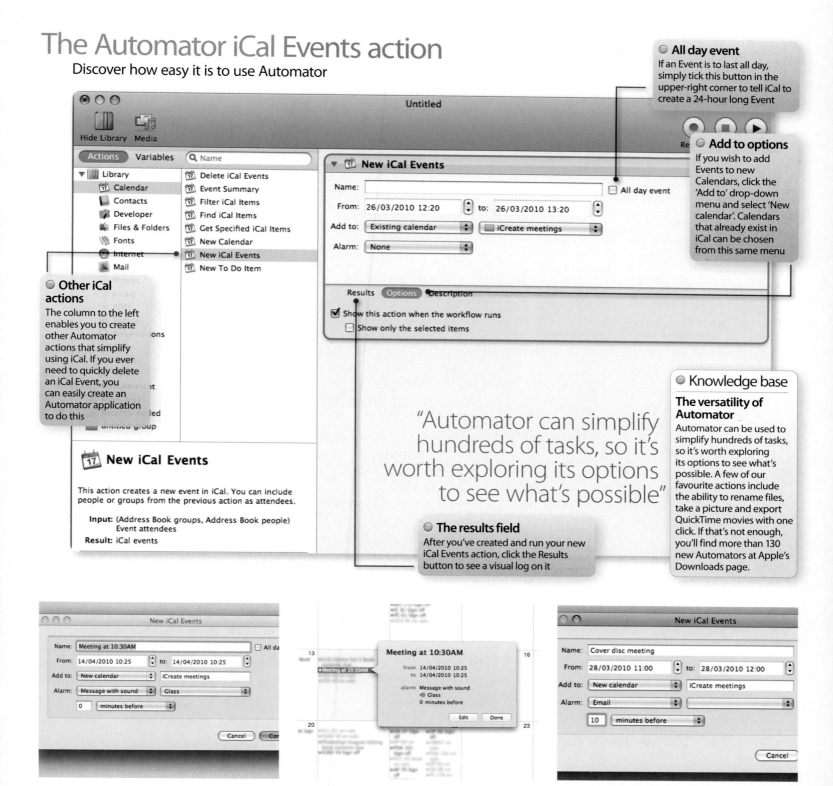

○ All day event
If an Event is to last all day, simply tick this button in the upper-right corner to tell iCal to create a 24-hour long Event

○ Add to options
If you wish to add Events to new Calendars, click the 'Add to' drop-down menu and select 'New calendar'. Calendars that already exist in iCal can be chosen from this same menu

○ Other iCal actions
The column to the left enables you to create other Automator actions that simplify using iCal. If you ever need to quickly delete an iCal Event, you can easily create an Automator application to do this

New iCal Events

This action creates a new event in iCal. You can include people or groups from the previous action as attendees.

Input: (Address Book groups, Address Book people) Event attendees
Result: iCal events

"Automator can simplify hundreds of tasks, so it's worth exploring its options to see what's possible"

○ The results field
After you've created and run your new iCal Events action, click the Results button to see a visual log on it

○ Knowledge base

The versatility of Automator
Automator can be used to simplify hundreds of tasks, so it's worth exploring its options to see what's possible. A few of our favourite actions include the ability to rename files, take a picture and export QuickTime movies with one click. If that's not enough, you'll find more than 130 new Automators at Apple's Downloads page.

7: Testing
You have now created your own custom application that adds new Events to iCal. Test it by closing both iCal and Automator, and running the application.

8: Event added!
Once you've entered the details into the application window, click the Continue button and the Event will be added to iCal.

9: Finer details
It's not possible to add attendees, URLs or attachments via this method, but it's still a great way to add simple Events without opening iCal.

Check your preferences

If you don't see connected servers in the Shared section of the sidebar when you mount a remote drive, make sure Connected Servers is selected in the Finder Preferences

Careful where you drag

If you drag a file or folder over an item in the Devices or Shared sections of the sidebar, the file or folder will be copied to the device or shared item

Knowledge base

Single-click behaviour
Applications and folders in the sidebar and toolbar behave differently to how they normally work on the desktop. For example, you double-click a folder or application to open or launch it in the desktop, but single-click on the icon of a file or application in a Finder window sidebar.

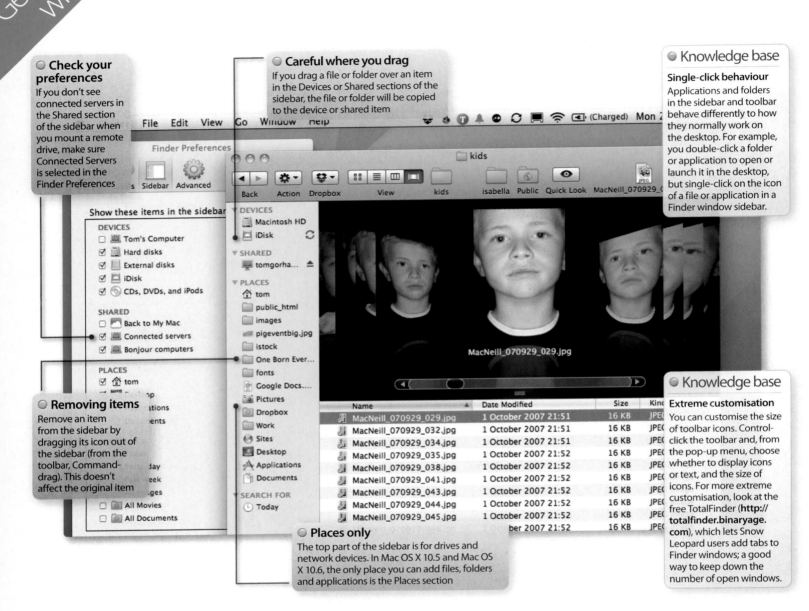

Removing items

Remove an item from the sidebar by dragging its icon out of the sidebar (from the toolbar, Command-drag). This doesn't affect the original item

Places only

The top part of the sidebar is for drives and network devices. In Mac OS X 10.5 and Mac OS X 10.6, the only place you can add files, folders and applications is the Places section

Knowledge base

Extreme customisation
You can customise the size of toolbar icons. Control-click the toolbar and, from the pop-up menu, choose whether to display icons or text, and the size of icons. For more extreme customisation, look at the free TotalFinder (**http://totalfinder.binaryage.com**), which lets Snow Leopard users add tabs to Finder windows; a good way to keep down the number of open windows.

Tutorial: Add locations to Finder windows

Finder windows are more useful than you might think – not only can they provide shortcuts, but they make it easier to mount remote servers

Task: Add shortcuts to files in Finder windows

Difficulty: Beginner

Time needed: 10 minutes

Mac OS X's Finder is often criticised by users who complain it's difficult to navigate, which makes it awkward to find files or folders. Yes, it could be improved, but it's already more flexible than many think. In particular, Finder windows can be customised to make file navigation a cinch. Keeping links to files and folders in a Finder window sidebar is a great timesaver, particularly in the Finder's Column view. Instead of navigating multiple folder windows to move files, you can just put a commonly used folder in the sidebar and drag files to it from the Finder window.

Storing remote folders from a network server or an FTP site in the sidebar gives a near-persistent connection. If you store your login details in your Mac's keychain, opening a remote folder in the sidebar will log you in to the server.

Step-by-step | Finder Add locations to Finder windows

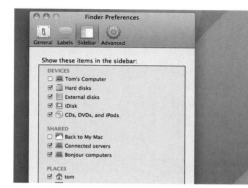

1: Configure the sidebar
In the Finder choose Finder>Preferences. Click the Sidebar tab and remove the checkmarks from any items you don't want to see in the window's sidebar.

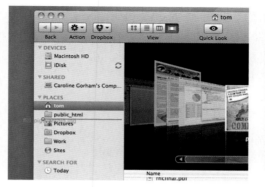

2: Add sidebar items
To add files, folders and applications to the sidebar, open a Finder window and drag the item to the Places section of the sidebar.

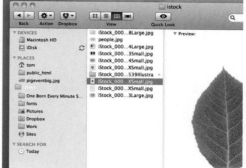

3: Reordering
You can rearrange the items in the sidebar by dragging them. The horizontal line indicates the location the item will occupy when you release the mouse button.

4: Use the toolbar too
You can also add items to the toolbar above the Finder window. Just click and drag files, folders or applications to the toolbar to add them.

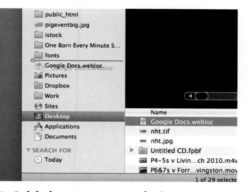

5: Add shortcuts to websites
Drag the icon from a browser's URL field to the desktop and, from there, to the sidebar or toolbar. When you click it you'll go to that site in the browser.

6: Connect remotely
Connect to a local server or remote network drive. In the Finder, select Go>Connect To Server. If prompted, store any login information in your Mac's keychain.

7: Add to Places
The drive will appear under the Shared section. But you should also drag a folder from the shared drive to the Places section of the Finder window.

8: Persistent connection
Now, even when the remote drive is disconnected, the folder will remain in the sidebar. With the password stored, it connects to the drive when you click it.

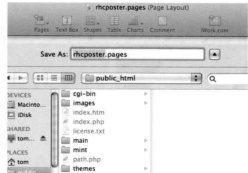

9: Connect within applications
This is handy if you want to save items to a remote drive from within apps. The folder appears in Open and Save dialogs and can log in when selected.

Update your TomTom

Put your Mac to good use by updating your sat nav with new maps, points of interest, voices and more

Task: Use the TomTom HOME app for Mac OS X
Difficulty: Beginner
Time needed: 20 minutes

Satellite navigation systems have transformed the way we drive cars these days. Now we blindly follow our sat nav units the wrong way up one-way streets, into muddy fields only fit for a farmer's tractor, down country lanes too narrow to fit through, and into streams that the device swears is a ford that will only come half-way up the wheels. Joking aside, sat nav systems are really useful devices, and they help us get to wherever we want to go without having to stop and try to read a map or rely on your partner's dodgy map-reading skills. Sat nav systems can be updated with the latest maps and corrections, and even with brand new maps covering different areas. They can have extra information added to them, such as points of interest, various attractions, theme parks and shopping centres. They can also have extra voices installed, new graphics, and so on. All this is achieved by plugging the device into your Mac and using free software from TomTom's website.

Step-by-step | TomTom HOME Getting started with the TomTom HOME software

1: Download the software
Start Safari and enter www.tomtom.com/home into the address box. Follow the links to the download for TomTom HOME and click the Apple Mac software link.

2: Install the app
Open the Downloads folder and choose the 'TomTom HOME.dmg' file. To install it simply drag it to the Applications folder in the usual way for Mac apps.

3: First steps
Double-click TomTom HOME in the Applications folder. You will be asked to select the country and agree to the license agreement. Click 'I agree' to continue.

4: Create an account
You can browse the products and services, but to download or use them you need an account. Click the Log In button and choose Create Account.

5: Enter your details
Enter your email address and a password for your account. When you have created your account you will automatically be logged in next time.

6: Plug in the TomTom
Connect the TomTom by plugging in the USB cable and then turn it on. A message on the TomTom screen asks if you want to connect to the computer. Press Yes.

Update your sat nav with Mac OS X

Going abroad this summer? Add a map of the country to your sat nav

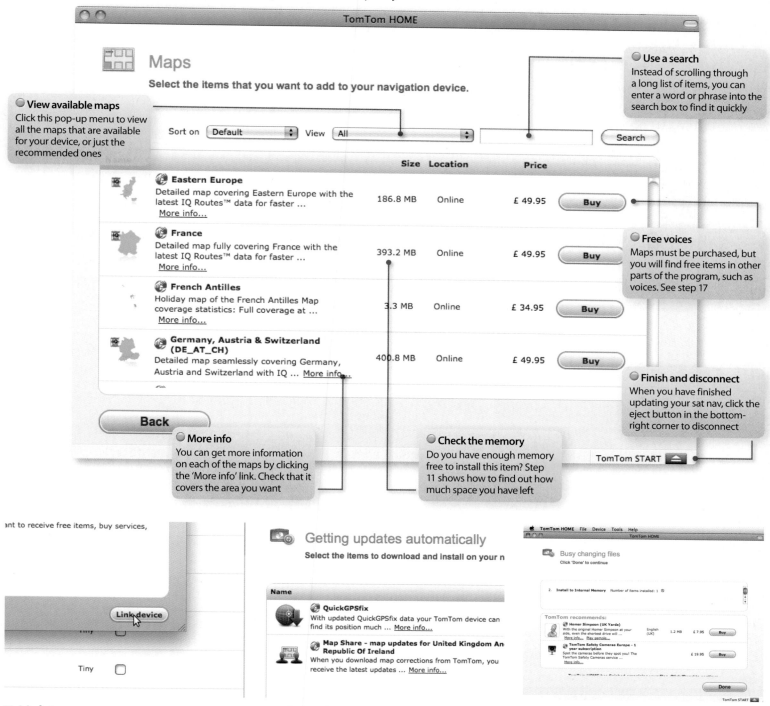

Use a search
Instead of scrolling through a long list of items, you can enter a word or phrase into the search box to find it quickly

View available maps
Click this pop-up menu to view all the maps that are available for your device, or just the recommended ones

TomTom HOME

Maps

Select the items that you want to add to your navigation device.

Sort on [Default ▼] View [All ▼] [ ] [Search]

		Size	Location	Price	
	Eastern Europe Detailed map covering Eastern Europe with the latest IQ Routes™ data for faster ... More info...	186.8 MB	Online	£ 49.95	[Buy]
	France Detailed map fully covering France with the latest IQ Routes™ data for faster ... More info...	393.2 MB	Online	£ 49.95	[Buy]
	French Antilles Holiday map of the French Antilles Map coverage statistics: Full coverage at ... More info...	3.3 MB	Online	£ 34.95	[Buy]
	Germany, Austria & Switzerland (DE_AT_CH) Detailed map seamlessly covering Germany, Austria and Switzerland with IQ ... More info...	400.8 MB	Online	£ 49.95	[Buy]

Free voices
Maps must be purchased, but you will find free items in other parts of the program, such as voices. See step 17

Finish and disconnect
When you have finished updating your sat nav, click the eject button in the bottom-right corner to disconnect

[Back]

TomTom START [⏏]

More info
You can get more information on each of the maps by clicking the 'More info' link. Check that it covers the area you want

Check the memory
Do you have enough memory free to install this item? Step 11 shows how to find out how much space you have left

---

...nt to receive free items, buy services,

[Link device]

Tiny ☐

7: Link to your account
The device restarts and the Mac detects that the TomTom is connected. Click 'Link device' to link the sat nav that is connected to the account you created.

Getting updates automatically

Select the items to download and install on your n

Name	
	QuickGPSfix With updated QuickGPSfix data your TomTom device can find its position much ... More info...
	Map Share - map updates for United Kingdom An Republic Of Ireland When you download map corrections from TomTom, you receive the latest updates ... More info...

8: Check for updates
Each time you connect, you'll see a list of updates. You will probably find that a couple are ticked already, but tick any others you would like.

TomTom HOME File Device Tools Help
TomTom HOME

Busy changing files
Click 'Done' to continue

2. **Install to Internal Memory** Number of items installed: 1

TomTom recommends:

	Homer Simpson (UK Yards) With the original Homer Simpson at your side, even the shortest drive will ... More info... Play sample...	English (UK)	1.2 MB	£ 7.95	[Buy]
	TomTom Safety Cameras Europe - 1 year subscription Spot the cameras before they spot you! The TomTom Safety Cameras service ... More info...			£ 19.95	[Buy]

[Done]

TomTom START

9: Install the updates
Click the Update button for the items to be downloaded and installed. You'll then see a report and some recommendations.

10: Manage your device

There are two pages of items you can switch between by clicking the arrow. Go to page two and click the Manage My Start icon (we're using a TomTom Start).

11: What's on the device?

Select the 'Items on device' tab to see what is installed on your TomTom. The total device memory, the amount that's free and how much is used is shown.

12: Remove unwanted items

There's lots of free memory on a new device, but you might eventually run short of space. You can remove items to free up memory, such as some of the voices.

13: Copy to the Mac

Select all the foreign language voices and click 'Copy items to computer'. Return to Manage My Start and remove them (you'll see them in 'Items on computer').

14: Back up and restore

It's a good idea to back up the device, so return to the home page and click 'Back up and Restore'. Click 'Back up my device', then 'Back up now'.

15: Restore the data

Clicking 'Restore my device' doesn't give a choice of backups and only the most recent is restored. Click 'Restore Now' if you need the device back as it was.

16: Add extra content

Return to the home screen and click the Add Traffic, Voices, Safety Cameras icon. There are several sub-options, but let's try 'Points of interest'.

17: Browse the items

You can browse the items on offer – some are free, but others have to be purchased. Click the Buy or Add button next to the item you want to download.

18: Add new voices

Now click Back and choose the option to add voices. You'll find Homer Simpson, Knight Rider and John Cleese among others.

Change the search order in Spotlight

Make the search system in Mac OS X more efficient and tailored to your specific needs

Task: Change the search order of items indexed by Spotlight

Difficulty: Beginner

Time needed: 5 minutes

X It's a little known fact that everything on your Mac is indexed so that it can be searched for. This even includes pictures you've named in iPhoto as well as those pictures you've tagged using Faces and Places. It's also a little known fact that you can take control of Spotlight and make it work for your specific needs. Each time you run a search the entire system is checked, then Mac OS X presents the findings in a predetermined order. It's possible, in the System Preferences, to alter this order of results so it suits the things that you search for the most. The process is very simple and completely reversible, so if it's not working for you then you can revert back to the old system.

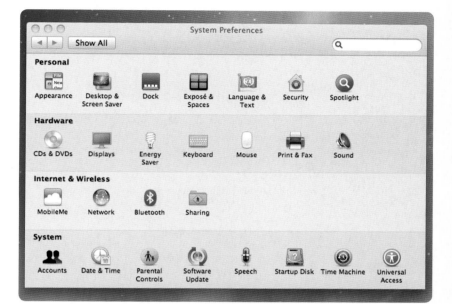

"Take control of Spotlight and make it work for your needs"

Step-by-step | Mac OS X Customise Spotlight

1: Lock and load

Start by loading System Preferences from the Dock, the Applications folder or from the Apple menu at the top of the screen. Now select the Spotlight option.

Spotlight helps you quickly find things on your computer. Spotlight is located at the top right corner of the screen.

	Search Results	Privacy	

Drag categories to change the order in which results appear.
Only selected categories will appear in Spotlight search results.

1	☑	Applications
2	☑	System Preferences
3	☑	Documents
4	☑	Folders
5	☑	Mail Messages
6	☑	Contacts
7	☑	Events & To Do Items
8	☑	Images
9	☑	PDF Documents
10	☑	Webpages
11	☑	Music
12	☑	Movies

2: Drag and drop

In the Search Results section you can now drag and drop the different categories into an order that suits you best. You can also untick the categories you do not wish to be shown.

Configure a Magic Mouse in Mac OS X

Learn how to apply the clicks and swipes that make your new mouse such a magical tool for your Mac

Task: Set up your Magic Mouse

Difficulty: Beginner

Time needed: 10 minutes

X If you're lucky enough to have one of the latest iMacs, you'll have been bestowed with one of the finest control devices Apple has ever created. For the rest of us, the Magic Mouse is a quick trip to the Apple Store away and, in our opinion, worth every penny. The touch controls across the back of the mouse mean that the swipes you're used to on an iPhone, iPod touch or iPad can be used when browsing the web or flicking through photos. When you become accustomed to such luxuries on your iPhone and iPod, and even on the new MacBook trackpads, it's a shame to have to go back to the old Mighty Mouse that was once seen as such a brilliant tool.

In this tutorial we'll show you how to make the most of your Magic Mouse, set the buttons up as you wish and make use of the swiping and scrolling features across its Multi-Touch surface. It's a simple task that requires a couple of clicks within your Mac's System Preferences and can make all the difference to the way you work.

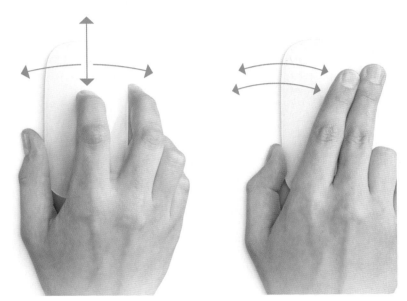

Step-by-step | Mac OS X Magic Mouse settings

1: Track, scroll & click
Under the Mouse section of System Preferences, the first set of sliders sets speed. Tracking determines the speed the cursor moves, Scrolling sets the scroll speed and Double-Click sets the speed for double clicks.

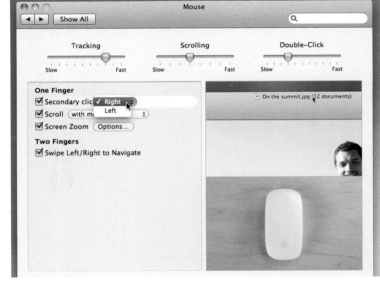

2: Right (or left) clicks
Using the drop-down menu below One Finger, under Secondary click, you can set which finger you will use to left- or right-click your mouse. The video on the right will show you your choice in action.

Magic Mouse Preferences
Customise the settings to suit your requirements

Scrolling momentum
Momentum means that you can flick a finger and let the display scroll freely rather than stop when you lift your finger. It also feels great to do!

Video preview
These little videos show you what changes you have made to your Magic Mouse and how to make use of them

Mouse speed
Using the sliders across the top of the display, you can adjust the speed your cursor moves and your mouse scrolls. You can also reduce or increase the delay between double clicks

Swiping
Two fingers sliding across the back of the Magic Mouse add even more control options, such as flipping through pictures and moving between pages in your web browser

Knowledge base

Available Magic Mouse functions
Click - One finger to select an item or button
Two-button click - Both fingers together makes a secondary click
360-degree scroll - Scroll in any direction using one finger
Screen zoom - One finger plus the Command key
Two-finger swipe - Two-finger swipe for web or image viewing

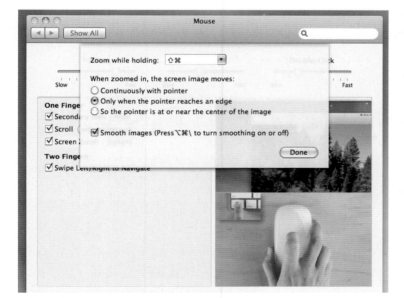

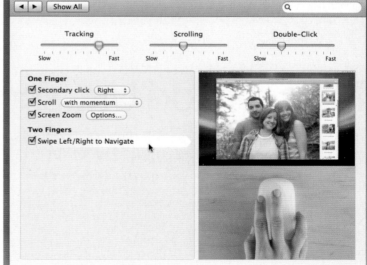

3: Screen zoom
Clicking Options next to Screen Zoom, you can determine which key you can hold down in order to zoom in on your entire screen. Further options allow you to focus your zoom by moving the cursor.

4: Swipe navigation
The Two Fingers section allows you to turn on the ability to swipe back and forth between pages in Safari, files in Cover Flow or across pictures in iPhoto. Many apps make use of this feature, so try it out.

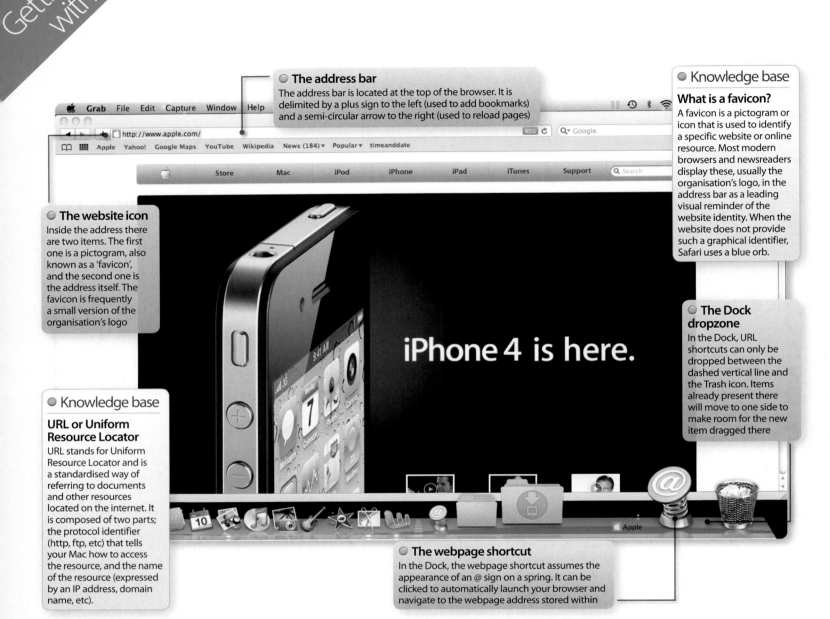

The address bar
The address bar is located at the top of the browser. It is delimited by a plus sign to the left (used to add bookmarks) and a semi-circular arrow to the right (used to reload pages)

Knowledge base

What is a favicon?
A favicon is a pictogram or icon that is used to identify a specific website or online resource. Most modern browsers and newsreaders display these, usually the organisation's logo, in the address bar as a leading visual reminder of the website identity. When the website does not provide such a graphical identifier, Safari uses a blue orb.

The website icon
Inside the address there are two items. The first one is a pictogram, also known as a 'favicon', and the second one is the address itself. The favicon is frequently a small version of the organisation's logo

The Dock dropzone
In the Dock, URL shortcuts can only be dropped between the dashed vertical line and the Trash icon. Items already present there will move to one side to make room for the new item dragged there

Knowledge base

URL or Uniform Resource Locator
URL stands for Uniform Resource Locator and is a standardised way of referring to documents and other resources located on the internet. It is composed of two parts; the protocol identifier (http, ftp, etc) that tells your Mac how to access the resource, and the name of the resource (expressed by an IP address, domain name, etc).

The webpage shortcut
In the Dock, the webpage shortcut assumes the appearance of an @ sign on a spring. It can be clicked to automatically launch your browser and navigate to the webpage address stored within

Tutorial: Add URL shortcuts to the Dock

We show you a simple and easy way to create URL Dock shortcuts to gain one-click access to your favourite and most-frequented websites

Task: Add a webpage shortcut to the Dock

Difficulty: Beginner

Time needed: 5 minutes

Do you require quick access to a specific website and need to open that online resource in just one click? Wouldn't it just be so convenient to be able to access that source of information quickly, without first having to open your browser and wade through your maze of bookmark folders?

Well, the Dock is here to help you achieve this. Indeed, this very elegant and beautiful feature of the Mac OS X interface cannot only help you access the most useful utilities and software in your system, but also offer you a very simple and quick way to access your favourite website.

Adding the webpage URL (Uniform Resource Locator) to the Dock and making it a clickable item is one of the easiest operations to carry out on your Mac. Furthermore, this is only a drag-and-drop away and will result in a neat '@ on a spring' icon sitting nicely in your Dock.

Step-by-step | Mac OS X Dock URL shortcuts in the Dock

1: Open your browser
Either from the Dock or the Applications folder, start Safari and, using your bookmark, open the website for which you wish to create a shortcut in the Dock.

2: Locate the Address bar
In Safari, the address bar is located at the top of your browser. It is the zone that contains the text starting with the URL of the website.

3: Locate the website 'favicon'
In the address bar, locate the favicon (it is situated between the plus sign and the website address). This is either a blue orb or a website-specific icon.

4: Locate the Dock target area
In the Dock, locate the area between the dash line separating the left side of the Dock and the Trash. It may already contain folders and website shortcuts.

5: Grab the address
Back in Safari, click on the website favicon in the address bar. Without releasing the favicon, start to move towards the bottom of your screen.

6: Drag the URL shortcut
Without releasing the click, continue moving towards the Dock target area identified in Step 4. Stop on top of it but do not release the click yet.

7: Make room for your shortcut
Make sure you drop the address being dragged into an empty space in the Dock. The items already present will move to one side to make room for it.

8: Drop the URL shortcut
Now complete the drag-and-drop move initiated in Step 5 and release the click. Completion will be indicated by the appearance of an '@ on a spring'.

9: Remove the URL Dock item
If the shortcut needs to be updated, click on it and, without releasing, move it out of the Dock. Release the item and it will disappear in a puff of smoke…

Access your own portable Wi-Fi with MiFi

There's nothing worse than not being able to access the web when you need it. The iPhone was our answer, but what about those of us with an iPod touch, an iPad or a MacBook? The answer is MiFi...

Task: Connect a MiFi to your Mac, iPod & iPad
Difficulty: Beginner
Time needed: 15 minutes

At the start of the internet revolution we were tied to our desk, Mac and modem, but then our laptops were freed by home wireless connections like Apple's AirPort. Now we've got a wealth of options, from free Wi-Fi hotspots at airports and coffee shops to wireless networks on planes and trains. Unfortunately, the world can be quite cruel and that usually means that when you really need a Wi-Fi signal away from your home, you won't be able to find one. Even worse is when you find a wireless hotspot and you're asked to pay for the privilege. The wireless world hasn't quite taken off on the scale we all expected, and so the iPhone has done a great job of helping us out with its Edge and 3G

connections, as well as Wi-Fi when it's available. But what about those of us with an iPod touch or an iPad that lacks the cellular data access? The answer is simple and is referred to on both sides of the Atlantic as MiFi. Offered by the 3 network in the UK (**www.three.co.uk**), the device connects to the network and transmits it to your computer, iPod or iPad as a Wi-Fi signal. 3's UK network is capable of a maximum speed of 3.6Mbps (although the company promotes 2.6Mbps as standard), which means a decent speed for email, web and even streaming and downloading on the move. You will need to buy a SIM card for your MiFi as part of a monthly plan or on a pay-as-you-go basis with very reasonable rates available. Here's how it works...

Step-by-step | MiFi Connect to a portable Wi-Fi network

1: Put it together
Before you start you'll need to insert the SIM card that shipped with your MiFi (or was bought separately) and also insert the battery into the device.

2: Charging time
It is recommended that you charge your MiFi for a full 12 hours before first use with the provided adaptor. The green battery light should blink until charged.

3: Power it up
Once you've charged your MiFi, you're ready to start it up. Hold down the power button for two seconds and wait for the signal light to turn green.

4: Ready for Wi-Fi
Once connected to the network, hold down the Wi-Fi button for two seconds. This allows you to connect your devices to the MiFi.

5: Connect
Holding down the connect key will now connect the dots and make sure your MiFi can connect to the network. A solid blue light means success.

6: Connect to a Mac
On the Mac you wish to connect your MiFi to, head to System Preferences via the Apple menu in the top-left of the screen and select the Network option.

Understanding MiFi

A quick look at the hardware involved

● Display
The screen shows a variety of lights to denote Signal, Mode, Battery, Wi-Fi and Roaming. The solid green and blue lights denote good connections

● Charging
The MiFi comes with a mains charger and USB cable, and can be charged via both methods. Mains charging is the fastest option

● Knowledge base

Monitor your usage
As a general rule, using 1GB of data on your MiFi will allow for the following:

• 10 hours web browsing
• Send 1,000 HTML emails
• Download 32 songs
• Download five four-minute videos

● Wi-Fi key
This button turns on the MiFi's Wi-Fi and allows it to be seen by your other devices and for them to connect to it

● Connect key
This button connects your MiFi to the network and begins sending the information to connected devices, such as laptops, iPods and iPads

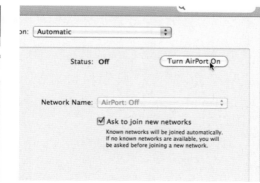

7: AirPort connection
If an AirPort connection isn't present in the side panel, click the plus button to add and name one. This is what you will use to connect to your MiFi.

8: AirPort on
Click on the AirPort option in the side panel to show AirPort network options. If AirPort is turned off, click the Turn AirPort On button.

9: Select your network
From the Network Name drop-down menu, select your MiFi. The default name is referred to as an SSID code and can be found on a card with your device.

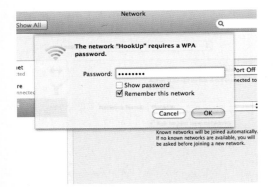

10: Enter the password
On the same card as your SSID name you will also find a default password, which you will be asked for when you connect to the network. Enter it now.

11: All done!
You should now be able to use Safari and other web-based tools using your MiFi connection. Head to any website to check your connection.

12: Connect to iPod and iPhone
It's even easier to connect your MiFi to an iPod touch or an iPhone. Start by heading to the Settings app on your homescreen.

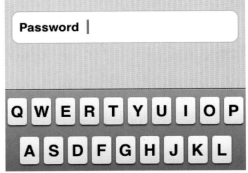

13: Select the Wi-Fi
There's a Wi-Fi option at the top of the list in Settings, which will allow you to find new networks. Click on it to access the menu.

14: Find your MiFi
As with the connection to your Mac, the MiFi will show up with its default SSID name on the menu. Use the same password as before when prompted.

15: Connect to iPad
On the homescreen of your iPad you can access the iPad's settings by clicking on the Settings app. From here, move into the Wi-Fi section of Settings.

16: Locate the MiFi
Your MiFi connection should appear on the list of available networks on your iPad. Select your MiFi's SSID name to connect to it.

17: Access the network
Use your unique Wi-Fi Key found on the card that came with your MiFi to log in to the network by entering it into the field that appears.

18: Time for 3
Once you have access to the web via your device you can access your own space at www.three.co.uk/my3 (UK users only) to check your account details.

iCandy
MacBook battery

MacBook battery No longer do MacBook users need to turn their laptop over to see how much juice they have left

61

20 Expert tips

Surf the web faster, avoid problems and speed up your Mac with this collection of top tips from the experts

Have you ever wondered how the experts use their Macs? What applications do they use, what techniques do they employ to speed up everyday tasks, solve problems and keep their computers running smoothly? We collected some of the top tips from three Mac experts, which has resulted in a diverse collection that covers a wide range of subjects. Some of the tips are quite straightforward and are useful to everyone, but a few are more advanced. Not everyone is a beginner, of course, and once you've learnt the basics you'll be keen to get to grips with some more advanced topics. So there's something for everyone here, and after employing these top tips you'll be using your Mac like an expert.

Meet the experts

Dave Hamilton is the president and CEO of The Mac Observer (**www.macobserver. com**) and co-founder of BackBeat Media (**www. backbeatmedia.com**). You can and listen to him every week on the Mac Geek Gab podcast or follow him on Twitter (**www.twitter.com/ davehamilton**).

Tina Roth Eisenberg runs Smissmiss (**www. swiss-miss.com**), a design blog and studio. She grew up in Switzerland and was influenced by Swiss design and fresh mountain air. She's now based in New York and has worked at several top design firms. Tina runs a simple browser-based to-do app called TeuxDeux.

Roland Waddilove was the editor of *Electron User* and *Atari St User* in the Eighties, the editor of *PC Today* and *PC Home* in the Nineties, and is now a freelance writer and occasional programmer. He also runs the RAW Computing website (**www. rawcomputing.co.uk**).

1. Restart your Mac

Dave Hamilton: "Reboot! Not daily (this ain't Windows after all), but at least once every two weeks." Some people use their Macs 24/7 for backups, as a media server, networking, and more. Or they simply put them to sleep rather than shutting down completely. That's okay and it won't do any harm, but restarting the Mac occasionally clears out the memory and breathes life into a slow machine.

2. Email pages and links

Tina Roth Eisenberg: Tina's most used application is Safari and it has lots of handy features. For example, if you want to email the web page you are currently looking at, press Cmd+I. But if all you want to do is send a link to the page, then press Cmd+Shift+I. You can also click and drag the URL from the address box, or click and drag a link on a web page and drop it on the Mail icon in the Dock to create a new email containing it.

"Restarting the Mac occasionally clears out the memory and breathes life into a slow machine"

3. Clean up with OnyX

Dave Hamilton: "Run OnyX every three months with all of the options ticked (except 'Display of folders content' and 'Web Browser Cache and History'). Keeping your Mac from getting bogged down and cleaning up the cruft can keep you happy forever." OnyX (**http://bit.ly/6f77vT**) is a free utility that provides lots of functions for cleaning up the Mac's hard disk drive and checking it for problems. It clears out caches, repairs permissions, rebuilds indexes and executes maintenance scripts. It may take a while to complete all the operations, but it's an essential tool that everyone should have.

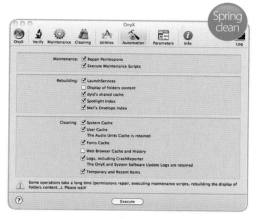

Spring clean

4. Window snapshots

Tina Roth Eisenberg: "To take a screenshot of an entire window with a drop shadow effect, hold down the Command+Shift+4 keys, then press the Spacebar. Instead of a cross-hair cursor, a small camera icon will appear. When you move this camera icon over the element you'd like to capture, that element will be highlighted. Now click your mouse or trackpad and you've captured a screenshot of just that element – with no further cleanup required." We used this capturing technique for the screenshots throughout this feature, and it worked brilliantly.

5. Multicoloured TextEdit

More fun

Roland Waddilove: "Changing a document's background colour in TextEdit isn't obvious. Go to the Format menu and select Font>Show Fonts. The fourth item along the Toolbar in the Fonts dialog is used for setting the document's background colour. Click it and the Color dialog will appear, and you can choose a colour from the palette."

6 Rectangular TextEdit blocks

Roland Waddilove: "Enter some text into TextEdit or load a text document into it. Hold down the Option key and you'll see the mouse cursor turn into crosshairs. Now you can click and drag a rectangle in the text to select it. Press Command+C and the text within the rectangle is copied. To confirm this, create a new TextEdit document and press Command+V to paste in the text. Notice that it retains its rectangular shape."

7. Monitor the CPU and RAM

More speed

Dave Hamilton: "Run iStatMenus or MenuMeters to monitor CPU and RAM usage. The former will let you see if you've got a process chewing up your processor's time, and the latter will tell you if you need to quit apps (or perhaps get more physical RAM)." iStatMenus (**www.islayer.com/apps**) and MenuMeters (**http://bit.ly/xxc3p**) add CPU, RAM usage, disk usage and internet usage meters to the desktop menu bar. They are very useful for monitoring the system and detecting when something is misbehaving, such as an app using up all the RAM or hogging the CPU. MenuMeters is free and iStatMenus is $16 (but there is a free Dashboard version available).

"Add CPU, RAM, disk and internet usage meters to the desktop"

8. Use the Console to solve problems

Cool code

Roland Waddilove: "Mac OS X creates log files that contain a record of every event that happens. This includes successfully completed tasks along with errors and crashes. The Console is an application that allows you to view these logs and you can use it to track down problems. Start the Console in the Applications/Utilities folder and you'll see a panel on the left with lots of categories of logs. Expand the sections and select the logs, and see what's displayed in the main pane on the right. The Console won't always tell you what is wrong or how to fix it, but with a bit of luck you might be able to spot the cause and do something about it."

Don't worry if you don't understand everything in the logs, just try to spot error messages. Useful logs are All Messages and Console Messages under Database Searches in the left panel. Another useful one is system.log under Files. If you see an error message about an application, see if there's an update from the supplier or try removing it and re-installing it.

9. Scan for wireless networks

Roland Waddilove: "iStumbler (**www.istumbler.net**) scans for networks and displays a list of every one found. It displays lots of useful information, like the security used, protocol, signal strength, noise, channel, and much more. It can even work out your location and display it on Google Maps. Armed with this information, you can easily see which networks you can log on to in public places and which has the best signal and least interference. At home, check the Channel column. Your wireless router should use a different one to your neighbours or the signals will clash and your wireless connection will be poor."

When there are two or more wireless networks, interference can cause reception problems. In public places or work you may have access to several Wi-Fi access points, and you should connect to the one with the strongest signal. At home, ensure the channel that your router uses isn't used by someone else. Pick a channel that's at least two away from your neighbours.

No cables

10. Test your internet connection

Roland Waddilove: "If you are having problems with your internet connection and want to test it to make sure it's working okay, there are two Terminal commands that will help: Ping and Host. Start Terminal in the Applications/Utilities folder and enter 'ping www.google.com'. Packets of information are sent to the URL entered and the website responds. Stop Ping by pressing Ctrl+C. If all packets are transmitted and received, your internet connection and the website are fine. If you enter 'host www.google.com', the result is the IP address of the web server and the Host command tests that the DNS server, usually run by your ISP, is working okay."

Ping tests whether a web server or computer is responding to requests and Host tests the system that turns URLs that we use into IP addresses that computers require. It's a handy tip for exerts.

Speed test

11. Create a copy

Dave Hamilton: "Clone your boot drive with SuperDuper (or Carbon Copy Cloner, though I use the former) daily. Having a Time Machine backup is also essential, but it could take several hours to restore from it and get back up and running. With a cloned drive, however, you simply hold down Option at boot, choose the clone, and you're back up and running as of your last clone." SuperDuper (**http://bit.ly/1q1uF3**) and Carbon Copy Cloner (**www.bombich.com**) are both free tools that can make an exact copy of your Mac's internal disk to a USB drive. In the event of a serious disk problem, you can simply boot from the USB drive and copy it back to the Mac's internal disk to be back to normal again.

Clone drives

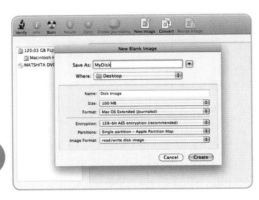

12. Secure your files

Roland Waddilove: "One way to secure your files and prevent others from seeing them is to store them in an encrypted disk image. Start Disk Utility in the Applications/Utilities folder and select File>New>Blank Disk Image. Enter a file name, choose the size and then set the Encryption to 128-bit AES. Click Create and enter a password. It's important that you clear the tick against 'Remember password in my keychain'. The disk image is created and you just double-click it to open it. Use it just like a disk drive and store any files you like."

13. Add security to PDFs

Roland Waddilove: "What if you already have unprotected PDF documents that you would like to protect? If you double-click a PDF file, it will open in Preview. You can then choose File>Save As and you'll see an Encrypt option in the Save dialog. It's better than nothing, but if you want the full security features then choose File>Print instead."

14. Faster web browsing

Roland Waddilove: "Switch to OpenDNS domain name servers and for a faster and more reliable internet. Go to System Preferences, click the Network icon and choose either AirPort or Ethernet depending on your connection type. Click the Advanced button and then the DNS tab. Click the plus button below the DNS Servers list and enter '208.67.222.222'. Now click the plus button again and enter '208.67.220.220'. Click OK and then Apply."

To test that this is working, go to **www.opendns.com/welcome**. To use Google's DNS servers enter '8.8.8.8' and '8.8.4.4' instead of the numbers above. Deleting the entries you added will restore the original DNS servers the Mac was using.

Rapid surfing

Show All

AirPort

AirPort | TCP/IP | DNS

DNS Servers:
208.67.222.222
208.67.220.220

> "Switch to OpenDNS domain name servers for a more reliable internet"

15. Customise the Finder toolbars

Roland Waddilove: "Most people know that they can customise the Finder toolbar and add or remove icons, but did you know that you can also add applications to it? Of course, you can add apps to the Dock, but if it's full just drag your favourites from the Applications folder to the Finder toolbar and drop them. You can start the app by clicking it or by dragging a file from a Finder window and dropping it on the icon."

Good looks

17. Clean up the disk

Dave Hamilton: "Run OmniDiskSweeper once every six months to find all those large files you didn't know were squatting on your drive. As always, if you don't know what something is, don't delete it until you do. Google is your friend, as are those great geeks over at the Mac Geek Gab podcast." OmniDiskSweeper (http://bit.ly/9oNgst) is a free app that displays the contents of the hard disk drive sorted by size. It's easy to find the biggest files and, if you're sure you no longer need them, you can delete them to free up disk space. It's essential when the disk is nearly full.

16. Secure your documents

Roland Waddilove: "In some cases you might want to password protect a document so it can't be opened, or you may want people to open it but not copy text and images out of it. You might even want to prevent people from printing it. All this is possible with the security features in PDF files, but start TextEdit, enter some text and select Save As PDF – and where are the security options? There aren't any! Select File>Print instead, and click the button in the bottom-left corner of the dialog to select Save As PDF. Click the Security Options button and you can set a password required to open the document, to copy text, images or other content, and print it out."

"You can set a password required to open the document or copy text and images"

18. Use Finder's title bar icon

Roland Waddilove: "Open a Finder window and, in the middle of the title bar at the top, is the icon for the folder. If you click it with the mouse you will notice that it highlights. This gives us a clue that it does something. However, left clicking just flashes the icon. If you left click (Ctrl+click) the icon, a pop-up list of folders is displayed. You can see the current folder, the parent, that folder's parent and so on. It goes right back to the top level. Click any of these locations to jump to that folder. Drag the folder off the title bar and drop it on the desktop or in another Finder window to move the currently displayed folder."

Don't do this with the Documents or Applications folders or they'll be moved, possibly causing problems. Try this with a folder containing your own files.

"Try this with a folder containing your files"

19. Auto-download torrents

Tina Roth Eisenberg: One of Tina's favourite apps is Dropbox (www.dropbox.com), which is used to keep files and folders in sync on multiple computers. A great trick some people use is to put an app like Transmission (www.transmissionbt.com) on their Mac at home and go to the Preferences>Directories section and set it to automatically download .torrents from the Dropbox folder. If you're out or at work and see a file you'd like to download, save the .torrent in your Dropbox and your home computer will automatically download it while you're out and about.

Share files

20. Sort Safari bookmarks

Roland Waddilove: "Show the Bookmarks in Safari and select Bookmarks Menu in the left panel. Now create a new folder on the desktop by right-clicking. Arrange the Safari and new folder windows next to each other. Click the first bookmark in the list, hold down Shift and click the last one to select them all. Drag them to the folder you created and drop them. Select the bookmarks again in Safari and drag them to the Trash to delete them. They're gone! Now click a bookmark in the desktop folder and Press Ctrl+A to select them all. Drag them to the empty Safari Bookmarks list and drop them. Safari imports the bookmarks in alphabetical order and the result is a sorted Bookmarks menu."

Discovering

The applications available in iLife will give you access to a world of creativity. Whether your passion is photography, movies, music or the web, the potential is massive…

Contents …

Feature: iLife journal 068
Whether you're new to iLife or a seasoned pro, a great way to get more from each app is to use third-party plug-ins. This guide will point you in the right direction

Feature: Create a website 077
One of the coolest things you can do with a Mac is to create your own website using iWeb. Learn how to get started and get yourself online here

Feature: Are you an artist? 176
We give you a run-down of all the apps you need to become an iLife artist. All you need is a creative spark, this guide and one or more of these applications

Feature: Missing iLife apps 186
Despite our love for all of the iLife apps, there are just some things they can't do. So, we've compiled a feature detailing the apps that Apple should have included in the suite

iPhoto:

Tutorial: Thank-you cards 084
Create incredible thank-you cards using your iPhoto library

Tutorial: Keywords in iPhoto 086
Organise your photos by giving them keywords which you can look up later

Tutorial: Keyword album 088
Create an album using the keywords you have used in iPhoto

Tutorial: Multiple libraries 090
You can keep photos apart by using separate libraries. Here's how to mange them…

Tutorial: Remove blemishes 092
Quickly correct images removing blemishes and even objects

Tutorial: Rate images 094
Another great way to organise your images in iPhoto is to rate them

Tutorial: Background images 096
Tailor your iPhoto images to be used as

Tutorial: Rotate images 098
Learn how to rotate a whole batch of photos in one very simple move

Tutorial: Themed keepsakes 100
Use iPhoto to create a themed album and then turn it into a keepsake

Tutorial: Multiple adjustments 102
Make the same changes to a batch of photos to save time and effort

Tutorial: Manage Places 104
Update images with no geotagging so they appear in your Places albums

iMovie:

Tutorial: Slow motion 106
Learn how to use one of the classic video effects to add flair to a movie

Tutorial: Continuous scenes 108
Use this editing trick to create what looks like one long continuous sequence

Tutorial: Video and stills 110
Combine both video and stills in your iMovie project for varied footage

Tutorial: High-speed action 112
Increase the drama with some high-speed action techniques

Tutorial: Underwater footage 114
Go sub-aqua with your video with this

Tutorial: Cross-processing 116
Use effects to add additional flair to your iMovie footage

Tutorial: Bleach bypass effect 118
Use the colour effects to create this traditional video effect in your projects

Tutorial: Animated titles 120
Make your project stand out by using slick animated titles

Tutorial: Crop, rotate and more 122
Even the most basic techniques can have a dramatic effect on your footage

Tutorial: Reduce size 124
Creating movies for specific mediums may require a change in movie size

Tutorial: Time Lapse 126
Create the illusion of time passing very quickly with time lapse video

Tutorial: Use keywords 128
Keep on top of your clips by organising them

iLife

Check out the contents of your free CD on page **258**

Tutorial: Insert a poll 156
Canvass the opinion of those that visit your website with an easy-to-add poll

GarageBand:

Tutorial: Magic GarageBand 158
Record and keep your GarageBand jamming session

Tutorial: Movie soundtrack 160
Create the perfect mood in your movie with the perfect music

Tutorial: Note velocity 162
Add the human touch to your composition by changing note velocities

Tutorial: Boost basslines 164
Add power and punch to the bottom end of your tracks with this guide

Tutorial: Vintage sound 166
Take advantage of effects to create a vintage sound in your next project

Tutorial: Create a ringtone 168
Customise your mobile phone with its very own GarageBand ringtone

Tutorial: Gated effects 170
Use the tremolo effect to recreate a gated sound to your instrument

Tutorial: Prepare a movie 172
Use GarageBand to prepare a movie you have created for scoring

Tutorial: Score a movie 174
Now score your movie using the professional tools in GarageBand

Tutorial: Holiday video 140
Create the ultimate holiday movie with these easy-to-use techniques

iWeb:

Tutorial: Web 2.0 footer 144
Use iWeb to create a stunning web 2.0 footer for your website

Tutorial: Navigation Bar 146
Customise the way your navigation bar looks and works in iWeb

Tutorial: Stream video 148
Show live video on your iWeb site by following this cool tutorial

Tutorial: 'Follow me' button 150
Get even more followers on Twitter by adding a 'follow me' button to your website

Tutorial: Play movies 152
Set iWeb up so that movies automatically play when visitors come to the site

Tutorial: Add a speech bubble 154
Add some fun to a website by using a speech bubble to interact with your visitors

Tutorial: Scrolling text 130
A very simple but very effective way of adding information to your footage

Tutorial: Control time 132
Use these editing techniques to show the passing of time

Tutorial: Transfer projects 134
Move your iMovie projects between Macs using this simple tutorial

Tutorial: Vintage effects 136
Use filter and effects to create a vintage style for your iMovie project

Tutorial: Combine sounds 138
Add a professional touch by using a combination of microphones in iMovie

iLife Journal

Add exciting new features and extend the functions and capabilities of this great suite of applications from Apple

iLife is a fantastic software suite, and it's arguably the best bundle of applications that you get with any computer. It's one of the major selling points of the Apple Mac and is probably the most-used software on the computer. You can organise and enhance photographs in iPhoto; make fascinating videos in iMovie and burn them to a DVD using iDVD; create music by simply pointing, clicking and dragging in GarageBand; and create fun or even commercial websites in iWeb. It's simply brilliant.

Although the applications themselves are excellent, many can be extended with new features, functions and capabilities added to them. For example, there are plug-ins that add new features to iPhoto that enable you to post directly to Twitter or email your snapshots via Google Mail. There are tools that help you to manage multiple iPhoto libraries and to discover duplicates of images that waste space and are unnecessary. GarageBand enables you to create music

from short sound loops and you can add a variety of instruments and electronic sounds. This has stimulated a whole industry dedicated to creating sound loops for this powerful audio-editing tool. There are countless loop packs you can buy, but if funds are tight you will also find lots of free samples too – and it's not difficult to find several hundred to add to the ones that are already bundled with GarageBand.

iWeb builds websites from templates that are based on themes, and there are some attractive designs included with this application. There are even more

online and you can buy extra templates created by expert designers for just a few pounds. Some are free to download

to use in your own projects. An unusual and professional design will make your website stand out from the crowd. There are extras to be found for iMovie and iDVD too, and these enable you to apply new themes for your movies and more.

If you have only ever used the stock applications, bundled themes and features then you're missing out on some great extras. Take a look at the items we've highlighted here and give your iLife applications a boost - then watch as your creative projects take a leap in quality and innovation. You'll find that the extras can offer a gateway

into features that mimmic and in some cases exceed the features of professional grade software packages.

> "If you have only ever used the stock applications, bundled themes and features then you're missing out on some great extras. Take a look..."

Audacity £4.41

Editing a video and trimming the start and end of it is easy enough, but what about the audio track? The editing facilities are limited to say the least, so you might choose to enhance it outside of iMovie. Audacity will do the job quite nicely. In iMovie, select Share>Export Using QuickTime and select the option to export the sound as an AIFF file. You can then load it into Audacity and use the various filters and tools to enhance the audio – but don't change the length. Now you can export this as an AIFF file. In iMovie, select Edit>Detach Audio and then delete the audio track. Now just drag the AIFF file from a Finder window or the desktop and drop it on the Project window when it turns green. You now have the enhanced audio track in your iMovie project ready

Slick plug-ins for iMovie $30

Slick 1 Overview

Transitions

Slick 1 Transition Gallery

Effects

Slick 1 Effect Gallery

Slick Transitions and Effects
Volume One

Make your movies into masterpieces with over 50 new transitions and effects for iMovie HD. This collection of plug-ins provides the digital wizardry once available only in expensive and complex editing programs. Now it comes to you with the simplicity and ease of use of iMovie.

Select an effect or transition to the left to preview or see Transitions Movie **or** Effects Movie

Over 40 new transitions
- Page Peels and Curls
- Barn Doors, Doors, Blinds
- Rotate, Spin and Tumbles
- Zoom
- Heart and Star shapes
- Any many more

16 new Effects
- Film Noise ... aged look with scratches, dust, color fade
- Mosaic ... pixelated tile look
- Diffusion ... less-focused impressionistic effect
- Emboss ... 3-D metallic look
- Posterize, Solarize, X-Ray and more

Great value
$29.95 as a digital download (CD also available)

System requirements:
iMovie HD 6, iMovie HD 5, iMovie 4
Mac OSX 10.3.9, 10.4 (Tiger) ,10.5 (Leopard)
Macintosh with PowerPC G3, G4 or G5 processor
Macs with Intel processor

iMovie '08 does not support any plug-ins. To use Slick, get iMovie HD 6 for free. See more info here.

Slick now Universal Binary

Unfortunately, the latest version of iMovie does not support plug-ins, but if you have an old version of iMovie – which some people consider to be more powerful – then there are ten packs of plug-ins on offer at the GeeThree website. There's a pack with over 50 transitions, key frame controls, draw on top of video, create a video wall, page curls, aperture blends, blue screen, picture in picture and much more. Some of the packs have as many as 100 plug-ins and there are some fantastic effects. Just check out their website to see what's on offer.

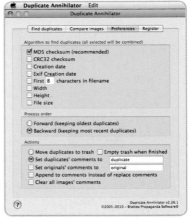

More plug-ins, tools and add-ons for iPhoto

Product	Price	URL
Impression	£8.96	www.bluecrowbar.com/software/impression
LightBrush	£8.96	www.bluecrowbar.com/software/lightbrush
iPhoto Library Manager	Free	www.fatcatsoftware.com
Downsize	$19.95	www.stuntsoftware.com/downsize
dupeGuru	$24.95	www.hardcoded.net/dupeguru_pe

www.bluecrowbar.com/software

iPhoto2Twitter £4.41

If you're a fan of Twitter then this plug-in for iPhoto is a handy tool for posting photos. It enables you to tweet from within iPhoto and post your snaps. Just download and install the plug-in from Blue Crowbar Software and then start iPhoto. Select the photo you wish to post and then choose File>Export. You will see a new iPhoto2Twitter tab, and the first time you use it you must click Setup and enter your username and password. Now you can type in the message, choose the size option and click Export. It's ultra simple yet very useful, and it sends photos to TwitPic or Mobypicture. From Mobypicture you can also upload your photo to Facebook.

http://iphoto2gmail.notoptimal.net

iPhoto2Gmail Free

Of course, we are all big fans of MobileMe here at iCreate and have email accounts there, but there's no denying that Gmail has its uses too. If you have a Gmail account and want to send photos directly from within iPhoto then this plug-in is right up your street. It's free to download and easy to use. You simply select the photo that you want to email and then choose File>Export. Select the iPhoto2Gmail tab (the first time you do this you will need to enter your Gmail account details). From then on you can just pick a photo, type a message and send it to friends and family without needing to run Safari and attach photos. Simple!

www.iphotobuddy.com

iPhoto Buddy Free

It is possible to create multiple libraries in iPhoto so that you can keep your images organised. For example, you might have work and personal folders, separate libraries for each year, or have images organised by a common theme. iPhoto doesn't make it easy to select a library and switch between them, and so iPhoto Buddy is ideal. It enables you to add iPhoto libraries and presents them in a list. Run iPhoto Buddy, select a library, then click the iPhoto button. iPhoto will load with the right library.

"It enables you to tweet from within iPhoto and post your snaps. Just download and install"

www.brattoo.com

Duplicate Annihilator $7.95

As your iPhoto library grows ever larger you can accidentally end up with multiple copies of some photos. You may have copies of images yourself or you could have imported photos twice without realising. This makes iPhoto bloated and inefficient. Duplicate Annihilator comes to the rescue by searching through your iPhoto library and finding the duplicates. There are several methods of detecting duplicates and it is possible to send them straight to the Trash or you can simply add a comment to them, pointing out that they are duplicates. You can then choose whether to keep it or delete them and they are also easy to find much later on when you have a clear out.

GarageBand Jam Packs £69

Your first port of call when looking to supercharge GarageBand is (of course) Apple, and there are five Jam Packs to choose from. Voices contains 1,500 loops featuring professional soloists and choirs in multiple genres and styles, plus 20 software instruments and drum kits using the voice or body. If you need a backing band then check out the Rhythm Section Jam Pack. This Pack provides a drum construction kit, many playable instruments, ten strings, basses and drum kits. The World Music Pack contains music styles and instruments from all over the world. Remix Tools is for electronic dance fans and there are beat kits, sound effects, synths and more available. Maybe Symphony Orchestra is more your cup of tea though, and there are strings, woodwind instruments and so on available here.

"Maybe Symphony Orchestra is more your cup of tea though"

XRB Free/$49

XRB contains 2,057 samples for GarageBand, which includes sounds from kick drums to robot noises. It's basically a massive library of sound samples that you can use to build your compositions from. The full product is a 543MB download, so you need a fast and reliable internet connection, but there is a link to a smaller version of the product on the web page that's just 37MB and is free of charge. Download it, install it and then select XRB Free in the Loops pop-up list on the right in GarageBand. Just drag and drop them onto a track in the usual way.

Vinyl Free

Producing music electronically on a computer is easy, but it can lead to perfect yet sterile music that is lifeless and unlike the real deal. This plug-in enables you to modify the sound so that it's like the audio experience you'd get if a track was on a vinyl record on an old record player. You can add mechanical and electrical noise, wear, dust, and even scratches for that truly authentic sound. Download and install the plug-in and then start GarageBand. You'll be prompted to register at the website to get a free reg code. Select an instrument in the Tracks list and press Cmd+i. Select the Edit tab, click an empty Effects slot and choose the Vinyl plug-in.

Drum loops and samples Free

If you want 100 per cent royalty-free drum loops for your musical creation then fire up Safari and head on over to Silicon Beats' website. You'll find lots of drum loop packs to buy, but before you hand over any money you should download the free samples. There are a dozen or more demo loops from each pack that you can download and use free of charge. They are in MP3, WAV, REX2 and AIF file formats. MP3s are good for a quick preview, but AIF are the ones to use in GarageBand. There are several hundred to choose from and they are all professionally recorded so they sound great. With so many sounds on offer, you're bound to find something you like! These are the perfect way to add an extra dimension to your creative music projects.

Platinumloops Free

www.platinumloops.com

Platinumloops is a great source of loops for GarageBand, and there is a wide range of packs to buy – including the five-DVD Max Producer Set containing 22,000 audio files in multiple formats. That's 13GB of loops for $499. If that is beyond your budget though, check out the individual packs and you'll find free samples with each one. There are around a dozen with each and the packs include Trance Loops; Fender Strat Guitar Multisamples; Slap Bass Loops; Ska and Reggae Guitar loops; Double Bass Samples; Violin String Samples; Keyboard Samples; Saxophone, Clarinet, Piccolo, Flute and Trumpet Samples, and dozens more.

Goldbaby free stuff Free

www.goldbaby.co.nz/freestuff.html

You'll find lots of downloads available at the Goldbaby website. Not all of them are useful, but there is bound to be something that you'll like so it is definitely worth a visit. For example, there's an MR-16 drum machine recorded on two different tape machines, a Roland TR606 recorded on a half-inch valve tape machine, vintage home keyboard loops, and many more. You'll spend a few minutes downloading them, but they are very easy to add to GarageBand. Just unzip them, move them to your Home/Music folder, then drag the folder to the Loops explorer in GarageBand and try them out.

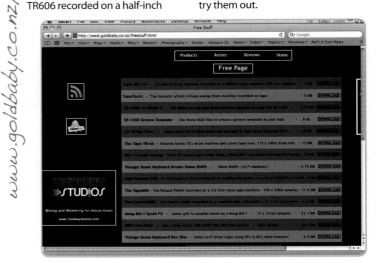

iWeb Templates

Free/$10

www.iwebtemplate.com

If you can't find exactly what you need in the collection of templates bundled with iWeb, it's worth visiting the obviously named **iwebtemplates. com**. There are lots of templates here and they're organised into categories like Family, Garden, Photography and Sport. Templates are a reasonable $10, but there is also a Free category that contains six interesting designs, such as a cat theme, treasure and others. Some work with iWeb '09 on Snow Leopard, but others are for older versions of iWeb and Mac OS X. There's something for everyone.

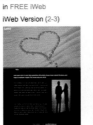

More plug-ins, tools and add-ons for iWeb

Product	Price	URL
iWeb Themes	Free	www.jumsoft.com/goodies
Miamiou Megapack	£31.49	www.miamiou.com
iWeb Buddy	$25	www.zarrastudios.com/ZDS/iWebBuddy.html
iWeb themes	$14.95	www.11mystics.com/store
iWeb Suite	$70	www.ipresentee.com/iPresentee

www.echoone.com

Analytics and Automator Free

Google Analytics (**www.google. com/analytics**) is a free service that enables you to view detailed information about your website. For example, you can view the number of visitors, see how many pages they viewed, which page they entered via and so on. It's very useful for anyone with a website. This software adds

Google Analytics code to every page of websites created with iWeb. You simply publish your site, run this Automator script and the job's done. It's not obvious how to set it up, so it is essential that you read the guide found on the website before you start. And you'll need a Google Analytics account, of course.

flashalbumexporter.home.comcast.net

Flash Album Exporter Free

This is actually an iPhoto plug-in, but it is more useful to iWeb users. If you select some photos in iPhoto and then choose File>Export, you'll see a new FAExporter tab that enables you to create a cool Flash application on a web page. The files are saved to a folder, which should then be uploaded to your web space.

You link to it from a page in your iWeb site or, if you're an expert user, embed it using an iFrame. The installation instructions are for iPhoto '08, so for '09 you must right-click iPhoto in the Applications folder and select Show Package Contents. Open the Contents folder and copy the plug-in to the plug-ins folder.

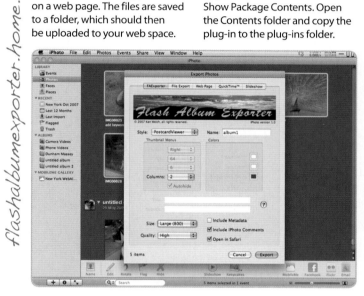

www.ziggysoft.com

iWeb Valet £17.09

Although iWeb makes it easy to create attractive page designs using text and images, it's not perfect and the pages could end up being static and dull. iWeb Valet solves this problem by enabling you to add widgets to the page, such as a calendar, clock, days remaining, a drop-down

menu, scrolling news and more. It also enables you to add meta tags that help search engines to index your site, and there's a 'search and replace' that works across all the pages in your site. Run iWeb and iWeb Valet at the same time so you can copy widgets from Valet and paste them into iWeb pages.

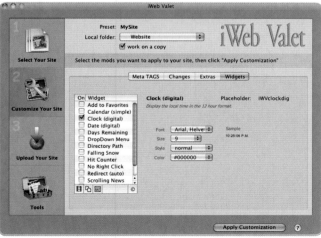

www.iPresentee.com

iWeb Themes 7.0 $25

There are lots of themes available for iWeb from various online companies, but what makes this pack from iPresentee stand out from the crowd is that, in addition to containing standard templates, it also has ones for the iPhone too. Lots of people use their iPhone or iPod touch to browse the web, and if you want to make it easier for them to browse the content on your site then these iWeb themes for the iPhone and iPod touch are a great idea. There's Blue Style, Shining Star, Greenish Style, Tango and Developer themes available, with 11 standard templates and ten iPhone/iPod touch templates each.

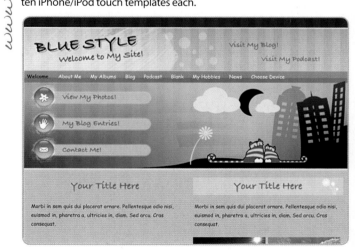

ThemePAK Free

There are dozens of brand new and exciting themes for iDVD at this site, and you can buy single themes for as little as $7.95 to packs of themes costing $150 or more. There is also a free ThemePAK that you can download and install, which gives you seven new themes for iDVD. After downloading and installing them, you'll find them on the Theme pop-up menu. There's BabyCake, ConcreteZone, Concrete, Brick, FoliaOrgana and several more. Just select one and it is applied to the currently loaded project in the usual way. It's excellent and will give you new ideas for your projects and a fresh look to your DVDs.

www.dvdthemepak.com/free.html

"There is also a free ThemePAK that you can download"

iDVD Themes Free

Themes hidden within iDVD!

If you have Snow Leopard and iDVD '09 (version 7), you'll find a short list of themes displayed when the Themes tab is selected. By default, only version 7 themes are displayed – but if you click the pop-up menu at the top and select the 'All' option, the theme list is greatly expanded. You'll find that there are a lot of themes towards the end of the list that are greyed out, but if you click one to select it you'll be offered the opportunity to download a themes pack for iDVD. Go ahead and grab it, it's well worth it – but be aware that it's a 500MB+ download, so make sure you're using a fast internet connection and have enough hard disk space.

DiscLabel £25.70

www.smileonmymac.com

After creating your DVD project and burning it to a disc, you will then need to create the artwork for the box or jewel case along with a disc label. DiscLabel is a great program for designing the artwork to accompany your DVD. It's a standalone application that isn't specifically for iDVD, but it does have a clever trick up its sleeve; it can pull in artwork from iDVD templates, which means that you can create a box sleeve using the same artwork as on the DVD. That's really useful when you're making your DVD sleeves. You don't have to use iDVD artwork though and there are lots of ready-made templates to use, and it can pull in iPhoto images too.

iLife & iWork '09

So many new features and endless creative possibilities await the user of Apple's new iLife and iWork suites

iCandy
Mac Mini

Mac Mini
The new Mac Mini is now crafted entirely from aluminium using Apple's unibody technique

Welcome

Welcome to Our Site

UTAH TABLE

Lorem ipsum dolor sit amet

Ligula suspendisse nulla pretium, rhoncus tempor placerat fermentum, enim integer ad vestibulum volutpat. Nisl rhoncus turpis est, vel elit, congue wisi enim nunc ultricies sit, magna tincidunt. Maecenas aliquam maecenas ligula nostra, accumsan taciti. Sociis mauris in integer, a dolor netus non dui aliquet, sagittis felis sodales, dolor sociis mauris, vel eu libero cras.

Made on a Mac

Akira, just after bringing him home.

Create your own

Website

Building a site has never been easier. Find out how today...

Coming up with a killer idea for a website – whether personal blog, portfolio or small business site – is the simple bit. It's easy to overlook what happens after. Once you've gone through the inevitable hassle of buying a suitable domain name and web space, you're plunged into wrestling with design tools such as Dreamweaver or Coda, and what quickly becomes the chore of editing and uploading content. No wonder most start-up websites flounder within a few months.

Of course, there are simpler ways of getting your message across. Hosted blogs like WordPress (**www. wordpress.com**) or Blogger (**www.blogger.com**) are great if you just want to keep a simple online journal. But as your site develops they begin to lose their luster. Adjusting the appearance of a WordPress-hosted site means either adopting a standard template or building your own from scratch. And as there's no visual preview of the changes you make, you won't have much of an

idea of how good it looks until it's actually published. And versatility can be a problem too. To add extras such as discussion forums, you can come up against the limitations of the service.

But what are the alternatives? Fortunately there are affordable tools that not only make setting up and publishing your own website easy, but also don't require a degree in web design to make the sites they create look good. In this feature we'll look at three of the most polished web-authoring applications on the market: Apple's iWeb, Squarespace and Moonfruit.

These three services all make it easy to create, edit and upload content, although they approach it in markedly different ways. For example, while Moonfruit and Squarespace are hosted services, which means that all data is stored on the service's server and you edit content directly on the hosted website, iWeb is a desktop application. Here, content is stored on your Mac and only sent online when you publish it. Both approaches have their merits, but what's best for you

depends on how you're going to update your web presence. iWeb may be a sensible choice if you're only ever going to edit your site from one Mac, and storing the content locally may be useful if you are worried about a third party being responsible for all your data. Or, if you think you need access from other locations, the web-based Squarespace and Moonfruit are more suitable. Squarespace even offers a free iPhone app to let you update and manage your site on the move.

iWeb's links to iLife also make it a good choice if you're creating portfolios or you want to add your own videos, images or audio to web pages. Both Squarespace and Moonfruit counter with advantages of their own, such as the ability to create discussion forums and web forms, or the ability to create a membership-driven site, allowing you to choose who has access to your site.

Over the next few pages we'll examine the features of all three options and show you examples of the websites each can produce.

The default Squarespace site may look like a standard blog page, but once you've got the hang of the way the service works, you can create astoundingly powerful and versatile sites.

Squarespace sites are made up of sections that hold pages – these can comprise journals, picture galleries, or even basic HTML pages – or widgets. Widgets are made up of similar content to pages, but hold their content in a sidebar.

You add and edit pages and widgets in one of Squarespace's three main editing modes, displayed above the current page when you're logged in. To add a widget just click the 'Add widget' button on the sidebar, choose the widget from a lengthy list of options, then configure and enable it, dragging it to reposition. From this Structure Editing mode you can quickly switch to a Content Editing mode, where you add or edit code in an HTML page or pen entries in a journal page. The other main editing mode, Style Editing, governs the appearance of your site. Your choice here can be as basic as choosing the look of a template to adjusting navigation and layout, and even coding your own CSS (cascading style sheets) – something that isn't possible with iWeb or Moonfruit.

When it comes to creating content, Squarespace's features rival those of popular content management systems such as WordPress. You can store journal entries as drafts and set entries to publish at a specified time, which is something you can't do with iWeb. Nor can iWeb match Squarespace's list of features, like the way you can drag-and-drop items such as forms (always a pain to build from scratch), mailing lists and journal archives onto a sidebar or page.

Like iWeb's blog page, entries or comments can be syndicated as RSS feeds so visitors can subscribe to updates. That's some compensation for the fact that, in contrast to Moonfruit, you can't add music or video directly to a website. But Squarespace does offer similar member management features as those provided by Moonfruit, with the added ability to block specific internet addresses.

One real plus for those who have cut their blogging teeth on a service like Blogger and want to move to something more powerful is the way Squarespace can import content from many popular blogging services. The feature that sets Squarespace apart, however, is its free iPhone app. This not only lets you preview the site, but gives access to visitor and subscription information. And you can even create new posts accompanied by pictures that you take on your iPhone. It's a publishing system in the palm of your hand. That's not to say that Squarespace isn't without its disadvantages, though. Unlike iWeb, you're restricted to a Squarespace account, so you can't use the spare web space provided by your internet provider. And Squarespace isn't cheap. But at under £5 a month it represents excellent value for those seeking a customisable yet powerful web presence.

www.squarespace.com

Squarespace is a powerful blogging system that also offers powerful layout and design tools

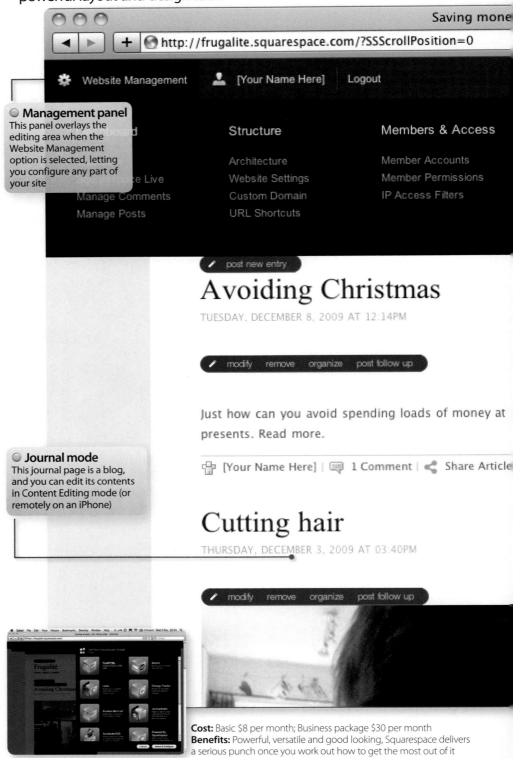

Management panel
This panel overlays the editing area when the Website Management option is selected, letting you configure any part of your site

Journal mode
This journal page is a blog, and you can edit its contents in Content Editing mode (or remotely on an iPhone)

Cost: Basic $8 per month; Business package $30 per month
Benefits: Powerful, versatile and good looking, Squarespace delivers a serious punch once you work out how to get the most out of it

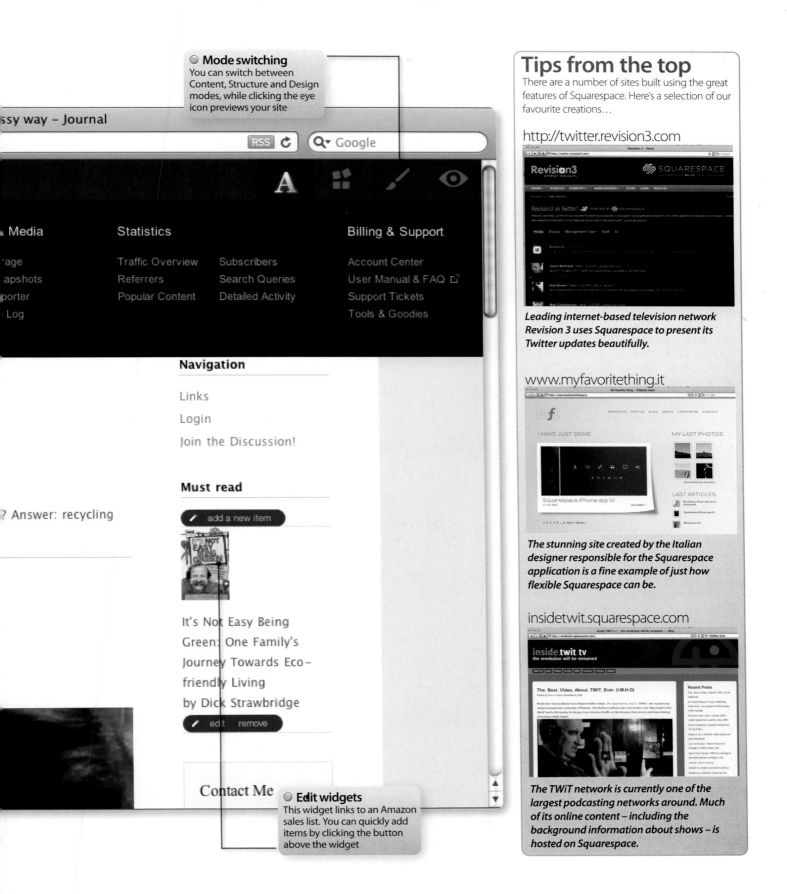

Mode switching
You can switch between Content, Structure and Design modes, while clicking the eye icon previews your site

ssy way – Journal

RSS C | Q▾ Google

A

& Media

rage
apshots
porter
Log

Statistics

Traffic Overview
Referrers
Popular Content

Subscribers
Search Queries
Detailed Activity

Billing & Support

Account Center
User Manual & FAQ
Support Tickets
Tools & Goodies

Navigation

Links

Login

Join the Discussion!

Must read

add a new item

It's Not Easy Being Green: One Family's Journey Towards Eco-friendly Living by Dick Strawbridge

edit   remove

? Answer: recycling

Contact Me

Edit widgets
This widget links to an Amazon sales list. You can quickly add items by clicking the button above the widget

Tips from the top

There are a number of sites built using the great features of Squarespace. Here's a selection of our favourite creations…

http://twitter.revision3.com

Leading internet-based television network Revision 3 uses Squarespace to present its Twitter updates beautifully.

www.myfavoritething.it

The stunning site created by the Italian designer responsible for the Squarespace application is a fine example of just how flexible Squarespace can be.

insidetwit.squarespace.com

The TWiT network is currently one of the largest podcasting networks around. Much of its online content – including the background information about shows – is hosted on Squarespace.

For one-click web publishing, there's little that comes close to Apple's iWeb. Its easy-to-use tools let you create a good-looking site in minutes. The secret to iWeb's success lies in its template-based system and its ties to iLife. When you create a new site you choose from nearly 30 different themes – each of which include individual page templates dedicated to specific purposes, such as podcasts, photo albums, and blogs.

iWeb is extremely easy to use. The sites (unlike Moonfruit and Squarespace, there's no restriction to the number you can manage) and pages are organised through a Source list on the left. All editing takes place within a single window, and iWeb automatically handles each page's navigation as you add or remove pages.

You add text by entering it on the page or into text placeholders, while images, audio and video can be dragged from a Media browser pane that links to your iLife media. And if you drag content onto placeholders it's automatically resized for you. The templates are well tuned to their purpose; the Photos template's grid not only organises images and adds a navigation menu if needed, but even includes a slideshow button so users can browse hosted images as a slideshow. And the Podcast page makes it a cinch to publish your podcasts. Such ease of use extends beyond creating to publishing; as a single Publish Site button sends everything to a MobileMe or FTP website.

iWeb comes with a number of drag-and-drop widgets, including YouTube videos and Google Maps, that let you add interactivity to your pages. An RSS feed widget lets you embed news or Twitter feeds from other sites, while the iSight Camera widget instantly adds photos or video taken with your iSight camera to your page.

iWeb's disadvantages relate to its lack of flexibility. Its HTML widget lets you add small HTML clips to a page, but there's no way to directly edit the underlying code of its parent page. And as the site can only be edited in iWeb, you can't make adjustments or post entries when you're away from your Mac. There's no doubt too that the pages generated by iWeb can be clunky, and each page generates its own, non-editable CSS file. And although sites hosted on MobileMe can be password-protected, it lacks the membership management features available in rival applications.

Still, iWeb has good value written all over it. As part of the iLife suite, it's pre-installed on new Macs or available with the other iLife applications off the shelf for under £69. And you don't need a MobileMe account to use iWeb; as long as you have FTP access to any web space account, iWeb will happily upload to it. There are still minor advantages to a MobileMe account, such as the healthy web space it offers and that fact that if you create a MobileMe gallery in iPhoto or iMovie, you can add this directly to your iWeb pages via a widget. The bottom line is, if you need a no-fuss website quickly, iWeb could fit the bill.

www.apple.com/mobileme

Apple's iWeb has some surprisingly powerful tools in its arsenal and is more flexible than people realise

Multiple site management
iWeb can handle many sites and these – and the pages within them – are all managed in a single window

Quick publish
You edit an iWeb site on the Mac rather than the web, but publishing is as simple as clicking this button

Cost: Part of iLife (£69 inc VAT). Some features require MobileMe (£58 inc VAT)
Benefits: Unlimited sites, easy editing

iLife integration
iWeb's selling point is the way it links to iLife. Add your favourite movies, audio or images in a second

new

Audio | Photos | Movies | Widgets

MobileMe Gallery

YouTube

Google Maps

Google AdSense

iSight Photo

iSight Movie

:42
Countdown

RSS
RSS Feed

HTML
HTML Snippet

Adjust   Inspector

ing hair ticks all the
ent there is – while you
of £20 spent on a pair of
urs when you consider
es on the High Street will

Widget heaven
iWeb doesn't have many widgets, but those it has are easy to add to a page by dragging onto it

Tips from the top

The uncomplicated tools found in iWeb have been harnessed to make some incredible online creations. Here are some of the best…

www.shelbeyhunt.com

Eclectic iWeb-based website from young filmmaker Shelbey Hunt includes embedded links to video and links to more details about other projects he's working on.

www.dickstrawbridge.com

Well-known British TV presenter Dick Strawbridge – he of the famous moustache – might be expected to leave the design of his site to an expensive designer, but iWeb does the job effectively.

www.joshpix.com

JF Photo's stunningly designed portfolio site is a great example of how far you can get away from the standard template look when producing a site with iWeb.

W hile Moonfruit is another system built on templates – here divided into personal, professional, clubs and groups categories – it differs from the others in one significant way: it's built on Adobe's Flash. This offers some advantages. Although it's hosted entirely on a remote server, editing content in Moonfruit looks just like you're working in a desktop application.

Just like iWeb, Moonfruit offers a single-window editing environment that lets you directly edit objects. To move, rotate or resize text or images, you just click once on its bounding box, while double-clicking a text box lets you add text directly. A floating Editor palette acts like an cut-down version of iWeb's Inspector window, showing details for any selected object.

Above the main editing window sits a standard toolbar that, as well as basic editing functions, offers wider site management, with contextual options appearing in a pane on the left of the window. Under its Design tab, for example, you can adjust default page size, menus and fonts. In Pages mode not only can you add pages to a site pre-built with galleries, video pages, forums and so on, but you can define a master that pages on your site can follow, and add metadata – title and keywords – to each page. A file manager makes it easy to upload images from your Mac either singly or in bulk.

You can drag tables, forms and files to the page from the left-hand pane, adjusting their size on page to fit the available space. Adding forums, Twitter feeds and comments is just a matter of clicking an option in the left-hand pane and doing a little configuring. Moonfruit websites can also host video, whether it's embedded YouTube video or using its own player, although any video you upload will have to be converted to Flash-native FLV format first.

There are also options for setting up Google's Analytics statistics package, although there's a perfectly decent basic site statistics tool under the Admin tab. In this Admin area you can also examine your disk space usage, which is a handy tool as the free version of the service comes with a limit of 20MB of space.

Another very impressive part of Moonfruit is the way you can set members and groups, and have permissions for individual pages based on this. You can even restrict the whole site to members only, so you know exactly who's viewing your site.

The big downside to Moonfruit's dependence on Flash is that it means you won't be able to edit your site on your iPhone without Flash installed. But visitors without Flash can still see your site – they'll just get a much simpler, non-Flash view. The Flash environment also makes launching the editing environment more sluggish than iWeb or Squarespace. Moonfruit does offer a free version of its service. This lacks some of the features of its more expensive versions, but if you're on a budget then it's hard to beat.

www.moonfruit.com

Moonfruit lets you edit pages in a visual way, dragging boxes to arrange them and editing directly in a box

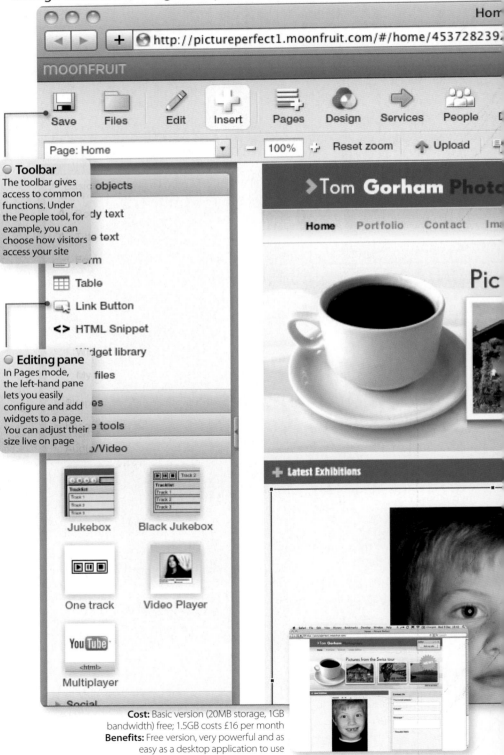

Toolbar
The toolbar gives access to common functions. Under the People tool, for example, you can choose how visitors access your site

Editing pane
In Pages mode, the left-hand pane lets you easily configure and add widgets to a page. You can adjust their size live on page

Cost: Basic version (20MB storage, 1GB bandwidth) free; 1.5GB costs £16 per month
Benefits: Free version, very powerful and as easy as a desktop application to use

e Perfect

Google

Upgrade your free site   Welcome tomgorham12 | logout

Admin

View my site

Help

from the Swiss tour

NEW!

LES PLEÏADE
VEVEY · ALT 1440

Click to see more...

itor

nfo | Image | Setup | Style

ptions

Add images   Width 450

Organise   Height 350

Advanced   Apply

ntact Us

ur email address *

Subject *

Message *

Editor window
Once you select an object on the page you can edit its contents – adding images and so on – in the Editor window

Form-filling
Moonfruit can automatically create forms for visitors to fill in. You can resize them on the page to suit your layout

Tips from the top
Check out the fruits of other people's labour using this quality blog-creation software. There's a host of different sites out there…

www.latinoscoffee.co.uk

The Latino's Coffee website illustrates what's possible with Moonfruit, and uses audio and video to help sell the product.

www.louiseredknapp.net

This Louise Redknapp-approved website shows just how easy it is to get professional looking material on a website. Here embedded video is married to a comments module to promote interactivity.

www.myecho.co.uk

My Echo are an unsigned band, and their website – hosted on Moonfruit – helps promote their work with links to embedded YouTube video as well as an audio player.

Tutorial: Create a thank-you card in iPhoto

iPhoto's card creation suite is fun to use and can allow you to produce some stunning cards, ranging from holiday tributes to tokens of appreciation – which is exactly what we are going to show you here

Task: Generate a thank-you card in iPhoto

Difficulty: Beginner

Time needed: 30 minutes

iPhoto's card creation feature is one of the most popular aspects of the application's DNA and, with such a wholesome range of template options available, it's not hard to see why.

In this tutorial we will be discussing how to create a thank-you card, but the very same process can be applied to any of the other samples on offer – whether it's for a birthday, Christmas, a new born, good luck, postcards or the year in review, the workshop is still relevant.

Thank-you cards are a perfect token for anyone and everyone. In fact, you could simply create a thank-you card just to experience the service. Is there somebody you forgot to thank for a gift or a party over the holiday season? If so, there's no better way to express your gratitude. So grab a few images from your photo collection and let's get creating!

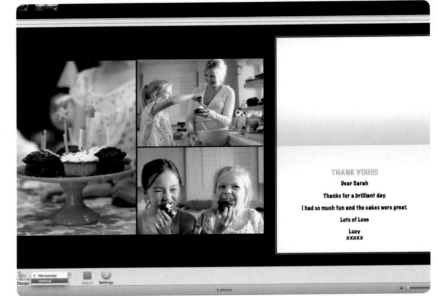

Step-by-step | iPhoto Use the card creation suite

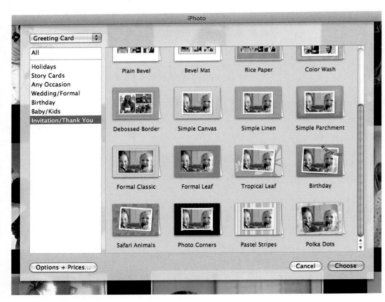

1: Get started
Open iPhoto and select an image or selection of pictures you would like to use to create your card. With these highlighted, hit the Greeting Card icon. Now select Invitation/Thank You and pick your favourite design.

2: Drag and drop
In the card creation suite the images you highlighted will appear in the browser. Drag and drop the image files to the relevant areas. Use the functions at the bottom of the screen to change the style of your card.

Use iPhoto's card creation suite

Make an attractive thank-you card in iPhoto

● Photo browser

The photo browser stores images that have been loaded into the card creator. Simply drag-and-drop these into position. When an image has been used in the template a white tick will appear on the thumbnail

● Knowledge base

iPhoto card prices

Apple's iPhoto cards are produced at a size of 13 x 18cm and cost £1.32 each when you order between 1 and 24 cards. However, the price is reduced to £1.21 when 25 to 49 cards are bought and only £1.09 when 50 or more items are obtained.

● Enter text

Tap the text frame and simply enter the message you wish to write. To alter the styling of the font, travel to the Settings icon

● Saved

Your card is saved in the Source list, so name it and revert to it later if you would rather complete your project in stages. You can also add more images to the browser by exiting the creation suite, going into Photos and dragging new files on to the card in the Source list

● Edit controls

Click on an image you wish to adjust. Across the top a ledge of controls will appear. Plump for the Hand tool and then drag the image around the frame to change its position, or slide the Zoom left or right to zoom in or out

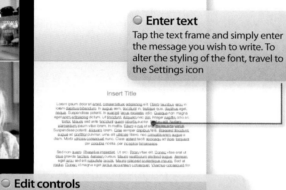

3: Editing

If you feel an image isn't up to scratch, double-click the frame and adjust it in the Edit suite. Alternatively, click the image in the card template once and use the Hand tool to move the composition or the Zoom tool.

4: Finishing touches

The thank-you card templates allow you to add text. Once you've finished entering and styling your text, and the arrangement is exactly how you want it, travel over to the Buy Card button to finish up and pay.

Tutorial: Add keywords to iPhoto images

With an overflowing library of photos, it can be a wise manoeuvre to utilise iPhoto's keywords for an enhanced workflow. We show you how…

Task: Add keywords to optimise workflow in iPhoto

Difficulty: Beginner

Time needed: 10 minutes

If you've been a fan of iPhoto for some time you'll have no doubt collected an expansive library of images, so much so that the idea of organising your workflow may intimidate rather than excite. But nevertheless, organise you must.

An organised bank of images can help you search for a selection of shots from one particular area, location, genre, person or activity. Furthermore, by assigning keywords to your frames you can isolate your search down to a single frame, and by adding and later selecting specific keywords – such as a name, activity, place and props – you could narrow the search down to one result. For example, your son Perry on horseback in New Zealand, wearing a cowboy hat. As you can create your own keywords the possibilities are endless, so round up your no-name frames and follow these four steps.

Step-by-step | iPhoto Add keywords to your photos

1: Show me the keywords
Load up iPhoto and head to View on the Menu bar. From this drop-down menu select Keywords, or use the shortcut Shift+Cmd+K. By doing this, the keywords already assigned to images will appear.

2: Enter new keywords
Isolate an image you wish to add keywords to and, in the keyword-dedicated area under the frame, add new keywords. These can be anything that describes the image. Press Enter after each entry.

Use keywords to maximise efficiency
Understand more about iPhoto's keywords

● View
To reveal the keywords listed under the images simply select Shift+Cmd+K

● Window
To reveal all the keywords currently being used, or to shortcut keywords, head to the Menu bar's Window option and select the Show Keywords option

● Knowledge base
Add keywords to Quick Group
Another way to add a keyword to the Quick Group pick list is to simply drag the keyword into the 'Quick Pick List' field. This will automatically assign the word a shortcut. This can save valuable time in tracking and assigning keywords to images – especially when you're using tools such as Batch Change.

● Keywords
The list of words written underneath an image are the image's keywords. They can help you to organise and track images

● Keyword search
Change the search method at the bottom of the interface to 'Keyword', which is represented by a small key. Now enter the keyword on your mind to track down a frame

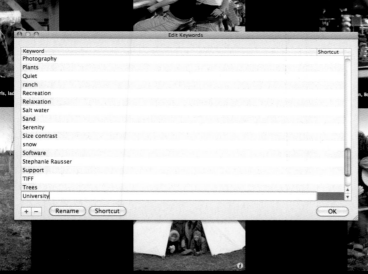

3: Create a keyword shortcut
Mac users can create shortcuts to save time when it comes to entering keywords. Do this by visiting the Window menu and hitting Show Keywords. A pop-up box featuring your keywords will now appear.

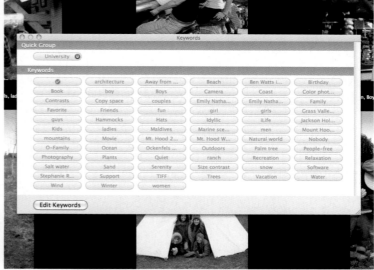

4: Quick Group keywords
Select a word, or hit the plus icon to create a new keyword. With this highlighted hit the Shortcut button, followed by OK. The shortcuts with the relevant command will now appear in the Quick Group section.

Tutorial: Create an album from keywords

Now that you've mastered assigning keywords to your images, come with us as we show you how to create an album from them…

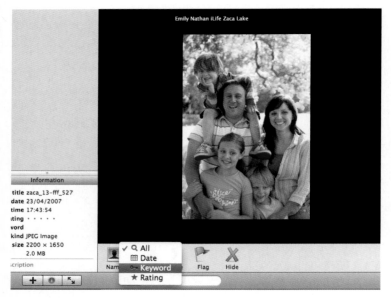

Task: Create an album just by using keywords

Difficulty: Beginner

Time needed: 10 minutes

We admit that keywording images isn't as exciting as some of iPhoto's more lavish editing functions, or as fun and enjoyable as book or calendar creation. But it is essential for maintaining a ship-shape system, which will ultimately streamline other operations – such as locating, editing and utilising frames.

In this tutorial we'll guide you in creating albums using keywords. By using the preceding four-step workshop you should now be accomplished in labelling your shots and have a selection of frames waiting to be assigned to an album. Once you have created an album using this method, you may want to edit the gathered batch or transport the album into the book creation suite and generate a tome from the pictures. Whatever the purpose, keywording can really help you achieve your goals faster and easier.

Step-by-step | iPhoto Use keywords to create an album

1: Recap
After following the previous iPhoto workshop in this issue, you'll now be au fait with adding keywords to an image. To recap, all you need to do is key Shift+Cmd+K and add appropriate name tags.

2: Search
Head to the search field at the bottom of the app's interface and select to search using keywords from the icon drop-down menu (shown as a key). A pop-up panel, stacking all of the utilised keywords, will appear.

Use keywords to create an iPhoto album

Discover how to utilise keywords to speed up your workflow

Hit and search
With the panel of keywords active, hit on relevant keyword buttons to narrow the search. Only those images matching all the selected and highlighted keywords will remain in few

Search for keywords
The search field's search orientation can be changed to suit your purpose. We have it set to Keyword to track matching pictures

Keywords added
The words that are listed under the images in iPhoto are the keywords already assigned. Hit this part of the interface to delete or add new items

Knowledge base

Preferences
Another way to change the keywords default list is to change it in Preferences. Travel up to iPhoto in the Menu bar and opt for Preferences. With the panel open, select the Keywords tab. With this active, punch the plus icon and add new keywords. To delete a word, select it and choose the minus icon.

Number of photos
As users select more keywords from this panel the search will narrow. Hover over the panel and iPhoto will notify the user how many images are left in the search

3: Select
You can select one or a series of keywords to narrow down the search, or type the word in the search field. With all of the matching frames on screen, key Cmd+A to select all and drag the files to the Source panel.

4: Name that album
You'll notice a new untitled folder appear. Click on the folder and enter a new appropriate name, and that's it. With the album selected you can hit the Edit or the Book icon to take this album elsewhere.

Tutorial: Manage multiple libraries in iPhoto

We show you how simple it is to both create and manage multiple libraries in iPhoto…

Task: Learn how to create multiple iPhoto libraries

Difficulty: Beginner

Time needed: 15 minutes

It may well have escaped most Mac users, but from iLife '08 onwards it has been possible to have multiple iPhoto libraries in use on the same computer linked to the same copy of iPhoto. You might be wondering why you might want to do this. Well, maybe you want to maintain one library for your party and holiday snaps and another for more serious photography? Or perhaps you and your partner have a camera each and want to keep your images separate? Whatever the reason, it's quite handy to know that you have the freedom to break away from the rigidity of only having one library. So if this seems like an appealing idea, here's how easy it is to set it up.

Step-by-step | iPhoto Create and manage multiple libraries in iPhoto

1: Option-launch iPhoto
Hold down the Alt key while clicking iPhoto's icon in the Dock. It can take a while as your Mac scans your hard drive, so be patient.

2: Create new library
To begin the process of creating your alternate library, click the Create New button from the dialog box that appears.

3: Name it
Now type a name for your new library that will make it easy to identify when you come to select it from the list.

4: Set location
Specify a different file location if desired – the default option is your Pictures folder, but you can save it anywhere, even on an external drive.

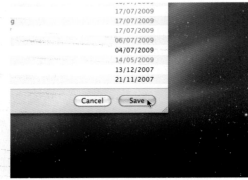

5: Save it
Finish the process off by clicking the Save button to create the new library in the location you have previously selected.

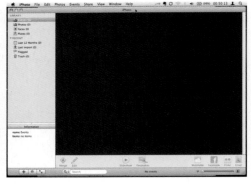

6: Presto chango
iPhoto will open with a blank library containing no images. Don't worry, your other library is still safe on your hard drive, even though you can't see it.

Use iPhoto to create multiple libraries

Use different libraries for different occasions

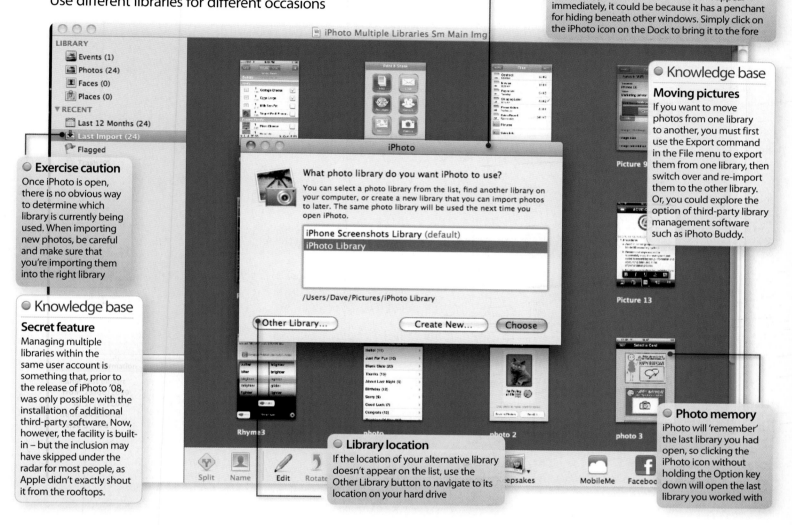

Hide and seek
If the library selection window doesn't appear immediately, it could be because it has a penchant for hiding beneath other windows. Simply click on the iPhoto icon on the Dock to bring it to the fore

Knowledge base

Moving pictures
If you want to move photos from one library to another, you must first use the Export command in the File menu to export them from one library, then switch over and re-import them to the other library. Or, you could explore the option of third-party library management software such as iPhoto Buddy.

Exercise caution
Once iPhoto is open, there is no obvious way to determine which library is currently being used. When importing new photos, be careful and make sure that you're importing them into the right library

Knowledge base

Secret feature
Managing multiple libraries within the same user account is something that, prior to the release of iPhoto '08, was only possible with the installation of additional third-party software. Now, however, the facility is built-in – but the inclusion may have skipped under the radar for most people, as Apple didn't exactly shout it from the rooftops.

What photo library do you want iPhoto to use?
You can select a photo library from the list, find another library on your computer, or create a new library that you can import photos to later. The same photo library will be used the next time you open iPhoto.

iPhone Screenshots Library (default)
iPhoto Library

/Users/Dave/Pictures/iPhoto Library

Other Library...   Create New...   Choose

Library location
If the location of your alternative library doesn't appear on the list, use the Other Library button to navigate to its location on your hard drive

Photo memory
iPhoto will 'remember' the last library you had open, so clicking the iPhoto icon without holding the Option key down will open the last library you worked with

7: Import images
You can now import pictures as you would normally, either by connecting a camera or by using the 'Import to Library' command in the File menu.

8: Switch back
To switch between libraries, simply quit iPhoto then relaunch with the Alt key held down once more to bring up the library selection window.

9: Select original
From this window, select your original library from the list and click Choose. iPhoto will load up your library in all its former glory.

Remove blemishes and objects in iPhoto

iPhoto includes professional-level editing techniques to remove unwanted objects from your photos

Task: Remove unwanted objects from a photo

Difficulty: Beginner

Time needed: 10 minutes

Each new iteration of iPhoto brings with it new features and improvements. iPhoto '09 introduces themed slideshows, travel maps, online sharing, faces, places and enhanced editing. It's this latter feature that we're going to investigate in this tutorial, in particular the Retouch brush. It now includes an edge detector, which means you can remove spots and blemishes that overlap other objects without losing any solid edges. It's the type of technology you'd expect to see in professional-level software, but is incredibly easy to use. With this new tool, every Mac user has the ability to perfect their holiday snaps without buying expensive software.

Step-by-step | iPhoto Remove blemishes and objects from your photos

1: Load up your image
Import a photo that needs retouching. Don't worry about using the image we've chosen here – any photo with an unwanted object or blemish will do.

2: The Edit tools
Click the Edit button at the bottom of the screen. A selection of controls will appear that include Rotate, Crop, Straighten, Enhance, Red-Eye and Retouch.

3: Zoom in for extra detail
Move your cursor over the area you want to edit and press '1' on the keyboard. This will zoom the screen into the troublesome area.

4: Custom sized tools
Click on the Retouch tool at the bottom of the screen. You can shrink and increase the size of the brush using the size slider that will appear.

5: Paint out those blemishes
Once you're happy with the brush size, simply draw over the object that you wish to remove. iPhone will automatically remove the object.

6: Comparing results
You can press the Shift key to switch between the original image and the edited version. This is a great way to ensure you haven't lost any key details.

Use iPhoto to create an iPad wallpaper
Personalise your iPad with a unique backdrop

● Knowledge base

The central square
iPhoto makes it easy to help you place the most important part of your image in the centre, since this will be the section that will always be seen no matter which orientation your iPad's currently set to. As you drag the current selection when cropping your photo, you can see faint lines inside the highlighted part. Place the crucial part of your image in the central square.

● **Effects**
When adding visual effects, try to avoid any that alter the corners like Matte, Vignette or Edge Blur since these parts will always be cut off from the iPad no matter which orientation is set

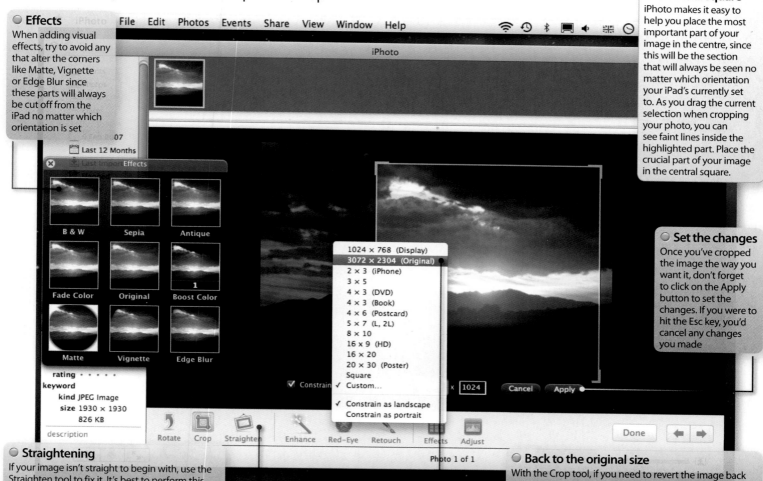

● **Set the changes**
Once you've cropped the image the way you want it, don't forget to click on the Apply button to set the changes. If you were to hit the Esc key, you'd cancel any changes you made

● **Straightening**
If your image isn't straight to begin with, use the Straighten tool to fix it. It's best to perform this action before you proceed to cropping the photo

● **Back to the original size**
With the Crop tool, if you need to revert the image back to its original size and start again you can either click on Cancel or select Original from this pop-up menu

7: Connect to iPad
You can create multiple photos in this way. When you're done, connect your iPad to your Mac and sync it with iTunes.

8: The photo in iPad
In your iPad, go to the Photos app and find the image you just created. Select the square icon with a curved arrow going out of it, top-right of the screen.

9: Set the wallpaper
Choose 'Use as Wallpaper', decide if it's going to be for your locked screen, the home screens or both, and tap on the relevant button.

Tutorial: Rotate multiple images in iPhoto

If you've imported some photos that are the wrong way up, here's an easy way to sort them out without lots of tedious clicking

Task: Rotate multiple photos with one click

Difficulty: Beginner

Time needed: 10 minutes

iPhoto's 'Import to Library' routine is fairly intelligent for the most part but sometimes, when importing a bunch of images, you can end up with several that are offset by 90-degrees. There may be a number of possible causes for this, but it's usually to do with the way that the camera was held when the shots were taken. iPhoto features a handy Rotate button that can be used to correct the problem, but if you have a large number of photos that need to be corrected, it can be a chore to have to rotate them one at a time.

Luckily, the simple technique shown here can be employed to correct the orientation of multiple photos at once. When you select a range of shots to adjust, however, be careful that only the images you want to rotate are visible in iPhoto's main window, as the Cmd+A keyboard shortcut can select all the images in your entire library if you don't select the right folder first!

Step-by-step | iPhoto Rotate multiple images in iPhoto

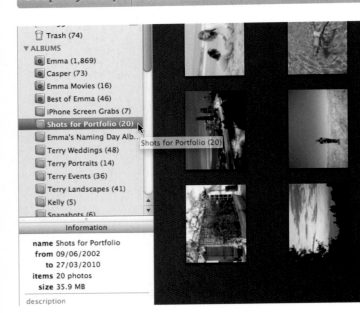

1: Select album
In iPhoto, select the album, folder or event that contains the images you want to work with. The images will be displayed in the main window. Again, make sure that only the images you want to affect are displayed.

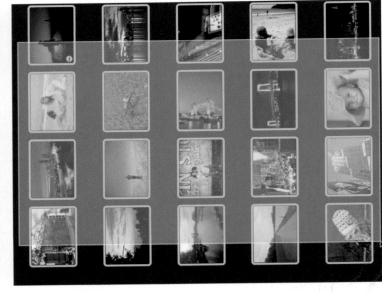

2: Select all images
Highlight all the images in the folder, either by dragging a selection window around them or using the Cmd+A keyboard shortcut. Selected images are shown with a yellow border.

Rotate your images in iPhoto
Edit multiple photos with one click

Spin decision
The default direction for the Rotate button can be set in the General pane of iPhoto's Preferences. Each click of the button spins the selected images through 90-degrees, and you can choose between clockwise and anti-clockwise rotation

Knowledge base

Copy protection

A photo's orientation is stored as part of the image file. This means that if you rotate an image, it alters its appearance in the photo library and in every album, slideshow, book, calendar, or card in which it appears. Therefore, if you want to leave the original file unaffected, make a copy of the image first and then rotate the copy.

Shortcut to success
Instead of using the Rotate button, you can use the Cmd+R keyboard shortcut as an alternative. Alt+Cmd+R rotates the selected images in the opposite direction

Engage reverse
To temporarily reverse the direction of the Rotate button without opening the Preferences, hold down the Option (Alt) key. The button's arrow icon changes to indicate the new direction

3: Deselect stragglers
If the folder contains any images that don't need to be rotated, you can remove them from the selection by holding down the Cmd key as you click on them.

4: Rotate images
Now you can rotate all the highlighted images through 90-degrees with a single click of the Rotate button, which is found towards the left of the toolbar at the bottom of the window.

Turn an iPhoto album into keepsakes

Use iPhoto effects to create a retro-style album and turn it into a top-quality calendar or photobook…

Task: Turn a retro album into a gift or keepsake

Difficulty: Beginner

Time needed: 30 minutes

Besides being a superb organiser, iPhoto is the gateway to Apple's quality print products. The idea is to use your photos to design a calendar, card or photobook, then print and share it with others. At the bottom of the main iPhoto screen you will find icons for Slideshow, Book, Calendar and Card. A click on any of these brings up templates, themes and relevant tools to guide you through to the purchase stage. From a personal family greeting card to an impressive photobook, the end product can be as simple or elaborate as you wish. There are many choices of colour, font, templates and themes, as well as end product type and size.

Step-by-step | iPhoto From iPhoto to an Apple print product

1: The album
In iPhoto, choose the photos to include in your album. In the main menu go to File>New Album From Selection and name your album

2: Retro look 1
Your album is now listed under Albums. Click on an album to display images within it. Select a photo and go to Edit>Effects. Click on the B&W effect.

3: Retro look 2
Go to Effects Palette>Fade Color. Click several times to brighten up the photo. Repeat with Antique to reach the desired level.

4: Retro album
Select another photo from the album and apply the same effects. Repeat the process for all photos until all of them have the same look.

5: Book type
With your album selected, click the Book icon. In the palette, choose from Hardcover, Softcover or Wire Bound, as well as the book's size.

6: Book design
Click Show Transitions Browser. Drag a classic Cross Dissolve between the clips. Use the Inspector to change the Transition Duration to 2:00 seconds.

Use iPhoto images to create keepsakes

Turn your images into cards, calendars and photobooks

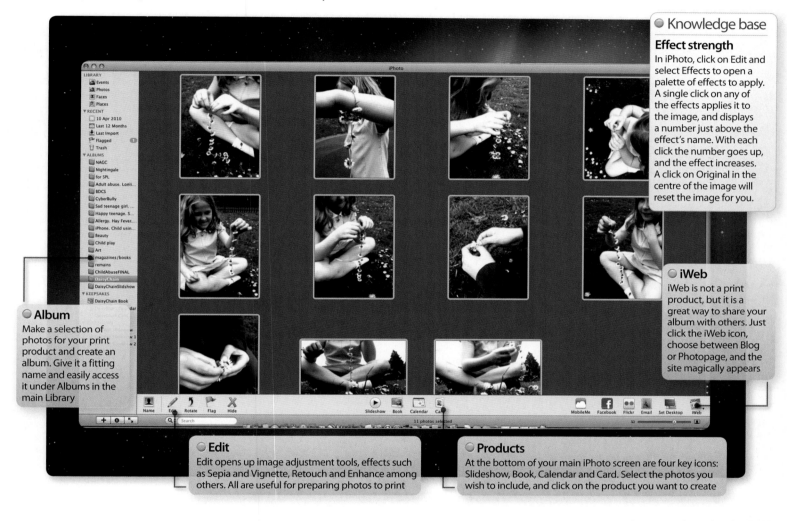

Knowledge base

Effect strength

In iPhoto, click on Edit and select Effects to open a palette of effects to apply. A single click on any of the effects applies it to the image, and displays a number just above the effect's name. With each click the number goes up, and the effect increases. A click on Original in the centre of the image will reset the image for you.

iWeb

iWeb is not a print product, but it is a great way to share your album with others. Just click the iWeb icon, choose between Blog or Photopage, and the site magically appears

Album

Make a selection of photos for your print product and create an album. Give it a fitting name and easily access it under Albums in the main Library

Edit

Edit opens up image adjustment tools, effects such as Sepia and Vignette, Retouch and Enhance among others. All are useful for preparing photos to print

Products

At the bottom of your main iPhoto screen are four key icons: Slideshow, Book, Calendar and Card. Select the photos you wish to include, and click on the product you want to create

7: Calendar

With your album selected, click Calendar. Enter details including the start date, which national holidays to show and the iCal calendars to import.

8: Card

From your album, select a photo for a greeting card and click the Card option. From the list on the left, choose card type. Click Settings to change the font.

9: Purchase your creation

As with all iPhoto print products, click Buy to open the Order palette. If you do not have an Apple account, you will need to set one up.

Apply multiple adjustments in iPhoto

It's possible to add the same adjustments to multiple photos. You can even do this in Full Screen mode, as we'll be showing you in this tutorial…

Task: Add the same adjustments to multiple images in iPhoto

Difficulty: Beginner

Time needed: 10 minutes

More often than not, if you have to make adjustments to a photo, you may find you need to also apply the same changes to other shots taken at the same time. Thinking that you have to manually alter each image in the same way over and over again may put you off the idea, or at the very least convince you to just alter the best photos and leave the others untouched. Thankfully, the iPhoto designers had considered this eventuality and thought of a way to simplify this process greatly – thereby not only saving you a considerable amount of time, but making sure all your photos look their best with very little effort.

We'll be showing you how this process works over the next two pages, but rather than working from the regular interface we'll also be taking a trip into Full Screen mode. Start by selecting an Event or Album, choose a photo and then go to View> Full Screen from the Menu Bar.

Step-by-step | iPhoto Apply adjustments to multiple photos

1: Multiple images

In Full Screen, you can only see one photo at a time by default. However, move the cursor to the top to reveal more thumbnails. Command-click on others to see them as well.

2: The Adjust window

With all your photos selected, you need to modify them. You can do this by moving the cursor to the bottom of the screen to reveal your tools. Click on the Adjust icon to bring up a floating window.

Adjust multiple iPhoto images

Add adjustments to your photos in Full Screen mode

● Thumbnails
Top of the screen are the thumbnails for the currently selected Event or Album. Any thumbnail surrounded by brown is currently displayed in the main body of the interface

● Effects
Although you can easily apply effects to your selected image, you cannot copy and paste them between stills. The Adjustments parameters are the only ones you can easily transfer to another photo

● Tools
All the tools you'll need to edit your image are shown when you mouse over the bottom of the screen. They're all the ones you would expect from iPhoto when not in Full Screen mode

● Knowledge base

White balance
You can apply a white balance to your image by selecting the Adjust window's eyedropper button and clicking on an area in the highlighted image that should actually be white (or light grey). Doing this will rebalance the colours to match what is expected. However, you cannot choose an area on another picture, only on the one you're currently working on.

● Adjustments
You can apply many adjustments to your photo from this window. To revert back to the original, click on the Reset button. To quickly switch between the original and the new look, hold down the Shift key

3: One at a time
Even though many photos are displayed, you can only modify one image at a time. Whichever one is currently selected will be affected by your modifications. Alter a photo until it looks just right.

4: Applying to others
Once you're happy with the alterations you've made, it's time to apply those changes to the other photos. Click on the Copy button, select another shot and click Paste. Repeat for your other images.

Tutorial: Manage Places manually

Not everyone's got a GPS-enabled camera, but that doesn't mean you can't use the Places feature…

Task: Use the Places feature for all your photos

Difficulty: Intermediate

Time needed: 25 minutes

When iPhoto introduced Places in 2009, it no doubt made a lot of iPhone users very happy, since the device has a built-in GPS antenna and can record the exact location of where any photo was taken. But the iPhone isn't the only product capable of doing this; many high-end cameras have this capability too, so all you have to do is connect it to your Mac and upload the pictures, then the map in Places gets filled with little red pins automatically. Sadly, most cameras are unable to store this information and you're left with regular digital photos with no idea where they were taken. But it is possible to manually add where in the world a shot was taken.

Step-by-step | iPhoto Add Places information to your photos

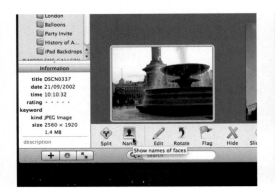

1: The interface
Select an album or Event of your choice. Looking at the interface, there isn't an obvious button you can use to set its Place, unlike the Faces button.

2: More information
Mouse over one of your photos and a small 'i' will appear, lower-right of the thumbnail. Click on it to reveal info about the image in a new window.

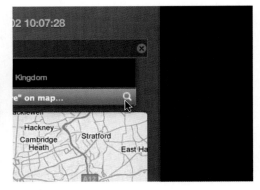

3: The photo place
You can use this window to rate your photo, rename it and add comments, but you can also add a location to it. Click on 'photo place' to highlight it.

4: Typing town
Start typing your city's name and a list of matching locations will appear. Select the correct one and the world map will be replaced with one from Google.

5: No possible alteration
You can zoom in and out of the map using the '+' and '-' buttons respectively. If you want to be more precise, you need to do something different…

6: The magnifying glass
Tap on your location to edit it. This time, enter a more precise location of where the shot was taken and click on the magnifying glass icon.

Manually use Places in iPhoto

Add your images to iPhoto's Places feature

Pin details
Mouse over a pin and its name will be revealed, along with a small arrow. Click on the arrow to see all the photos taken at that location

Knowledge base

List View in Places
The Places section has two views available. One is the Map (which is selected by default), the other is a list view. You can choose either by clicking on their respective icons, lower-left of the interface. In List view you can, for instance, select a country, county, town or address to only see the photos taken at that specific location.

Knowledge base

Managing Places
You can get to the window shown in Step 7 via Window>Manage My Places. You can rename your pins or alter their location. To add a new place, click on the 'Google Search' tab, find the new location then tap on its very small '+' button. When you get back to the My Places tab, you'll find it at the top of the list.

Switching views
These buttons let you switch between the world and list views, which display your photos in very different ways. The default option is world view

Zoom and drag
To zoom in and out of the map, use this slider. Once you've zoomed in, you can drag the cursor along the map to navigate across it. Double-click on a pin to zoom straight to it

Photos within view
To see all photos taken within the map's viewable area, click on this button. Places will then display all the images linked to all the visible pins

7: Add a new place
This reveals the 'Add New Place' window. Again, you can zoom in or out, but this time you can reposition the pin and alter the purple circle.

8: Assigning a place
When done, click on 'Assign to Photo'. You'll notice that the map's position will have changed in your photo to match the place you just added.

9: Stored in memory
When you need to add the same place to other photos, all you'll need to do is start typing that address. iPhoto will recognise it immediately.

Tutorial: Use slow motion effects in iMovie

Enhance the drama in a scene by slowing down time and creating your own action replays

iMovie enables you to tinker with time. By slowing down the action in your footage you can analyse a fast-moving event like horse riding at a more leisurely pace. We'll show you how to cut from real time to slow motion (and back to full speed) in one seamless sequence by using iMovie's clip splitting and re-timing tools, creating action replay style shots. By slowing down the video you'll also slow down the clip's sound, which can make speech sound strange. We'll show you how to replace the re-timed audio with the original sound and add dramatic music to link all the re-timed clips together.

Task: Adjust a scene's speed to have more of an impact

Difficulty: Beginner

Time needed: 10 minutes

Step-by-step | iMovie Change a clip's speed for dramatic effect

1: Import assets
Go to File>New Project. Create a project with a 16:9 aspect ratio. Choose File>Import Movie and add the Jumping and Driving clips into a new event.

2: Add to project
Drag the imported clip into the Project browser. Drag the number of frames per thumbnail slider to the left to see more of the shot's frames.

3: Split the clip
Scrub forward through the clip until the horse's front feet leave the ground. Right-click and choose Split Clip from the pop-up list of options.

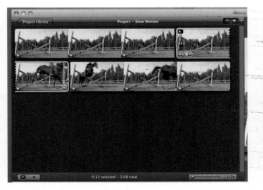

4: Split again
Split the clip again as soon as the front feet land on the ground. You now have three chunks of footage that still flow seamlessly together.

5: Convert clip
To change the middle section's speed double-click on the clip to open the Inspector. Click Convert Entire Clip from the Speed section.

6: Slow down
Drag the Speed slider towards the tortoise icon on the left to slow the speed of the clip down to 25%. Click Done to apply the change.

Add slow motion in iMovie
Introduce dramatic effects to your footage

Real time
The start and end clips in our sequence run at the normal speed. Only the middle section has been slowed down

Sound
To avoid the re-timed clip's slowed-down speech from sounding slurred we replaced it by inserting audio from the original clip

Action replay
Slowing down part of a clip is a brilliant way of analysing action that is normally over in a fraction of a second. Slow motion can also enhance dramatic sequences

Knowledge base

Invisible edit
This is a video editing term that refers to clips that appear to run as a single shot but actually contain several cuts. Our footage was cut to isolate the bit where the horse leaves the ground. We then slowed down the middle segment, but the invisible edits still let the footage flow smoothly as a single shot.

Slow down
Once you've converted a clip so that its speed can be altered use the Inspector's Speed slider to slow down the action

7: Playback
Part of the girl's speech has been slowed down. Press Command+A to select the clips. Go to the Inspector's Audio pane and reduce Volume to 0%.

8: Replace sound
Drag the clip from the Event browser onto the clip in the Project browser. Choose Sound Only from the pop-up menu. An audio track will appear.

9: Fine-tune sound
Drag the audio track right so the girl says "Good Boy!" after the horse jumps. Use Dramatic Accent 01 to add some sound at the start.

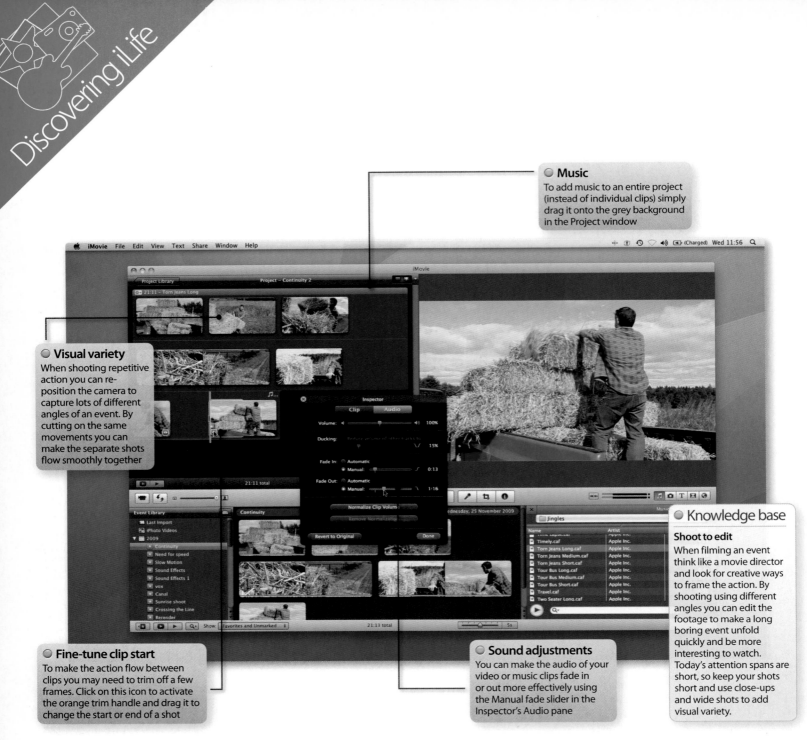

Music
To add music to an entire project (instead of individual clips) simply drag it onto the grey background in the Project window

Visual variety
When shooting repetitive action you can re-position the camera to capture lots of different angles of an event. By cutting on the same movements you can make the separate shots flow smoothly together

Knowledge base

Shoot to edit
When filming an event think like a movie director and look for creative ways to frame the action. By shooting using different angles you can edit the footage to make a long boring event unfold quickly and be more interesting to watch. Today's attention spans are short, so keep your shots short and use close-ups and wide shots to add visual variety.

Fine-tune clip start
To make the action flow between clips you may need to trim off a few frames. Click on this icon to activate the orange trim handle and drag it to change the start or end of a shot

Sound adjustments
You can make the audio of your video or music clips fade in or out more effectively using the Manual fade slider in the Inspector's Audio pane

Tutorial: Shoot & edit continuous sequences

Shoot your footage so that you can cut between multiple shots to produce an apparently continuous sequence

When we watch film or TV we tend to forget that we're watching an edited sequence, even though we know that between each shot the camera often stops recording and is repositioned to get a different angle. A minute of screen time may take an hour to film, but thanks to the magic of editing we believe that the action is happening in real time.

With some careful camera work we can record an event as separate shots and edit the clips together into a tight, 'real time' style sequence in iMovie. Our raw footage on the disc this issue shows a farmer loading up bales of hay onto a truck, but you can apply our shooting and editing tips to any activity you wish to shoot and edit yourself. Follow the steps over the page to create your own 'continuous' sequence in iMovie.

Task: Shoot and edit footage that flows
Difficulty: Intermediate
Time needed: 10 minutes

Click to fine tune clip start

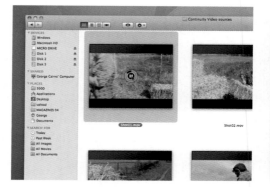

1: Review footage
Play the clips in the Continuity Source video folder to become familiar with the raw footage. We've labelled the clips according to the order in which they will cut.

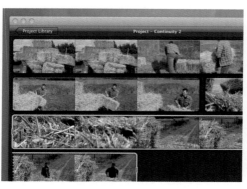

2: Import assets
Create a new 16:9 project. Import the clips. iMovie places them in the Event browser in chronological order, which is the same order in which we'll cut them.

3: Exit frame left
Drag 'Shot01' into the Project window. Here we let the actor walk out of the frame. This enables us to cut to him in 'Shot02' without a nasty jump cut.

4: Repetitive action
In 'Shot03' the actor dumps another hay bale on the truck. Filming repetitive actions helps you add a variety of different camera angles to your project.

5: Transition
By craning up from the hay ('Shot04') we create a natural transition to a later time in the sequence. This is an alternative to using iMovie's transitions.

6: Mid to wide
In 'Shot05' the actor climbs onto the truck. We filmed this as a close-up. We then cut to a wider version of the scene by cutting on the repetitive action in 'Shot06'.

7: Quick trim
Click the Fine-tune Clip start icon on 'Shot06'. Drag the handle to the right two frames so that the bale's position matches the bale in 'Shot05'.

8: Struck dumb
The sound changes in each shot, which highlights the cuts. Press Cmd+A in the Project window and choose Edit>Mute Clips.

9: Fade music
Drop the Torn Jeans Long jingle onto the Project window. As it cuts off abruptly, manually fade it out over 1:16 seconds using the Audio Inspector.

Tutorial: Combine video and stills in iMovie

Create a slideshow that mixes video and stills to produce a video sequence with different textures

Task: Create a slideshow with video and stills
Difficulty: Intermediate
Time needed: 10 minutes

When we film an event on our camcorder we may also take a few stills with our digital camera at the same time. We can use these stills to enhance our video programmes with a slideshow-style sequence in iMovie; with the combination of the still and moving images adding some variety to our programme.

SLR cameras produce a much higher resolution image than video footage does, which enables us to use iMovie's rostrum camera-mimicking abilities to zoom into objects in the photo without a drop in quality. A slideshow is also a good way to add a change of pace to your video production – not to mention the fact it can hide dodgy camera work, as you'll see in our walkthrough! Follow our nine easy steps to effectively combine your footage in iMovie.

Step-by-step | iMovie Combine a series of still cutaways with video footage

1: Into iPhoto
Drag the Slideshow Sources folder from the free disc onto the iPhoto icon. The video footage and stills will be imported into a new iPhoto event.

2: Access photos
Open iMovie. To access the stills click on the Show Photos Browser icon and double-click on the Slideshow Sources Event icon to see the shots.

3: Access movie
To see the imported video clip click on the iPhoto Videos icon and scroll through your movies to find it. Create a new project called Slideshow.

4: Add movie
Drag the movie into the Project window. The footage starts off okay but becomes wobbly. We'll replace the wobbles with stills, but retain the audio.

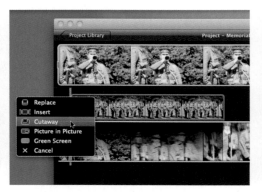

5: Add still
Drag a still from the Photos browser onto the video clip (before the camera starts to wobble). Choose Cutaway to preserve the video clip's sound.

6: Trim photo
The photo's default duration of four seconds is too long. Drag the end of the still to the left to shorten it to around 1:19 seconds.

Create a slideshow

Combine video footage and stills

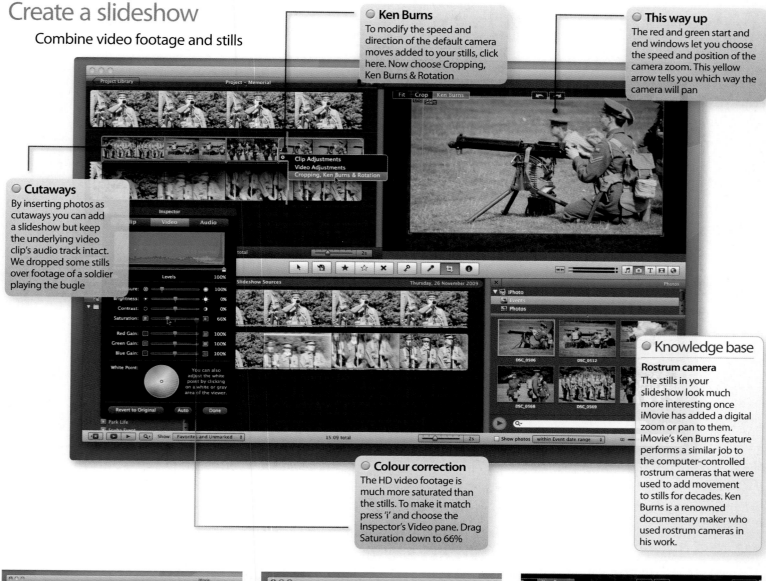

Ken Burns
To modify the speed and direction of the default camera moves added to your stills, click here. Now choose Cropping, Ken Burns & Rotation

This way up
The red and green start and end windows let you choose the speed and position of the camera zoom. This yellow arrow tells you which way the camera will pan

Cutaways
By inserting photos as cutaways you can add a slideshow but keep the underlying video clip's audio track intact. We dropped some stills over footage of a soldier playing the bugle

Knowledge base

Rostrum camera
The stills in your slideshow look much more interesting once iMovie has added a digital zoom or pan to them. iMovie's Ken Burns feature performs a similar job to the computer-controlled rostrum cameras that were used to add movement to stills for decades. Ken Burns is a renowned documentary maker who used rostrum cameras in his work.

Colour correction
The HD video footage is much more saturated than the stills. To make it match press 'i' and choose the Inspector's Video pane. Drag Saturation down to 66%

7: Add more stills
Drop in a few more photos as cutaways. Trim them and slide them to hide any of the wobbly video footage. Play back the slideshow.

8: Modify movement
By default the slides are zoomed to give them movement. Click a photo's Gear icon and choose Cropping, Ken Burns & Rotation.

9: Rostrum camera
Position the green square to indicate the start of the rostrum camera move. Now place the red square to indicate the end.

Tutorial: Create high-speed action in iMovie

Enhance your road movies with exciting high-speed driving scenes and iron out bumps in the re-timed footage with help from iMovie's picture-advanced Stabilization tool...

Task: Speed up driving footage in iMovie

Difficulty: Intermediate

Time needed: 10 minutes

Thanks to iMovie's ability to speed up HD (High Definition) or SD (Standard Definition) footage, you can add dramatic Hollywood-style driving scenes to your programmes without breaking the speed limit! However, by speeding up handheld driving footage you can run the risk of exaggerating wobbles caused by bumps in the road or excessive camera shake. Professional filmmakers can avoid camera shake by mounting their camera onto a rig strapped to the bonnet of the car, but we're unlikely to have access to such specialist kit. Luckily, we have iMovie to smooth out the bumps in our re-timed footage, which means we can produce a smooth high-speed shot. Just follow the steps to find out how.

Step-by-step | iMovie Shoot and edit smooth high-speed driving footage

1: Establishing shot
Find somewhere scenic and film your car driving past to place it in a location. A low-angle camera shot will produce a more cinematic look

2: Ride shotgun
All driving movies need a protagonist to put his foot down, so sit in the passenger seat and film the driver for a few seconds.

3: Round the bend
To capture dramatic road footage tilt the camera and lean into the bend, then straighten it up once you hit a straight road.

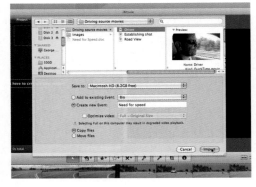

4: Import assets
Create a new 16:9 project and choose File>Import Movies. Import the HD clips from the Driving Source Movies folder on the disc.

5: Edit clips
Drag the clips onto the timeline in the Project window. Place the establishing shot first, then add the driver and drag in the road footage.

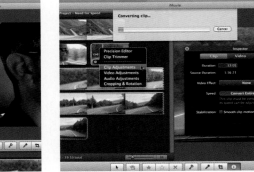

6: Convert clip
Click on the third clip's gear icon and choose Clip Adjustments. Click the Convert Entire Clip button next to the Speed option.

Shoot & edit high-speed footage
Speed up your driving footage in iMovie

Grading
To create a stronger contrast and produce more vivid-looking colours, adjust the Contrast and Saturation sliders in the Inspector's Video pane

Knowledge base

Fade it down
When you speed up your video footage it speeds up the sound too, creating comical high-pitched sounds. Go to the Audio pane in the Inspector and reduce the volume of speeded up footage to 0%. You can now replace the original audio with sound from other clips, or raid the Transportation folder in the iLife Library for suitable sound effects.

Turbo charger
To make your car drive faster drag the Clip Inspector's Speed slider to the right. Try and resist pushing it to the max or the high-speed footage will look unrealistically fast!

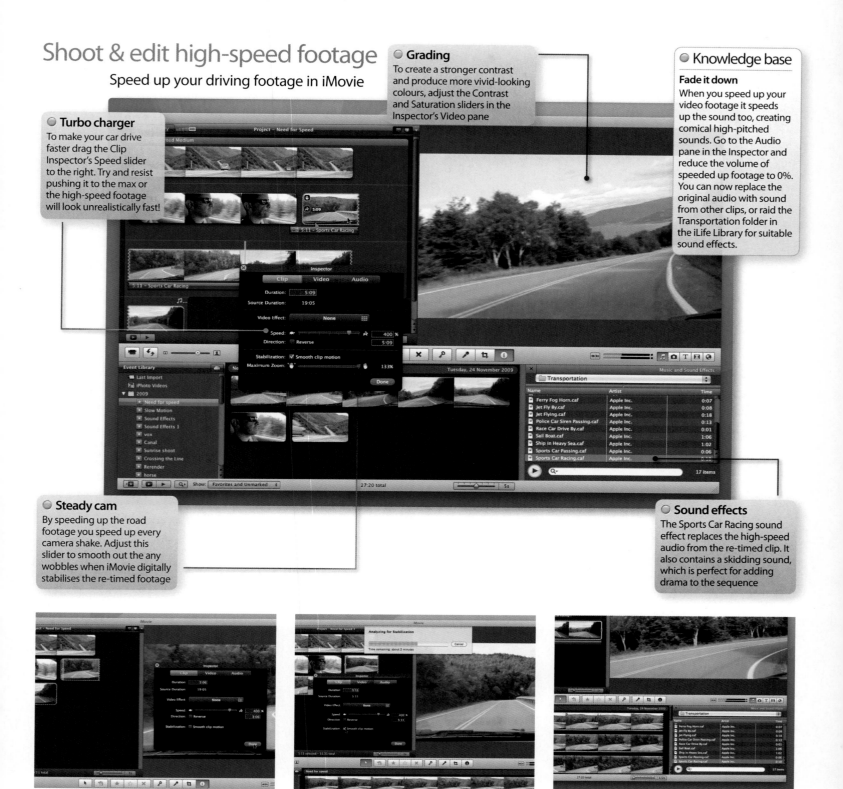

Steady cam
By speeding up the road footage you speed up every camera shake. Adjust this slider to smooth out the any wobbles when iMovie digitally stabilises the re-timed footage

Sound effects
The Sports Car Racing sound effect replaces the high-speed audio from the re-timed clip. It also contains a skidding sound, which is perfect for adding drama to the sequence

7: Speed up
Drag the Speed slider right (towards the nippy hare icon) to speed up the clip by 400%. This will make the clip's duration much shorter.

8: Digital suspension
Play back the re-timed footage. It's a little wobbly! Press 'i' to open the Clip Inspector. Tick the 'Smooth clip motion' box. Click Done.

9: Sound effects
Go to the Transportation folder in the Music & Sound Effects browser and use Sports Car Racing to enhance the high-speed footage.

Tutorial: Shoot and edit underwater footage

Capture holiday activities above and below the water line, then edit your shots into a documentary-style sequence

Task: Shoot and edit underwater footage

Difficulty: Advanced

Time needed: 10 minutes

On previous holidays you may have bought a disposable waterproof stills camera to take snaps underwater. These film cameras tend to steam up with condensation, and you have to get the film processed before you can see the (often disappointing) results. In these digital days you can buy compact cameras that are at home above or below the water line. Because they can also shoot video, you can share your underwater experiences with friends and family from the comfort of dry land. To make your raw footage easier to consume here's our guide on ways to shoot clips that will cut together into a seamless sequence.

Step-by-step | **iMovie** Shoot and edit underwater clips into a smooth, flowing sequence

1: Right tool
The Olympus μ Tough range of compact cameras are great for shooting video or stills underwater. We put a Tough-8000 through its underwater paces.

2: Right mode
When shooting underwater it can be a challenge to get focus and exposure set correctly, but the Tough cameras have a range of preset underwater modes.

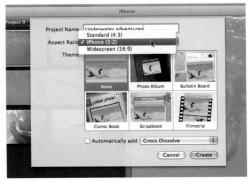

3: Create new project
Create a new project with an iPhone aspect ratio (the Tough-8000 produces the same 640 x 480 clips). Import the clips from the CD into a new Event.

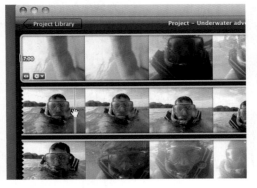

4: Select footage
Drag a yellow selection handle over the second half of clip two in the Event browser. Drag the selected footage into the Project window.

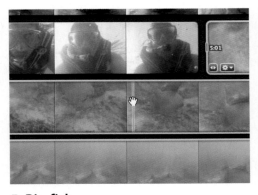

5: Big fish
Select the Event browser's third clip (the big fish swimming) and place that after the first clip in the Project window's timeline.

6: Adjust exposure
To give the underwater footage more contrast press 'i' to open the Inspector and click Video. Drag the shadow Levels slider to 14%. Click Done.

Sub-aqua shooting
Make a splash in iMovie

Create continuity
When shooting underwater you may not have planned how the clips will edit together. By flipping problem shots horizontally we can make the diver swim in the same direction all shots

Knowledge base

Choose your weapon
There's a range of compact waterproof cameras to choose from. The Olympus MJU Tough 8000 costs around £200, and you can use it to shoot as deep as ten metres. If you only plan to snorkel near the surface then the cheaper Olympus MJU 1050 SW will set you back around £130, and you can use it up to a depth of three metres.

Multiple sound effects
To add layers of sound to your silent project drag Ocean Surf to the Project's grey background. Drag Water Lake onto one of the clips, then stretch it out to cover the whole programme

Non-linear editing
We shot our diving and surfacing shots in a single clip, then popped the diving section of the footage at the start of the sequence and the surfacing section at the end

Adjust Contrast
Shooting underwater tends to produce clips with a flat, washed-out contrast. The Video Inspector's Levels sliders help as they produce a wider range of tones

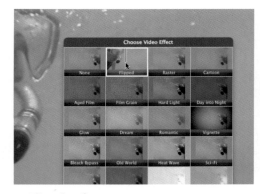

7: Flip the footage
Add the clip of the diver to the sequence. To make him swim in the correct direction use the Clip Inspector to flip the footage horizontally.

8: Add the flippers
You can film yourself to get close-up footage, then drop in a clip of a friend's flippers to fake a long shot of yourself underwater.

9: Back to the surface
To make the diver surface, drag the yellow selection handle over the first part of shot 2 in the Event browser and add that to the project.

Gain

The Video Inspector's colour Gain sliders enable you to make specific colours become more dominant. This slider helps turn the shot's blue sky a cross-processed style green

Colour continuity

It makes sense to adjust all of your clips using the same cross-processing settings. Before opening the Video Inspector press Command+A to select all of the clips in the Project window

Black levels

By dragging the shadow Levels slider right you can darken the shadows in the shot. Rich black shadows are typical in cross-processed clips and make the footage look more dramatic

Knowledge base

Cross-processing

This term comes from a traditional photography darkroom technique. If you process print film using slide film chemicals (or vice versa) you can produce striking shifts in colour hue. Fashion photographers often favour this effect. Traditional cross-processing is very hit and miss but iMovie lets you get the effect right every time (without having to mess around with any smelly chemicals!).

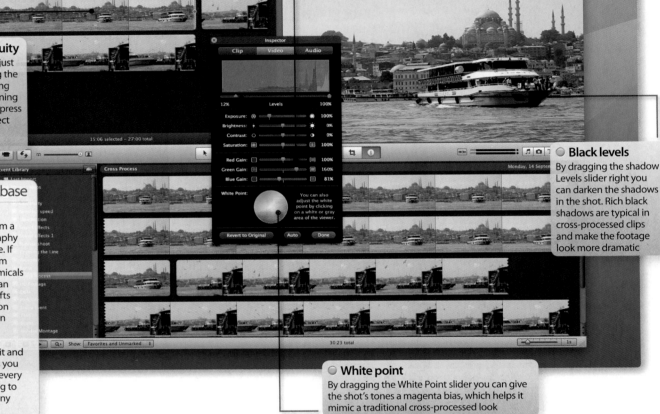

White point

By dragging the White Point slider you can give the shot's tones a magenta bias, which helps it mimic a traditional cross-processed look

Tutorial: Mimic cross-processing effects

You can adjust a shot's hues and tones in iMovie to make your ordinary footage look extraordinary. We show you how…

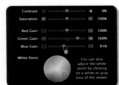

Task: Cross-process your clips in iMovie

Difficulty: Beginner

Time needed: 10 minutes

Professional filmmakers sometimes shoot on video for budgetary reasons, as film is more expensive. To make their humble video footage more interesting to watch they tend to tinker with colour and tone. It's quite fashionable to make video footage mimic the old-school cross-processed look favoured by fashion photographers. Cross-processed shots tend to feature green looking skies and have dark blues in the shadows. These distinctive colours are sure to make the shot get noticed. The shadows in cross-processed shots are often much darker than in normal exposures, causing the darkest details to become clipped (or hidden). Thanks to iMovie's wide range of colour tweaking commands, you can create eye-catching cross-processed style shots in minutes.

Step-by-step | iMovie Add customised animated titles to enhance your online production

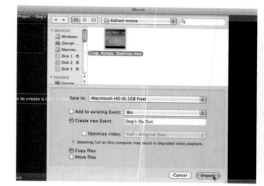

1: Create new project
Go to File>New Project. Create a project with a Standard 4:3 Aspect Ratio. Use File>Import>Movies to import 'Crop, Rotate, Stabilize.mov'.

2: Title browser
Press the Show Titles browser icon. You can preview the behaviour of each animated title by letting the mouse hover over its thumbnail.

3: Add a title
Now drag the Lens Flare thumbnail into the Project window. Drag the end of the title bar so that it overlaps the first shot.

4: Bigger preview
Double-click the Title bar, then click on Title: Lens Flare. You can explore much larger previews of all the titles in the main Viewer.

5: Tacky title
Click on Four Corners, as cheesy lens flares are a bit Nineties! Click Done. Now hit the Spacebar to preview the new title's movement.

6: Edit title
Type in some customised text in the main Viewer. You can click Show Fonts to fine-tune the size and colour of your text.

7: More impact
Fancy fonts, like this title's default Coolvetica, can date pretty quickly. A strong bold sans-serif font like Impact will be easier to read.

8: Neutral colour
The default colours make the text blend with the shot's greens and yellows, making it harder to read. A clean white makes the title stand out.

9: Giving it large
Some web galleries display footage in a small window. To make your titles more legible, bump up the font size to 6. Click Done and you're finished!

Tutorial: Crop, rotate and straighten in iMovie

Use iMovie's image adjustment tools to give you more editing options from your iPhone footage

It may take a special occasion to motivate you to dust off your camcorder, so you may miss the chance to record unexpected events. Since your iPhone is with you at all times, you can capture video opportunities as they occur. As the iPhone is lighter than a typical camcorder, it can cause your handheld footage to wobble. There's no zoom function either, so your subject may appear too small. And if you rotate the iPhone from a horizontal to vertical position, your footage will appear on its side when viewed on your Mac. Fortunately, iMovie's clever post-production tools can stabilise shake, crop shots and rotate clips to a correct orientation.

Task: Stabilise and rotate iPhone 3GS footage

Difficulty: Intermediate

Time needed: 15 minutes

Step-by-step | iMovie Crop, rotate and stabilise

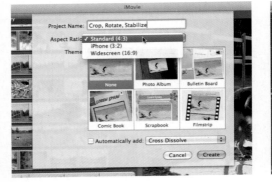

1: Create new project
Go to File>New Project. To avoid seeing black vertical bars (pillar boxing) at the edge of the 3:2 iPhone footage, choose Standard (4:3) Aspect Ratio.

2: Import footage
Go to File>Import>Movies. Browse to the six source files on the disc. Press Cmd+A to select them, create a new event and click Import.

3: Clip adjustments
Drag the fourth shot in the Event browser to the Project window. The clip's a bit wobbly, so click on its gear icon and choose Clip Adjustments.

4: Stabilise
In the Inspector tick the 'Smooth clip motion' box. This will cause iMovie to crop and move the clip so it can try and iron out some of the wobbles.

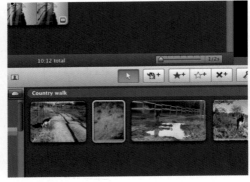

5: This way up
Drag the second shot from the Event browser to the Project window. This was captured when holding the iPhone vertically, so it needs to be rotated.

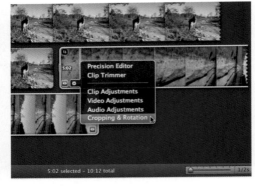

6: Rotate clip
Click the second clip's gear icon and choose Cropping & Rotation. In the main Viewer click the 'Rotate clip 90° counter-clockwise' icon.

Crop, rotate and stabilise footage

Overcome problems created when shooting on your handheld iPhone

Get in gear
Each clip's Gear icon will give you access to a selection of extra editing tools, like the handy Cropping & Rotation command

Crop
If you add a 16:9 HD shot to a 4:3 project then iMovie will automatically crop out the left and right edges of the clip. This avoids letter boxing (black bars along the top and bottom)

Our three-legged friend
While iMovie's stabilisation tools can help improve the footage, there's no substitute for using a tripod – as our project's final shot demonstrates

Steady on
iPhone clips can be a little shaky, so press 'i' to open the Inspector and tick here to smooth out the shakes. Some clips will respond better than others to this treatment

Knowledge base

Unstable
iMovie stabilises a shot by zooming in to lose the edges of the frame. It then tries to reposition the cropped clip's contents frame-by-frame to reduce shaking. You'll notice different clips have a different maximum zoom percentage. The wobblier the clip, the tighter iMovie has to zoom to hide the edges of the frame.

7: Add next clip
You can also choose a different colour for your links. Highlight one and go to the Text Inspector. Click the colour well and choose a different shade.

8: Digital zoom
The dog is too small in the frame. Go back to the Cropping & Rotation menu and draw a tighter green box around the hound. Click Done.

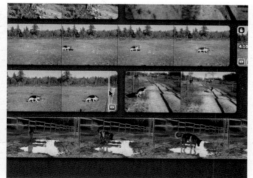

9: Tracking shot
The crop makes the dog walk out of frame, which lets us cut back to him in the following shot. The tighter you crop, the fuzzier the shot will look.

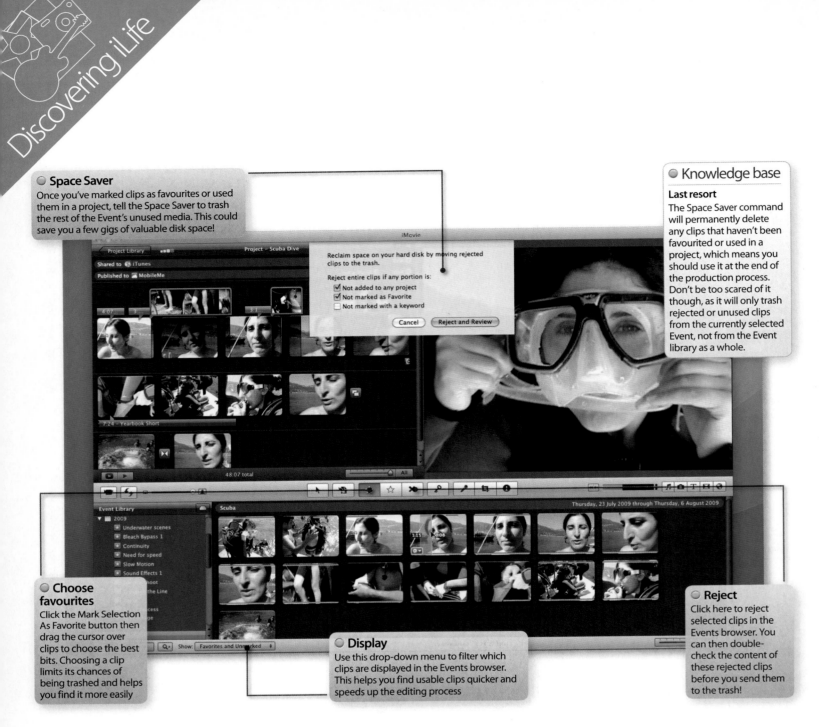

Space Saver
Once you've marked clips as favourites or used them in a project, tell the Space Saver to trash the rest of the Event's unused media. This could save you a few gigs of valuable disk space!

Knowledge base

Last resort
The Space Saver command will permanently delete any clips that haven't been favourited or used in a project, which means you should use it at the end of the production process. Don't be too scared of it though, as it will only trash rejected or unused clips from the currently selected Event, not from the Event library as a whole.

Choose favourites
Click the Mark Selection As Favorite button then drag the cursor over clips to choose the best bits. Choosing a clip limits its chances of being trashed and helps you find it more easily

Display
Use this drop-down menu to filter which clips are displayed in the Events browser. This helps you find usable clips quicker and speeds up the editing process

Reject
Click here to reject selected clips in the Events browser. You can then double-check the content of these rejected clips before you send them to the trash!

Reduce the size of your iMovie projects

By organising your projects more effectively you can work faster and save valuable disk space at the same time!

Task: Create tidier projects and save disk space
Difficulty: Beginner
Time needed: 10 minutes

Thanks to gadgets like your iPhone 3GS and the fact that you can shoot relatively inexpensive HD footage using camcorders (and even digital SLRs), you will soon find that your poor hard drive is beginning to groan under the weight of all that footage. As well as losing valuable disk space you will also find that asset management becomes a problem, as it can take ages for you to find specific clips – but by having 'favourite' and 'rejected' clips, finding specific clips becomes much easier.

Fortunately, iMovie has some handy tools to help you sort out the wheat from the chaff and make your projects tidier, not to mention saving some valuable disk space at the same time. So, follow the nine steps over the page and get ready to spring clean that hard drive!

Step-by-step | iMovie Save space on your hard drive

1: Organise your assets
When you import footage, iMovie places the clips in Events that are presented in chronological order. You can browse these clips in the Events library.

2: Choose your favourites
While watching clips highlight the best bits. Click a clip, select part of it and press the Mark Selection As Favorite button. A green line will appear.

3: Reject
If a clip (or part of a clip) is out of focus or suffers from dodgy camera work, press the Reject Selection button. The rejected clip will vanish.

4: Show and tell
To help you find the best clips (and ignore the rejects) you can set the Show button at the bottom to display Favorites Only.

5: Edit a project
Favouriting and rejecting clips helps you work out what's worth using. Clips that feature in a project have an orange line across the bottom.

6: One last chance
You can still use rejected clips by setting the Show drop-down menu to Rejected Clips. If you don't need them click Move Rejected To Trash.

7: Belt and braces
If you're accessing clips from an external drive, import the edited footage to your Mac before deleting anything. This ensures that the project will be playable.

8: Consolidate media
Choose File>Consolidate Media. By clicking Copy Clips you'll only import the footage that features in the project. You can trash the rest of the event later.

9: Space Saver
Go to File>Space Saver. Tick to reject clips that haven't made it into your project (or aren't favourites). Click Reject and Review, then click Move Rejected To Trash.

Use time lapse techniques in iMovie

Shoot a series of stills at regular intervals, then turn your footage into a high-speed movie

It's easy to forget when watching a movie that we're actually viewing a series of still images. Because these images whiz by at a rate of 25 images (or frames) per second, the footage appears to run in 'real time'. However, if you capture just one image every second (instead of the usual 25) then play the shots back at the usual rate, you'll see a dramatic increase in the speed at which time passes. This technique is called time lapse photography, and you can produce it using an iPhone and iMovie. You need to capture a series of shots at regular intervals so they flow smoothly. Here's how to capture and edit your time lapse sequence…

Task: Shoot and edit time lapse footage in iMovie

Difficulty: Intermediate

Time needed: 10 minutes

Step-by-step | iMovie Shoot and edit time lapse footage

1: Suitable software
To shoot a series of stills, download the free Gorillacam app and pop it on your iPhone. You can set it to shoot 100 shots at intervals of 5 seconds.

2: Stay steady
The Gorillamobile tripod is a great way to keep your iPhone stable. Trigger Gorillacam then sit back and relax while it automatically shoots a series of stills.

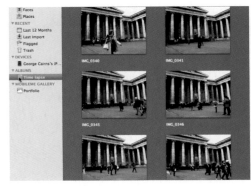

3: Import photos
Import the shots from the Time Lapse source folder from this issue's CD into iPhoto. Pop the photos into a new album called 'Time Lapse'.

4: Open iMovie
In iMovie, create a new project called Time Lapse. Choose a Standard Aspect Ratio. Click the Show Photos icon and select the Time Lapse folder.

5: Play sequence
Drag the Time Lapse album into the Project window. Play the project. At this stage each still lasts four seconds and has a default Ken Burns transition.

6: Remove Ken Burns
Press Cmd+A to select all the stills. Click on a still's gear icon and choose Cropping, Ken Burns & Rotation. Click Fit to remove the movement.

Edit time lapse footage in iMovie

Condense minutes into seconds with this time-travelling technique

Sound
A suitable music track helps knit the separate stills into a smooth flowing time lapse sequence

Knowledge base

Shooting the stills

The great thing about shooting your time lapse stills using an iPhone is the fact that you're almost invisible. When shooting using an SLR camera and a large tripod you'd soon get questioned by police or security personnel (and be asked to move on). To help you shoot unnoticed, don't stare at the screen while the software automatically snaps away.

Stay still
By default, iMovie slaps a random camera move on each still. Use the Ken Burns menu to make every shot fit into the frame and lose this unwanted movement

Import albums
Your imported time lapse iPhone frames will start off in iPhoto. If you pop them into a labelled album then it's a doddle to import them into iMovie

Change duration
Imported stills run for four seconds, which creates a jerky and slow time lapse sequence. Change the duration to four frames per second

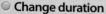

7: Change duration
Press 'i' to open the Video Inspector. Set Duration to 0:04. Tick the 'Applies to all stills' box. Click OK and play the time lapse sequence.

8: Boost exposure
Because the weather can change during a time lapse shoot, you may get an under-exposed frame. Use the Inspector to boost the Exposure of still 49.

9: Music
To link all the shots together pop to the Music browser and drag the tinkling Time Lapse jingle onto the Project window.

Use Keywords for organisation in iMovie

Discover how to assign keywords to your clips and find your footage faster!

Task: Add and search by keywords in iMovie

Difficulty: Beginner

Time needed: 10 minutes

Most photographers realise the importance of keywords, as they have thousands of shots to wade through in iPhoto. Keywords help them find photos in seconds rather than minutes. Now that many of us carry a camcorder around (courtesy of our iPhone), we may have hours of footage to wade through. As our iMovie Event Library grows, it makes sense to add keywords to our collection of video clips, so that we don't have to waste time scrolling through events trying to remember when we shot a specific video. Luckily iMovie makes it a doddle to add keywords to bits of footage (or the entire clip) by ticking boxes.

Step-by-step | iMovie Assign keywords to help you find footage quicker

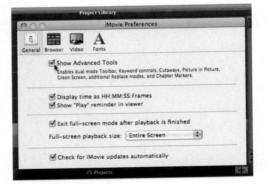

1: Advanced tools
To assign and search for keywords in iMovie you need to delve into iMovie>Preferences. In the General section tick Show Advanced Tools.

2: Keyword Tool
Click the Keyword Tool icon (or press 'K' to activate it). The Keywords window will appear containing a series of common keywords, like Pets or People.

3: Assign a keyword
Tick the keyword that you want to use. Drag the key-shaped cursor over a clip (or part of a clip) in the Event browser to assign it to that footage.

4: Thin blue line
You can apply multiple keywords to a clip at the same time – a label will indicate which keywords are being added. This footage contains a blue line.

5: Create keyword
Create more specific keywords by typing in the text field and clicking Add. Tick the new keyword's box and assign it to a clip in the usual way.

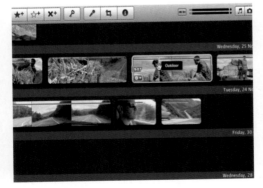

6: Shortcuts
Keywords have a number by them. You can select a clip in the Event browser and type '1' to assign a Landscape keyword, or '2' for Outdoor.

Add keywords to clips in iMovie

Find footage quicker in future by assigning keywords to it

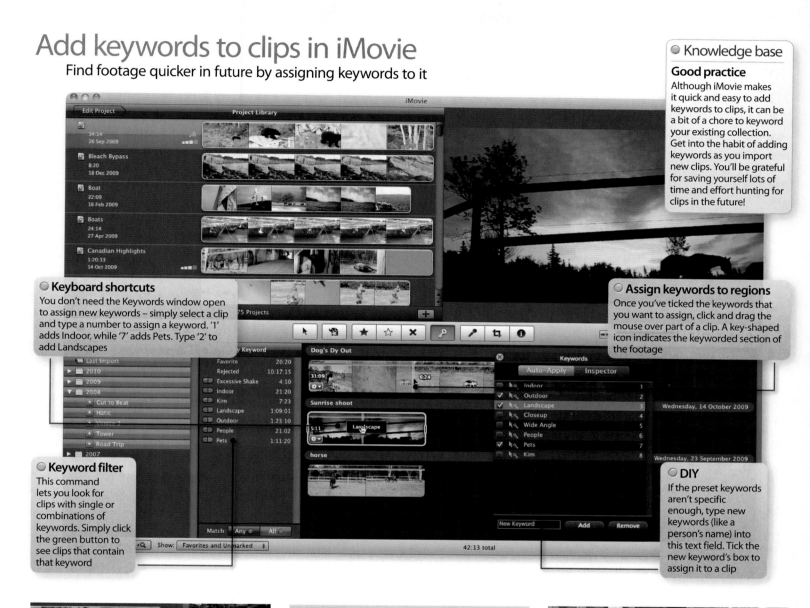

● Keyboard shortcuts

You don't need the Keywords window open to assign new keywords – simply select a clip and type a number to assign a keyword. '1' adds Indoor, while '7' adds Pets. Type '2' to add Landscapes

● Assign keywords to regions

Once you've ticked the keywords that you want to assign, click and drag the mouse over part of a clip. A key-shaped icon indicates the keyworded section of the footage

● Keyword filter

This command lets you look for clips with single or combinations of keywords. Simply click the green button to see clips that contain that keyword

● DIY

If the preset keywords aren't specific enough, type new keywords (like a person's name) into this text field. Tick the new keyword's box to assign it to a clip

7: Auto apply

Click on the Keywords Inspector tab. Select a clip by clicking on it. Now, when you tick a keyword or two, they will automatically be assigned to the clip.

8: Search keywords

Go to Window>Show Keyword Filter. Tick 'Filter by Keyword'. Click Match Any. Tick the green buttons to see clips that are Outdoors or feature Pets.

9: Fine-tune search

By ticking the Match All button you can make the Event browser display all shots that are outdoors and feature a pet.

Add a scrolling text effect

A video is incomplete without being top and tailed by a title and credits sequence. Here's how to make those credits roll!

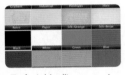

Task: Add rolling text using iMovie's Titles browser

Difficulty: Intermediate

Time needed: 5 minutes

Veterans of tape-to-tape video editing suites will remember the hassle of adding captions and titles to their films. You had to print your title or credits on a sheet of paper, use a vision mixer to invert the clip and turn black lettering to white, then key the text over the footage. To get the text to actually scroll involved splashing out cash on an expensive caption generator. Thanks to iMovie, we can add slick-looking text with ease (and customise font, colour and alignment to suit our footage). We can also make those credits scroll in a smooth and professional looking way.

Step-by-step | iMovie Create a rolling credits sequence

1: Import photos
Drag the photos from the Credits Stills folder into iPhoto. You can then import them (or some of your own assets) into iMovie.

2: Open iMovie
In iMovie create a new project. Click the Show Photo browser icon and click on Last Import. Drag the six stills into the Project window.

3: Change duration
By default each still runs for four seconds. To speed the sequence up select a clip and press 'i'. Type a Duration of 3:00. Tick 'Applies to all stills'.

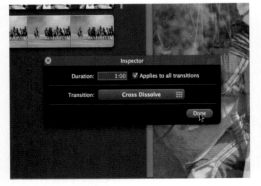

4: Add transitions
Each still is given a random camera move to make it more interesting. To blend the stills together, drag a Cross Dissolve transition between each image.

5: Scrolling text
Click on the Show Titles browser icon. Drag Scrolling Credits onto the first still. Drag the blue bar to extend the credits through the whole sequence.

6: Edit the text
Replace the placeholder text with something more relevant. Tap the Return key a few times to put some space between each credit.

Create a credits sequence in iMovie

Use iMovie's Titles browser to add rolling text to your footage

● **Knowledge base**

May the force be with you…
One of the most famous scrolling text sequences in a movie is the long intro at the beginning of the *Star Wars* films. This epic scrolling text slowly recedes into the distance over a star field backdrop. You can pay homage to this sequence by adding the Far Far Away title to your project. There's even a starscape backdrop in the Choose Background panel.

● **Alignment**
By aligning your font to the right (instead of the default central position) you can stop it from obscuring any of your onscreen footage

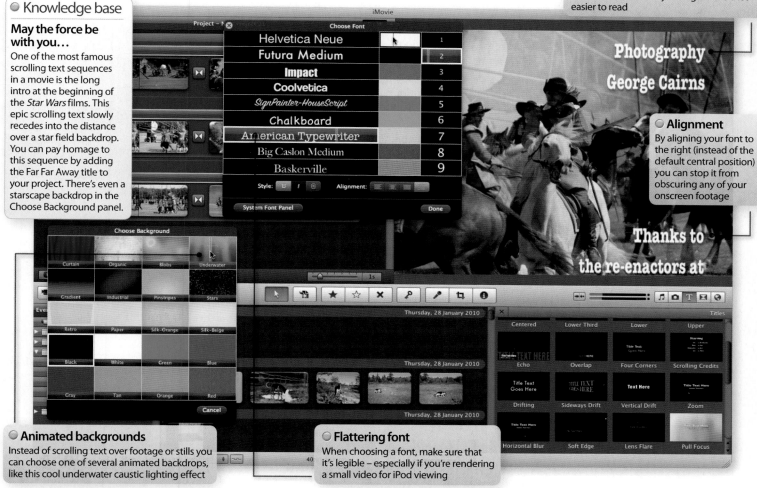

● **Animated backgrounds**
Instead of scrolling text over footage or stills you can choose one of several animated backdrops, like this cool underwater caustic lighting effect

● **Flattering font**
When choosing a font, make sure that it's legible – especially if you're rendering a small video for iPod viewing

7: Modify fonts
Click Show Fonts and choose a font to suit your footage. We picked a red to match the tunics of our riders and aligned the text to the right.

8: Quality control
You can add more credits at any time. iMovie will underline possible spelling mistakes to help your production look more professional.

9: Add music
Rolling credits look more professional with an accompanying score, so drag a suitable jingle (like Pursuit) into the Project window.

Control time in iMovie

Use a variety of editing tricks, techniques and effects to show the passing of time

Task: Evoke the passing of time in iMovie

Difficulty: Intermediate

Time needed: 15 minutes

If you watch a documentary from a couple of decades ago, the pace is much slower than the programmes we watch today. Old-school editors would let a shot run for longer, leading to a pace that can be frustrating and boring for modern viewers. For example, a traditional editor would wait for the camera to finish panning before cutting to the next shot. Modern editors will happily cut during a pan to tighten the pace of their programme. Thanks to iMovie's editing tools, slow-paced videos are a thing of the past. In this walkthrough you'll learn techniques to make time pass in a variety of ways, so the viewer will stay hooked.

Step-by-step | iMovie Use cuts, transitions and rendering effect to make time pass

1: Speed up time
Create a new Widescreen (16:9) project and use File>Import>Movies to add the 'Re-time.mov' to a new event. Label it 'Time Travel' and click Import.

2: Convert clip
Drag the clip into the Project window. The clouds move too slowly in real time. Click the clip and press 'i' to open the Inspector. Click Convert Entire Clip.

3: Detach audio
Before you speed up the shot, click on the clip and choose Edit>Detach Audio. This will enable you to re-time the video without altering the audio.

4: Increase speed
Open the Inspector and drag the Speed slider to the far right. This speeds up the clouds by 800%, making them streak across the sky. Click Done.

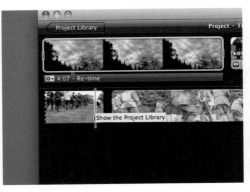

5: Disjointed cut
Add 'March.mov' and 'Battle.mov' to the project. There's a jarring jump between the march and the battle. A transition will make time pass smoother.

6: Smooth transition
Click Show Transitions Browser. Drag a classic Cross Dissolve between the clips. Use the Inspector to change the Transition Duration to 2:00 seconds.

Make time pass in iMovie

Take control of time and pace

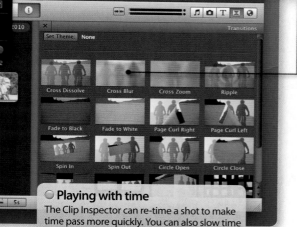

Detach audio

By detaching the audio from a clip, you can avoid speeding up the sound when you speed up the visuals. High-speed audio produces an unwanted comic effect

Knowledge base

What's a transition?

The most common way to show the passing of time is to add a transition between two clips. One of the oldest transitions is the cross dissolve (or mix). This gentle blend from one shot to another has been around since the earliest days of cinema. For that reason the Cross Dissolve is a timeless transition, and is less likely to make your footage look dated than a flashy Page Curl.

Transitions

The Transitions browser lets you mix or wipe between shots to indicate the passing of time. Hold the cursor over a transition to see a preview

Split clip

By splitting a single clip into several chunks you can make time run at a normal pace, then speed up or slow down using time ramps

Playing with time

The Clip Inspector can re-time a shot to make time pass more quickly. You can also slow down to highlight a particular moment

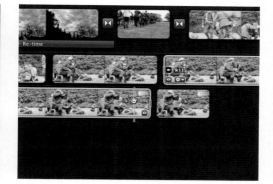

7: Slow down

Slowing down time can add drama. Add 'Shoot. mov' and scrub to where the soldier begins to raise his rifle. Right-click and choose Split Clip.

8: Let's split

Split the clip again after the soldier fires the shot. Use the Inspector to slow the middle section down to 25%. Click Done.

9: Time ramps

Play the sequence. Time slows down as the soldier fires, then returns to normal speed within the same clip. This is called a time ramp.

Transfer iMovie projects between Macs

Need to move an iMovie project and its clips from one Mac to another? We show you how…

| Zoo |
| 56s |
| 13 Jan 2009 |
| Disk 1 |
| Disk 2 |
| Disk 3 |
| Time Travel |
| 24s |
| 27 Apr 2010 |

Task: Move an iMovie project between Macs

Difficulty: Beginner

Time needed: 10 minutes

Video clips can take up lots of space on your Mac's hard drive, especially the footage in iMovie's Event Library. If you're shooting and editing while on the move, then your MacBook might find itself running out of storage space. But by transferring an iMovie project and footage to an external hard drive, you can free up valuable disk space on your MacBook. You can then edit the footage directly from the external hard drive, or choose to transfer it to another Mac – like a desktop Mac Pro or an iMac, for example. So follow our step-by-step guide to find out how to transfer your iMovie projects between Macs.

Step-by-step | iMovie Transfer projects and events to another Mac

1: External drive
Plug an external drive into your Mac. It will need to be formatted as Mac OS (Journaled) for iMovie to recognise it.

2: Choose a project
Click the Project Library button to see a list of your iMovie projects (like the Time Travel project we created on page 30).

3: Drag and drop
Scroll down to the bottom of the Project Library window to see the external disks. Hold Command and drag your project onto the disk's icon.

4: Copy project
Transfer the project and footage by clicking 'Move projects and events'. You'll see the size of the project's footage in brackets.

5: Transfer assets
A progress bar shows which clips are being transferred to your external disk. The project will now appear below the disk's icon.

6: On the disk
To edit the transferred project you'll need to have the external disk attached. If the disk is unavailable then the project and clips won't appear in iMovie.

Move your iMovie projects
Copy your project and clips to another Mac

Copy everything
To make sure that the transferred iMovie project will play on another Mac, click this option. All the clips associated with the project will be copied to the external disk

Two copies
When you copy an iMovie project from the external hard drive to another Mac you will have a backup of your project

External drive
By plugging in an external hard drive you can store iMovie projects and clips here, which will free up lots of space on your Mac's hard drive

Drag and drop
The attached external disk will appear here. You can drag projects to and from the disk with ease

Knowledge base

In command
When you hold the Command key while dragging a project to an external disk, you remove that project's video clips from your Mac's hard drive and transfer them to their new location. To copy the clips to the external drive without deleting them from your Mac, simply drag and drop without holding down the Command key.

"By plugging in an external hard drive you can store iMovie projects and clips"

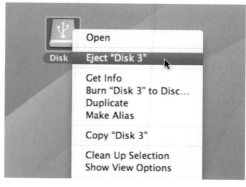

7: Plug and play
You've now freed up disk space on your Mac's hard drive. Quit iMovie, eject the external drive and plug it into another Mac.

8: View project
Open 'iMovie09' on your other Mac. By accessing the external disk from within the Project Library you can view and edit the footage.

9: Import project
By dragging the project from the external disk into iMovie's Project Library you can copy everything into your other Mac.

Give your footage a vintage effect in iMovie

Give your modern digital video footage a vintage film makeover!

Task: Create a vintage film effect in iMovie

Difficulty: Beginner

Time needed: 10 minutes

Most camcorders can produce high-quality video footage that has a wide range of tones and strong vibrant colours, so that what you see with the naked eye is what is captured on camera. By processing your crisp and clear modern video footage in iMovie, you can add vintage-style colours and tones to your clips, which helps give the footage an old-fashioned, film-like feel. This colour-grading effect is a great way to add texture and variety to your documentaries, or to turn back time and create faded monochrome film clips for your dramas. And by tinting your shots sepia you can make the footage look much older, which is a great way to add a romantic mood to your wedding videos, for example.

Kick off by finding a modern clip that looks like it could have been shot on an old film camera, or use the 'Vintage.avi' clip on your CD. You can then follow our simple step-by-step walkthrough and use iMovie's Effects filters to add vintage colours and tones in minutes.

Step-by-step | iMovie Add a vintage effect to your videos

1: Create new project

Open iMovie and choose File>New Project. Select a 16:9 aspect ratio to create a more cinematic shape. Go to File>Import>Movies. Browse to the 'Vintage01.avi' clip on your CD. Add the clip to a new event.

2: Add effect

Drag the clip to the Project window and double-click the footage to open the Clip Inspector. Click the Video Effect option and choose Aged Film. This produces film grain, tints the shot sepia and adds scratches.

Add a vintage effect in iMovie

Give your modern footage a vintage makeover

Vignette
By using the Vignette effect you can make the edges of your shot fade, adding a vintage-style lens artifact to the footage. This helps evoke a sense of faded memories

Video effects
Kick off by applying the Aged Film effect to your modern HD footage. As well as tinting the clip with a wash of sepia, it also adds vintage-film style artifacts (like grain and scratches) to your modern footage

Knowledge base

Vignette
Our filtered video's faded corners mimic the classic vignette effect produced by old-school film cameras. This corner fading was caused by the lens's inability to create an even exposure at the edges. Some vignetted corners could even be lighter than the rest of the shot. Modern lenses can still add a hint of vignette when fully zoomed out.

Unprocessed footage
Here's the modern footage with its wide range of colours and tones. The old-fashioned subject matter suits a retro makeover to flatten the contrast and desaturate the shot

Layer effects
By default, iMovie can only add one effect at a time. To add multiple effects you need to export a clip with the chosen effect, then re-import the footage before adding another effect to it

3: Desaturate the clip
To create an older looking monochrome image (and preserve the sepia tint) click the Video Inspector tab and set Saturation to 0%. Set Contrast to -39% for a washed-out range of tones. Now the shot looks even older.

4: Add a vignette
Export the clip to add more than one effect. Go to Share>Export Movie and choose the HD option. Re-import the movie with the added tint, scratches and contrast. Use the Inspector to add a Vignette Video Effect.

Comment Marker
This handy Comment Marker tells us where the speech in the HD clip begins. We can use the marker to help us sync up our iPhone audio with the HD camera's footage

Audio track
The high quality iPhone audio exists as a separate track. You can align the sound with the video by sliding the green bar left or right until it's perfectly in sync

Knowledge base

Sound advice
The earphone mic is only connected to the iPhone via a small mini-jack plug. If you put pressure on the plug while recording your audio you might add some crackling to your sound. Make sure that you play the iPhone movies back to check that the sound is okay. We had sound drop-out problems when we took the iPhone out of a pocket, for example.

iPhone footage
This video clip was recorded on an iPhone using an earphone mic to capture decent quality speech from our subject. It doesn't matter about video content as we only use the sound captured with the clip

Knowledge base

Now you see it…
If you're recording drama and want to hide your earphone mic, you can pop the cable up the back of your shirt and over your shoulder, then use a bit of tape to stick it to the inside of your shirt. You can leave the iPhone hidden in a back pocket.

"You can capture high-quality sound from a distant subject if they're using an iPhone"

HD footage
This wide shot of our subject talking was recorded on an HD camera. The sound is very poor due to the distance between the subject and the camera, but we can replace it with the high-quality audio from the iPhone footage!

Combine sounds in iMovie

Use iMovie to combine sound recorded on an iPhone with HD footage shot on a separate camcorder to turn your iPhone into a radio mic

These days it doesn't cost a fortune to shoot high-quality footage. Digital SLR cameras like the Nikon D90 or the Canon EOS 550D can record High Definition (HD) footage with ease. The downside of shooting with a DSLR or an HD camcorder is the lack of a decent microphone. If your subject is more than a few feet away from the camera then you'll barely be able to hear them talk. Most camcorders and DSLRs lack the option to plug in an external microphone, so capturing decent quality sound is a big challenge.

Fortunately you can capture high-quality sound from a distant subject if they're using an iPhone 3GS, and then synchronise this sound with your camcorder's HD footage using iMovie. In the following walkthrough we'll show you how to trim and reposition the iPhone-sourced sound so that it matches your HD footage perfectly – turning your iPhone into a wireless mic!

Task: Synchronise sound from one clip with video with another

Difficulty: Expert

Time needed: 20 minutes

Step-by-step | iMovie Improve your project's sound quality

1: Set up your iPhone
You'll need to plug some earphones with a built-in mic into your iPhone. You can pop an earphone in the subject's ear or hang the mic on a shirt button.

2: Record sound and vision
Set your iPhone to record a movie. The mic on the earphone cable will pick up your subject's voice. Set your HD camcorder to record them talking.

3: Import clips
Import the iPhone clip 'iPhoneSound.mov', and the camcorder footage 'HD Scene.mov' into iMovie. Drag HD Scene into a new project.

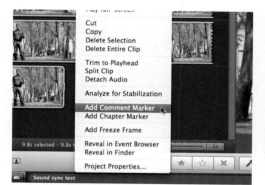

4: Add Comment Marker
Drag the cursor to scrub through the HD footage until you hear the subject speak. Right-click and choose Add Comment Marker from the menu.

5: Remove bad sound
Click on the clip's gear icon and choose Audio. In the Inspector's Audio pane set Volume to 0% to remove the clip's poor quality sound.

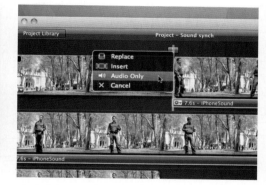

6: Add good sound
Drag the iPhone-sourced clip onto the Project window and choose Audio Only. You now have clearer sound, but it's out of sync with the picture.

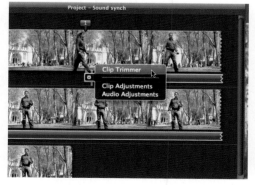

7: Trim audio
Click on the iPhone sound track's gear icon and choose Clip Trimmer. Drag the start and end handles to include just the speech. Click Done.

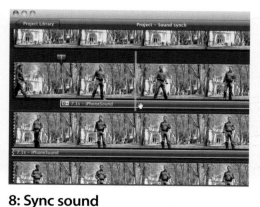

8: Sync sound
Drag the start of the trimmed clip under the Comment Marker. Play the clip. If the sound clip isn't synced you can slide it about until it matches up.

9: Ambient sound
To add a background sound to the edited clip, double-click the footage. Use the Audio Inspector to pop the original sound's volume up to 30%.

Tutorial: Use iMovie to create a holiday video

Combine HD video, iPhone-sourced clips and photos to share the highlights of your holiday with a slickly edited video in iMovie

Task: Combine different video formats with stills

Difficulty: Intermediate

Time needed: 20 minutes

Holidays provide a great opportunity to shoot video and photos, thanks to the combination of free time and many exciting photo opportunities. Indeed, you may come back from your holiday with a huge collection of stills and clips (or assets). One challenge you'll face is how to share these exciting holiday memories with friends and family back home, without forcing them to wade through hours of unedited footage and long boring photo slideshows. Another challenge is to find the best bits from your holiday, as clips and stills may be stored in a variety of places – like on your iPhone or on a digital camera's SD card, for example.

Fortunately, iMovie has all the tools you need to gather these various assets together in one place so you can present your holiday highlights in a movie that mixes stills, HD footage and iPhone clips. Your slickly edited holiday highlights video will leave your audience wanting more, courtesy of all the post-production bells and whistles that you'd expect to see on a professional production. We'll show you how to add animated transitions to take you from one scene to the next, plus captions that explain which location or event the viewer is watching. You'll learn how to customise an animated map that shows the viewer where your holiday scenes are set, so they can share your holiday experiences.

Step-by-step | iMovie Create a holiday highlights video

1: Create new project
Choose File>New Project. Choose the Standard (4:3) Aspect Ratio. This avoids enlarging low quality iPhone footage to fit a high definition format.

2: Import your clips
Go to File>Import>Movies. Select the Holiday Movies folder on your disc. Tick 'Create new Event'. Label the event 'Holiday Assets'. Tick Optimize Video and Import.

3: Organise your photos
To get photos into iMovie you have to pop them into iPhoto first. Drag the folder Holiday Stills onto iPhoto's icon. This will place them in an iPhoto event.

4: Browse photos
In iMovie, click on the Photos browser. Now click on the Last Import option to see your holiday photos. You now have access to all of your stills and videos.

5: Marvelous maps
To show the viewers of your video where the holiday took place, click on the Maps browser. Drag a template like Old World Map into the Project window.

6: Start and finish
Use the Inspector to type a start and end location for your holiday jaunt. Click Done. An animated red line will now show your journey across the map.

7: Establishing shot
Click on the traffic clip and drag it into the project. This wide shot introduces our holiday location. The 16:9 high definition clip is automatically cropped to fit.

8: Add a transition
To create a link from the map to the establishing shot, select the Transitions browser. Drag Page Curl Left between the two clips. Set a Duration of 1 second.

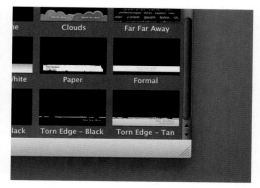

9: Add a title
To introduce the holiday location click on the Titles browser. Drag a template like 'Torn Edge – Tan' onto the second clip. Type in a caption.

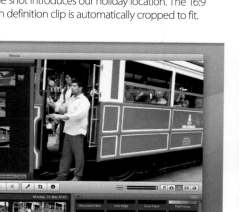

10: Add iPhone clip
Add the tram footage to the project. This iPhone movie doesn't need to be cropped as it matches the project's 4:3 Aspect Ratio.

11: Add a still
Drag the Exploring photo from the Photos browser into the Project. By default, iMovie adds random camera movement to the image to make it less static.

12: Adjust movement
Click on the still's gear icon and choose Ken Burns. Drag the green start rectangle to fit the whole image. Tighten the red rectangle to frame the group.

13: Zoom in
Click Done to change the camera move. Play back the sequence and the camera will zoom in on the holidaymakers, leading the viewer into the scene.

14: Insert sound
Drag the Tram clip from the event onto the people photo. Choose the Audio Only pop-up option. Drag the green bar so the tram's sound overlaps the photo.

15: Ambient sound
The overlapping tram sound helps make the animated photo blend in more effectively with the video footage. This is an alternative to using music.

16: Add camera tilt

Add the Shopping photo to the project and use the Ken Burns effect to tilt up from the girls to the lamps. This tells a story from a single still.

17: Change duration

By default, all stills last for four seconds. To speed things up, drag the end of the Shopping clip so it runs for two seconds. Press Cmd+B to 'Trim to Selection'.

18: Sightseeing

Add the footage of the pillars to the project. Drop in a photo taken at the same location. Mix between the two assets using a Mosaic transition.

19: Clip adjustments

Click on the photo's gear icon and choose Clip Adjustments. Set Duration to 2.0 seconds. Tick 'Applies to all stills' and click Done.

20: Montage sequence

Give a taste of your holiday activities by adding more stills and placing a Swap transition between them. This creates a Cover-Flow-style transition.

21: Add videos

Add the rest of the video clips to the holiday montage. For visual variety, pop in a Cube transition between the videos. Fade to black at the end of the programme.

22: Reduce volume

Shift-click to select the last three clips. Press 'i' to open the Inspector. Click Audio and reduce volume to 0%. Now the montage's stills and photos are silent.

23: Add music

Click on the Show Music browser and drag a jingle like Sanskrit onto the montage section of your project. This links the stills and video clips into a smooth sequence.

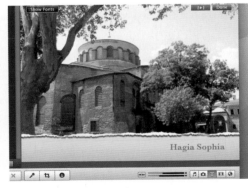

24: Finishing touches

Use the Titles browser to add any captions that the viewer might need to identify your holiday landmarks. Use the same template to create a unified look.

Show off your holiday highlights in iMovie
Create a slickly edited holiday movie with stills and video footage

Post-production effects
Thanks to iMovie's rich collection of titles and transitions, you can create a professional-looking production that is both entertaining and informative

Publish
iMovie is a one-stop-shop. As well as turning your holiday assets into a slickly edited video, it enables you to publish them online with ease so that others can enjoy your holiday highlights

Knowledge base

Optimise video
Some of our holiday footage was shot in HD format at a resolution of 1920 x 1080. By choosing to optimise the imported footage, you'll drop it down in size to a smaller resolution of 960 x 540. The smaller-sized clips will not look quite as good as the full-sized ones, but the quality drop should be fairly negligible, and you'll save lots of space on the Mac's hard drive.

Different sizes
Holiday videos can be shot on an HD camcorder and with a lower resolution iPhone. iMovie will automatically crop different video formats to fit the project's aspect ratio

Super stills
By importing holiday snaps from iPhoto you can add variety and texture to your holiday highlights video. As stills have a higher resolution than video, you can zoom in on them to highlight specific details

25: Sound effects
To enhance the opening graphic, go to the iMovie Sound Effects folder and drag the Jet Fly By sound onto the animated map.

26: Share your movie
To share the edited highlights go to Share>YouTube. Type in a suitable title. Tick the 'Make this movie personal' box so only friends and family can see it.

27: Publish
Now click Publish. iMovie will upload the video to your YouTube page and give you a link to share with family and friends.

Tutorial: Design a Web 2.0 footer in iWeb

Nothing completes your site like a well-designed footer – the perfect place to collate your contact information

Task: Design a Web 2.0-style footer for your site

Difficulty: Intermediate

Time needed: 90 minutes

It's tempting to concentrate all of your creative efforts on the top or your website. All to often the bells and whistles go into the site's top banner, leaving the pages tailing off towards the bottom. Take a look at many of the best-designed sites on the web and you'll see that the attention to detail continues all the way down to an info-packed footer at the bottom. Using iWeb, it's easy to create your own footer design - use it to advertise your contact details or list your social networking connections (like Facebook or Twitter). To use an official Twitter button, try our tutorial on page 44 once you've mastered footers in iWeb

Step-by-step | iWeb Design your Web 2.0-style footer

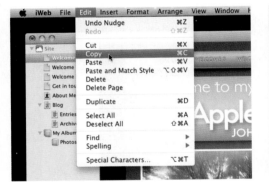

1: Matching the header
We've got a custom header banner for our site, so we're going to start by copying elements from that. You could always start by drawing a fresh rectangle.

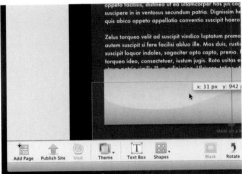

2: Drag it down
Drag the banner down the page until a light blue highlighted frame appears around the footer area – this means the element is locked into the footer.

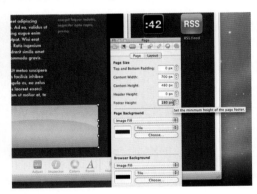

3: Big footer
You'll want a little space around your design, so open up the Inspector and click on the Layout tab. Increase the Footer Height.

4: Back to back
With the footer banner still selected, choose 'Send to Back' from the Arrange menu to send it behind the other elements of your page.

5: Steal from other themes
Create a new welcome page from the Travel theme. Click the wavy-edged frame behind the main photo and choose Copy from the Edit menu.

6: Paste and scale
Switch back to your webpage and choose Paste, again from the Edit menu. Drag the corner handle on the frame to make it smaller.

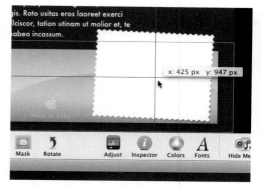

7: Down to the bottom

Drag the pasted and resized frame down into the footer area and position it over the right-hand corner of the footer banner.

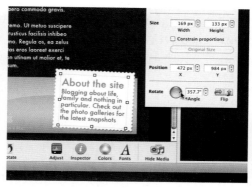

8: Shout about your site

Create a text box and position it over the frame. Add some text, styling it to suit the site, and then rotate the text box to match the angle of the frame.

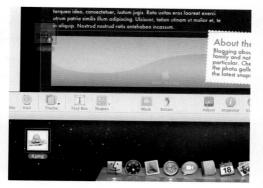

9: Badges of honour

You can download free badges for sites like Twitter. We got ours from **www.smashingmagazine.com**. Download one and drag it into the footer.

10: Get rid of the stroke

With the imported badge still selected, choose the Graphic pane of the Inspector and click on the Stroke menu. Choose 'None'.

11: Link to your profile

Now switch to the Link pane and click the 'Enable as a hyperlink' checkbox. Enter your direct Twitter URL (**www.twitter.com/username**) into the URL box.

12: Title it up

Create a new text box and enter a title for your footer bar. Size and style it to suit your site and position it in the centre of your footer.

13: Ready-made buttons

iWeb makes it easy to add an Email badge. Choose Button from the Insert menu, and then Email Me from the flyout menu.

14: Put it in its place

Drag the Email Me button down into the footer area and centre it in the banner. The blue guides that pop up will help you with the positioning.

15: A Facebook final touch

We've grabbed another badge from a collection on **www.smashingmagazine.com**, this time for Facebook. Link it directly to your Facebook profile.

Tutorial: Customise the Navigation bar

Learn how to customise the default elements of iWeb's built-in themes and you can quickly create individual looking websites without having to start from scratch

Task: Customise your site's Navigation bar

Difficulty: Intermediate

Time needed: 20 minutes

As lovely as iWeb's built-in templates are, there's one problem. There is a very good chance your website is going to look exactly the same as everyone else's (well, at least everyone else who uses iWeb anyway). But if you learn how to customise the template's elements, you can quickly eradicate those clues that give your site's origins away. Chief among those tell-tale signs is the Navigation bar that sits at the top of every page on your site. Sure, you can turn if off altogether, but then you have to build your site's navigation from scratch (and remember to include any new pages you add). It's a far better – and deceptively simple – idea to tweak and change the bar's appearance to suit your site's style. The tricky part is that Apple has locked most of the bar's styling options but – as with most things – there are ways around that, as you'll learn here…

Step-by-step | iWeb Give the Navigation bar a Web 2.0 makeover

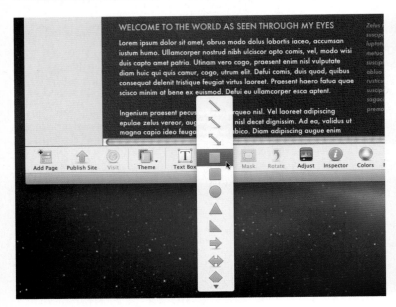

1: Throw some shapes
Click on the Shapes icon at the bottom of the screen and select the square shape. Open up the Inspector and click the Graphic icon at the top. Change the Stroke width to one point and colour it a mid grey.

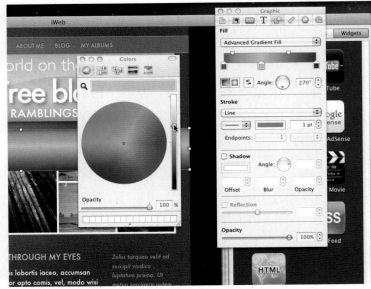

2: Shades of grey
Resize the box to fill the width of the page. From the Fill menu choose Advanced Gradient Fill. Click on each pointer in the bar and set them to dark grey. Click in between to create a new pointer and set it a lighter grey.

The elements of creating a Web 2.0 style

iWeb has plenty of tools to help you get that modern web sheen

Advanced Gradient fill
While the standard Gradient Fill only allows you to blend between two colours, the Advanced option allows you to add multiple colour stops

Mid-point sliders
These small triangles let you set where in the blend you want the mid-point, between the two colours, to be. This changes the sharpness of the gradient

The new Nav bar
Here's the freshly styled Navigation bar, with a grey sheen instead of the transparent bar you can see in the image to the left

Setting colour stops
These pointers set the colour of each stop. Click on one and the Color Picker (far left) will appear, allowing you to select the colour you want to add into the blend

The colour picker
When you click on the colour stops in the Gradient bar this picker will pop up. Drag in the circle to choose a colour, and drag up and down the bar on the right to set its brightness

Mix and match
Using these same techniques you can create or customise additional elements to accent your new web page styling

Adding colour stops
Click anywhere on the bar to add a new colour stop, which you can then drag left or right to fine-tune the gradient's blend

3: Move it into place
Click on the box and move it up into the Navigation bar's area (which will become highlighted with a blue outline). Line the top of the box up with the top of the Navigation bar and then resize it to the same height.

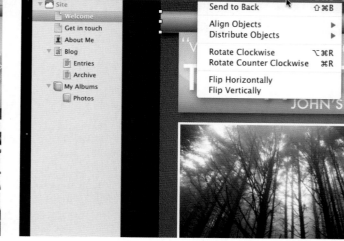

4: Send behind the bar
The Navigation bar will now be behind your new box, so with the box still selected choose Send Backward from the Arrange menu to send it behind the Navigation bar.

Stream live video to your iWeb site

Want to launch your own TV channel? Here's how to set up Ustream's free video streaming service on your iWeb site

Live video streaming services have been around for quite a few years now, but only recently has the average consumer internet connection become fast enough to make them truly viable for all. The idea is that you use a camera connected to your computer to transmit video in real time to the service, which then broadcasts your video live over the internet, or allows you to record events for streaming later. The really great part is that most services also provide an embed code for the live stream, enabling you to embed the feed into an iWeb page. So, if you fancy broadcasting your household news live as it happens from the kitchen table, read on to discover how.

Task: Set up a live video feed in iWeb using Ustream

Difficulty: Intermediate

Time needed: 30 minutes

Step-by-step | iWeb | Set up live video streaming

1: Visit Ustream
To begin, navigate to the Ustream website (**www.ustream.tv**) and click the Sign Up link in the top right-hand corner of the page.

2: Create new account
Enter the required details, like your chosen username and password, and click the Submit button to create your free account.

3: Name your show
After entering your profile information you'll need to type in a name for your live show. Now hit the Broadcast Now button.

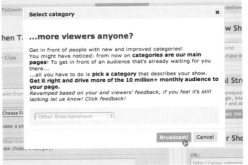

4: Select category
On the next screens, you can enter a description, some search engine tags and choose a category under which your show will appear. Hit Broadcast.

5: Allow access
A window appears asking you to grant Ustream access to your camera and microphone. Click 'Allow' then 'Start Broadcast' to begin sending video.

6: Copy embed code
Navigate back to the 'Your Shows' page and double-click the Live Embed window. Hit Cmd+C to copy the HTML code to your clipboard.

Transmit live video to your site

Let visitors see what's going on in your world

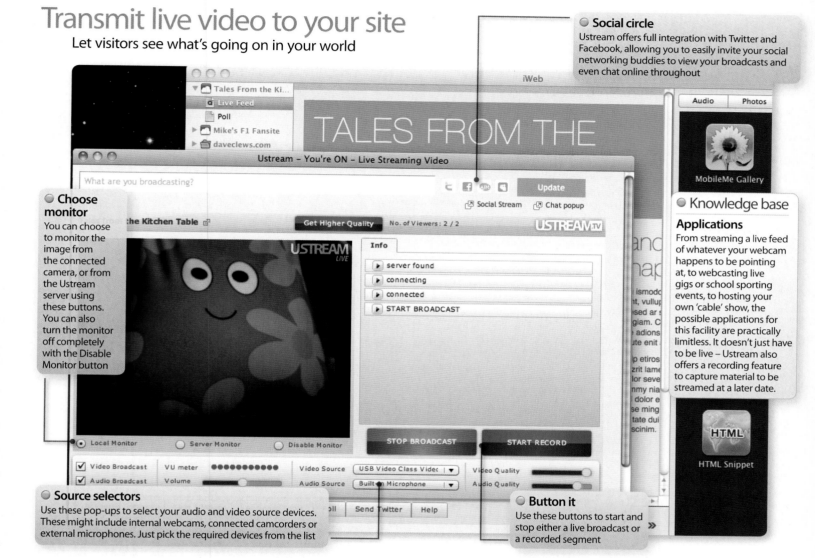

Social circle
Ustream offers full integration with Twitter and Facebook, allowing you to easily invite your social networking buddies to view your broadcasts and even chat online throughout

Choose monitor
You can choose to monitor the image from the connected camera, or from the Ustream server using these buttons. You can also turn the monitor off completely with the Disable Monitor button

Knowledge base

Applications
From streaming a live feed of whatever your webcam happens to be pointing at, to webcasting live gigs or school sporting events, to hosting your own 'cable' show, the possible applications for this facility are practically limitless. It doesn't just have to be live – Ustream also offers a recording feature to capture material to be streamed at a later date.

Source selectors
Use these pop-ups to select your audio and video source devices. These might include internal webcams, connected camcorders or external microphones. Just pick the required devices from the list

Button it
Use these buttons to start and stop either a live broadcast or a recorded segment

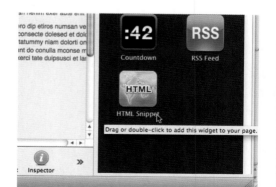

7: Drag widget
In iWeb, select the page that will host the video. Open the Media drawer and click the Widgets tab. Drag an HTML Snippet onto the desired location.

8: Paste code
Click once in the grey box to plant a text cursor, then hit the Cmd+V shortcut to paste the HTML code into the widget.

9: Apply
Click Apply to embed the video into your page. Once your site is published, you can visit it online and view your video streaming live on your page.

Tutorial: Add a Follow Me button for Twitter

Let your blog visitors know about your Twitter account by adding an official Follow Me button to your iWeb site to direct some traffic toward your tweets…

Task: Add a Twitter Follow Me button in iWeb

Difficulty: Beginner

Time needed: 5 minutes

The Twitter phenomenon is still going strong, with more and more users making use of the microblogging service than ever. While some have replaced their traditional blogs with these mini-posts, there's no reason the two can't work together. Bloggers regularly use Twitter to notify followers of updates on their main blog site, and your tweets can also provide a neat way to keep people up-to-date with goings on when a long blog post isn't necessary. It's for these reasons that it makes sense to add a Follow Me button to your iWeb site that will automatically take visitors to your Twitter feed once clicked. Fortunately, the process is very simple and can be completed in a matter of minutes. There are also a wide range of buttons available, so you can match your Follow Me button to your site design for a professional look. So, load up your iWeb site and read on…

Step-by-step | iWeb | Link to your Twitter feed

1: Start with the basics
Here we have our blog, and next to it is a small 'Contacts' box made using a rounded rectangle shape set to 48% Opacity. We've also added an Email Me button from the Insert menu.

2: Head to Twitter.com
Open Safari, navigate to **Twitter.com** and log in to your account. Now head to the bottom of the page and click on the Goodies link before clicking Buttons on the next page.

Direct site visitors to your tweets

Promote your site and gain new followers with Twitter

○ Twitter Button
Once live, your button will link from your site to your Twitter account and allow people to decide to follow you or not. Those clicking this button will need to sign up to Twitter in order to see your tweets

○ Shift the blog
To make room for our contacts box, we shifted the blog space across a little. This can be done in the same way as you would adjust the size of a shape; by selecting it and dragging it to fit

○ Knowledge base

Buttons and beyond
You will notice on the Twitter Goodies page you visited in step 3 that you can also add Twitter Widgets to your site that will display your recent tweets. These are added in the same way, by using HTML code that can be pasted into and a HTML Snippet Widget on your site.

○ HTML Snippet
This is where you paste your Twitter button code. If you want to change your button at any point, simply enter a new code into this box

○ Widgets
Drag this HTML Widget button onto your site in order to paste your Twitter button code into it. You can do this any number of times for different buttons and more

3: Pick your button
You'll now be presented with a selection of Twitter buttons in different sizes and colours. Click on the button you would like and copy the code that is displayed in the box above.

4: Paste your code
Now head back to your iWeb site and drag an HTML Snippet Widget from the Media browser (under the Widgets tab) to your page. Paste the Twitter button code into the box, click Apply and you're done!

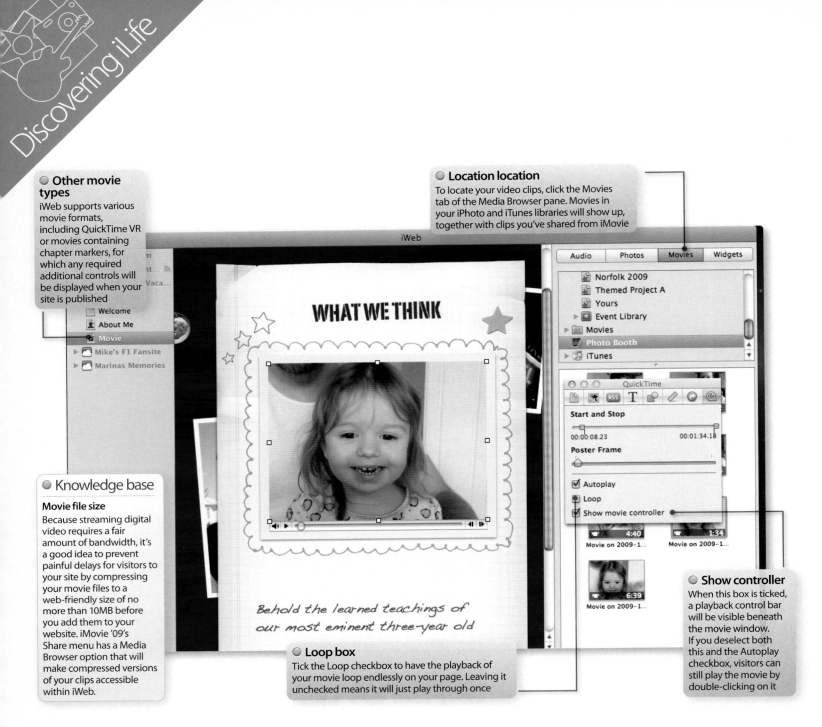

Other movie types

iWeb supports various movie formats, including QuickTime VR or movies containing chapter markers, for which any required additional controls will be displayed when your site is published

Location location

To locate your video clips, click the Movies tab of the Media Browser pane. Movies in your iPhoto and iTunes libraries will show up, together with clips you've shared from iMovie

iWeb

WHAT WE THINK

Behold the learned teachings of our most eminent three-year old

Knowledge base

Movie file size

Because streaming digital video requires a fair amount of bandwidth, it's a good idea to prevent painful delays for visitors to your site by compressing your movie files to a web-friendly size of no more than 10MB before you add them to your website. iMovie '09's Share menu has a Media Browser option that will make compressed versions of your clips accessible within iWeb.

Audio | Photos | Movies | Widgets

- Norfolk 2009
- Themed Project A
- Yours
- Event Library
- Movies
- Photo Booth
- iTunes

QuickTime

Start and Stop
00:00:08.23   00:01:34.18

Poster Frame

☑ Autoplay
◉ Loop
☑ Show movie controller

Movie on 2009-1...   4:40
Movie on 2009-1...   1:34

Movie on 2009-1...   6:39

Show controller

When this box is ticked, a playback control bar will be visible beneath the movie window. If you deselect both this and the Autoplay checkbox, visitors can still play the movie by double-clicking on it

Loop box

Tick the Loop checkbox to have the playback of your movie loop endlessly on your page. Leaving it unchecked means it will just play through once

Tutorial: Play movies automatically in iWeb

Putting movies onto your web pages is simple with iWeb '09. To play them automatically when the page loads, here's a simple way to do it

Task: Set movies to play automatically when pages load
Difficulty: Beginner
Time needed: 15 minutes

iWeb really does make it easy for even the least tech-savvy among us to produce crisp, professional-looking websites with minimum effort. Thanks to the Movie Page template, it's now simpler than ever to feature video clips on your web pages – but instead of taking the traditional route of having the viewer click a play button on a transport bar to play a movie, why not feature a clip that will play back automatically when the page loads? Its a fantastic way to draw visitors into a site and set the mood for the content they are about to look at. If the site is aimed at family members it could contain a greeting, or it could use music to create a mood. It's up to you. Whatever you choose, it will make an attention-grabbing centrepiece for your page and, as you'll see in this tutorial, is incredibly easy to do.

Step-by-step | iWeb Enable automatic movie playback in iWeb

1: Create a website
Start off by selecting one of the themes from iWeb's startup browser. Now you can add a few pages to create a basic website.

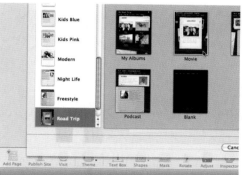

2: Add movie page
Click on the Add Page button to the left of the lower toolbar, then pick the Movie page template for your site's chosen theme.

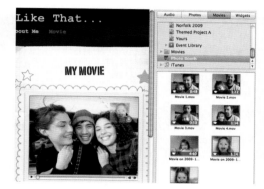

3: Insert movie
Click the Show Media button to reveal the Media Browser. Locate your desired video clip and drag it onto the page to replace the placeholder movie.

4: Customise text
You can replace the placeholder text by double-clicking to select the text and retyping your own caption straight over the top.

5: Reveal inspector
Click once on your movie to highlight it, then click the 'i' button to display the Inspector. Click the Q tab to reveal the QuickTime pane.

6: Trim up
Remove any unwanted footage from the beginning and end of the clip by using the sliders to select the start and end playback points.

7: Pick poster frame
The Poster Frame is the frame that's displayed on your page when the movie is not playing back. Use this slider to choose a suitable frame for the job.

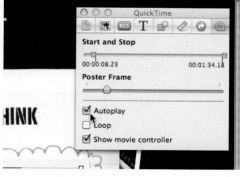

8: Autoplay away
Now for the key to the whole thing; checking the Autoplay box will enable automatic playback of your movie as soon as the page loads.

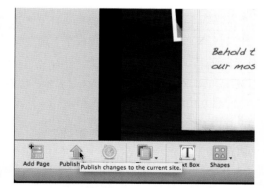

9: Check & publish
Once you're happy with the way your clip is behaving, upload your changes by clicking the Publish Site button in the toolbar.

Add a speech bubble to your iWeb site

Make your site more fun with a cartoon-esque speech bubble to add excitement to your images…

Task: Liven up your site with the Quote Bubble shape

Difficulty: Beginner

Time needed: 10 minutes

iWeb works perfectly with all of your images, and you can even edit them within the interface if you need to rather than jumping into iPhoto. It also borrows a number of features from Pages that allow you to introduce shapes into your website designs. In this tutorial we'll be working with a shape that Apple has handily included in iWeb: the speech bubble. Once inserted, a speech bubble not only enlivens your page, adds colour and a more personal feel, but can be manipulated as you wish with text and gradients. You can even adjust the shape and orientation of your speech bubble to make sure it fits perfectly on your site. If you have a 'welcome' or 'about me' page with a photo included, why not give this quick tutorial a try? There are many uses of the speech bubble beyond a simple hello, so see what you come up with using this comic book-esque technique.

Step-by-step | iWeb Apply the Quote Bubble shape

1: Add your bubble
Start by opening iWeb and selecting the page you wish to add your speech bubble to. Now head to the Insert menu and select Quote Bubble from the Shape section to add a bubble to the page.

2: Shape your bubble
Use the handles on the edge of the shape to adjust its size and select the blue circles to direct the speech bubble to your subject's mouth. Hold down the Apple key and drag the shape to rotate it.

Tweak your bubble
Take advantage of iWeb's tool set

● Moving the shape
Clicking anywhere on the shape will select it and allow you to drag it to any point on your site. Use this to position it near a face

● Knowledge base

What about a comic site?
There's a comic-style iWeb template available, as you can see from our main image on the left. Using this fun template, you could create an entire site in this style and add speech bubbles for each 'character' on your page. This could be your friends, family or even your pets.

● Colour and shape
Use the Inspector's Object pane to adjust the colour and style of your speech bubble. You also have the option to add a shadow to it and adjust the opacity if you wish

● Text Box option
You don't have to type directly into your speech bubble; you could add a Text Box over the top of it and type into that instead. Make sure you rotate the text to match the speech bubble

● Blue circle
Clicking and dragging this blue circle allows you to alter the shape of your bubble and move its point to the mouth

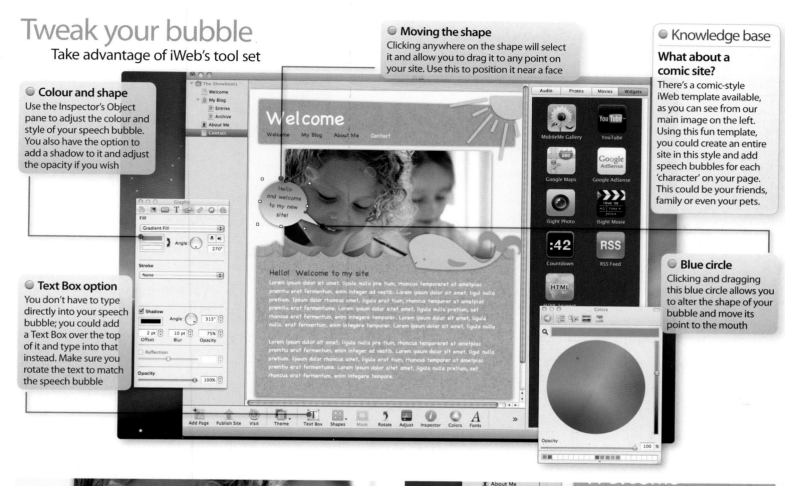

3: Add your text
Double-click in the middle of your speech bubble to add your text. Now select all of it by clicking and dragging across it. You can hit Apple+T to adjust the font, colour and size of it.

4: Introduce some colour
With the speech bubble selected, click on the Inspector button and select the Object tab. From here you can choose a solid colour or the gradient, like we have here.

Tutorial: Insert a poll in your iWeb site

Canvas your visitors' opinions on important matters using iWeb's HTML Snippets feature

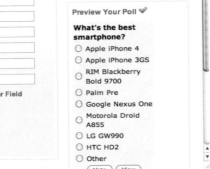

What's the best smartphone?
- Apple iPhone 4
- Apple iPhone 3GS
- RIM Blackberry Bold 9700
- Palm Pre
- Google Nexus One
- Motorola Droid A855
- LG GW990

Task: Create and insert a visitors' poll on your website

Difficulty: Beginner

Time needed: 20 minutes

Adding a poll to your website is a good way to gauge the opinion of your visitors on almost any topic you care to mention, from the best kind of TV to buy to what people think of England's performance in the World Cup. Furthermore, iWeb's HTML Snippet feature makes it a breeze to add one to your website. The first step is to track down the necessary HTML code for you to paste into your snippet, and doing a Google search for 'Free iWeb Poll' should present several alternatives. For the purposes of this tutorial, we're going to use Pollcode.com, a quick and easy service that allows you to create your poll free of charge.

Step-by-step | iWeb Create and embed your poll

1: Launch iWeb
Create the page on your site where you want your poll to appear. Click Show Media, then click the Widgets tab at the top of the Media drawer.

2: Pollcode.com
In a web browser, go to **http://pollcode.com** and enter a poll question or title of your choice into the box provided.

3: Enter answers
Add all the possible answers, one per box. You can increase or decrease the number of available answers by clicking the link in the bottom-right.

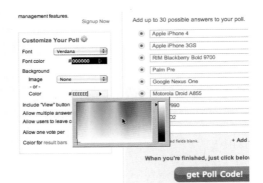

4: Choose style
You can select from a variety of options for font type, text colour and background colour. A preview of your poll appears on the right of the screen.

5: Other options
Select whether people can choose multiple answers, leave comments or view results, and also set the minimum time before they can vote again.

6: Get the code
You can check out how your choices will look with the preview. If you're happy with how it looks, click the 'get Poll Code!' button.

Put a poll on your iWeb page
Get your site visitors to share their views

View results
Once a visitor clicks the Vote button, they are taken to a section of the Pollcode.com website where the results of the poll are displayed as a bar chart

Spit and poll-ish
If you know a little HTML, the code in the grey box can be edited as much as you like to further personalise the appearance of your poll

Knowledge base

When polls go bad
If your poll doesn't appear on your page as planned, open the Metrics pane of iWeb's Inspector and check the width of the HTML Snippet you created, as it can sometimes end up wider than your page. If so, adjust the width value to around 250 pixels and the x-position to a positive value. You should now be able to see your poll.

Publish your site
Don't forget that, in order for your poll to appear online, you have to publish your site. You can do this by clicking the Publish Site button on the lower toolbar

Make a choice
Visitors cast their vote by clicking the button next to their favourite answer and clicking the Vote button

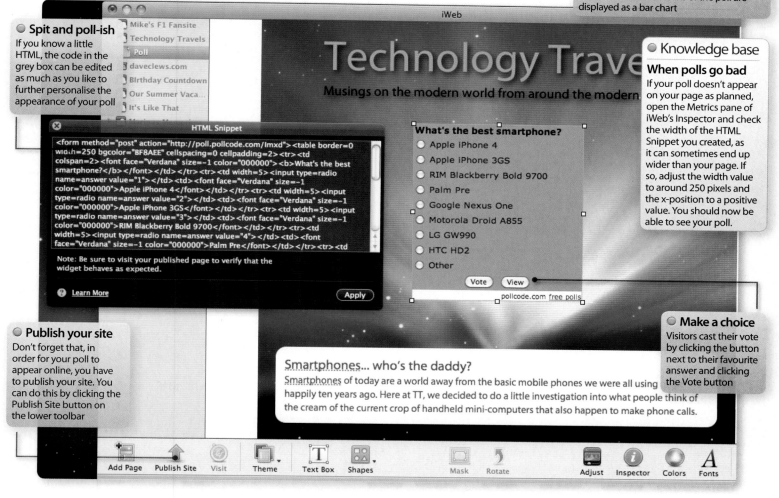

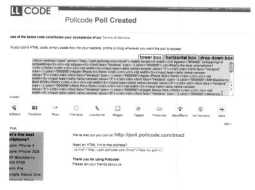

7: Copy to clipboard
The HTML code for the poll will appear in a window. Select all of the text with a triple-click and copy it to the clipboard with Cmd+C .

8: Poll position
Back in iWeb, drag an HTML Snippet widget from the Media drawer and drop it into position on your allotted page.

9: Embed code
Paste the copied poll code into the grey box with Cmd+V, then click the Apply button to embed the poll into your page.

Record and edit Magic GarageBand tracks

Not only is it possible to play along with Magic GarageBand, but you can edit the tracks too

Task: Edit your Magic GarageBand track

Difficulty: Beginner

Time needed: 30 minutes

If you are any kind of musician then you'll know that practice makes perfect. It's a universal rule and one that, if kept to, can improve your skills dramatically – even over a short period of time. As a Mac user you have a fantastic practice tool at your disposal in the form of GarageBand. The free music suite that comes pre-loaded on all new Macs is a total powerhouse, and one of the many unsung features is Magic GarageBand. Often regarded as a bit of a gimmick, Magic GarageBand actually has the power to be incredibly useful for musicians wishing to practice in a live situation without inviting the band or orchestra round to rehearse. It comes pre-loaded with nine styles for you to play along with and, as an added bonus, you can delve into any of these and edit them so they are tailored to suit your needs. As you would expect, the process is simplicity itself. Users of older Macs may find that Magic GarageBand takes a few minutes to load, but just be patient as the system is a little heavy on the processors.

Whirly

Step-by-step | GarageBand Edit Magic tracks

1: Lock and load
Launch GarageBand form your Dock or Applications folder. A window of options will appear. Click Magic GarageBand to be presented with your nine genres. Pick the one you want to play and then hit Choose.

2: Visualiser
In order to appear more simplistic, the Magic GarageBand system uses a visual system to show you the song. You can edit your own and all the other instruments from here; just click on an instrument to edit it.

Edit a Magic GarageBand jam
Add the professional touches to a great rehearsal

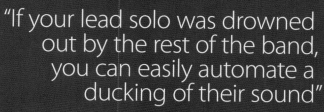

> "If your lead solo was drowned out by the rest of the band, you can easily automate a ducking of their sound"

Knowledge base

Replace too
You don't have to stick with the Magic GarageBand templates if you don't want to. You can easily drop other loops in and out in all of the other parts so that the song has the features you need to rehearse properly. Just remember to save the project…

Tweak the backing
If your lead solo was drowned out by the rest of the band, you can easily automate a ducking of their sound so your super shredding or quick keys stand out the right amount

Share it, learn it
From here you can Share your song to disk and load it onto your iPod or iPhone so you get to know the song and can mentally practice when away from your instrument

Your part
Once you've recorded your part, you can edit all the facets of its sound – including the panning and automation – from here

Record it all
With GarageBand you can keep on recording over and over again, and then choose the best take and use it in the final mix

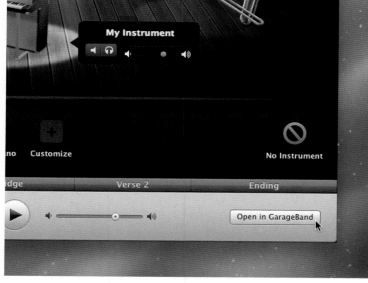

3: Ready to edit
Once you've played around with the settings, warmed up using your own instrument and are ready to edit, click the 'Open in GarageBand' button in the bottom right-hand corner of the screen.

4: Familiar interface
The song you have been playing will now be loaded and you can edit all the elements in the same way you would do any other song. You can also record your own part, adding effects and automation as you see fit.

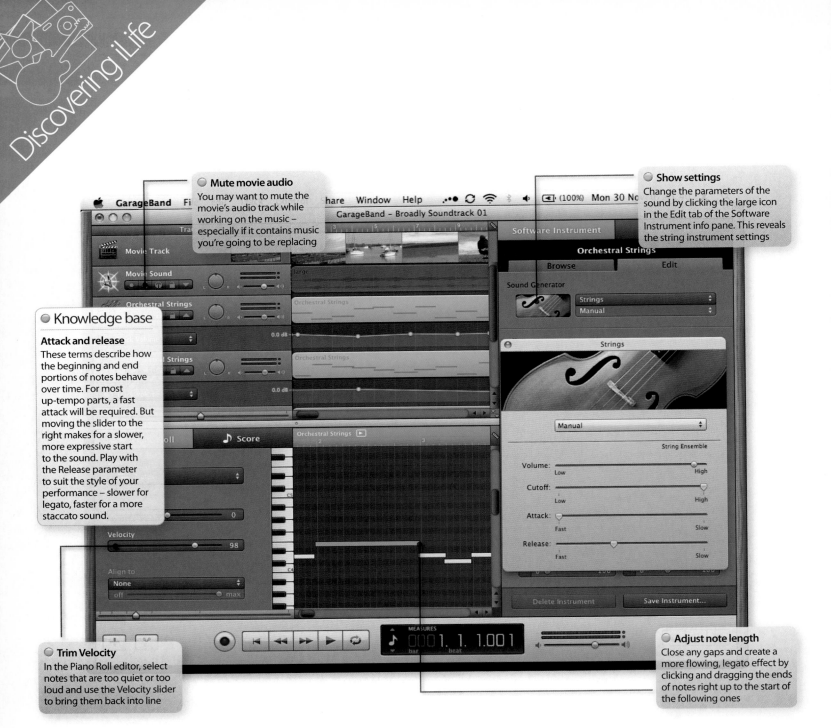

Mute movie audio
You may want to mute the movie's audio track while working on the music – especially if it contains music you're going to be replacing

Show settings
Change the parameters of the sound by clicking the large icon in the Edit tab of the Software Instrument info pane. This reveals the string instrument settings

Knowledge base

Attack and release
These terms describe how the beginning and end portions of notes behave over time. For most up-tempo parts, a fast attack will be required. But moving the slider to the right makes for a slower, more expressive start to the sound. Play with the Release parameter to suit the style of your performance – slower for legato, faster for a more staccato sound.

Trim Velocity
In the Piano Roll editor, select notes that are too quiet or too loud and use the Velocity slider to bring them back into line

Adjust note length
Close any gaps and create a more flowing, legato effect by clicking and dragging the ends of notes right up to the start of the following ones

Tutorial: Compose a movie soundtrack

Compose your own orchestral score for your iMovie projects with the use of GarageBand's strings

Task: Create a basic classical movie score

Difficulty: Intermediate

Time needed: 45 minutes

Adding background music and sound effects to your iMovie creations is all well and good, but to really give your movie the ultimate personal touch why not try your hand at producing your own orchestral score in GarageBand? Apple's free music creation software has its own template specifically created for this very purpose, but it's not that easy to spot (you have to scroll down past the first options in the New Project intro screen). The steps outlined will get you started on the process of creating a basic layered string soundtrack to accompany your movie, so – for the purposes of this tutorial – you'll ideally need a USB MIDI keyboard connected. Before you begin, you'll also need to make sure that your movie files are visible within GarageBand. You can do this by sharing them to the Media Browser from within iMovie.

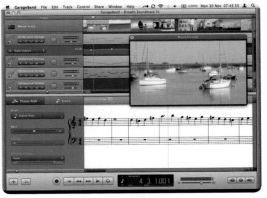

Step-by-step | GarageBand Score your movies with GarageBand

1: Select new movie project
Scroll down to locate the Movie option in the New Project dialog, then choose a name and a save location to create your project.

2: Drag in movie
Now drag in your target movie file and drop it on the movie track's timeline, where it says 'Drag Movies Here'.

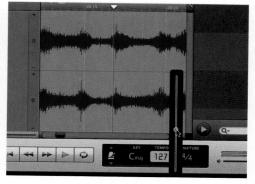

3: Set project tempo
Enable the metronome (Cmd+U) and play it alongside the movie. Select the Project display and adjust the tempo so that it fits the pace of the video.

4: Create new track
Create a new Software Instrument track and select the Orchestral Strings option from the preset library panel on the right.

5: Record first part
Enable Count In from the Control menu and click Record. Record in your part, using your keyboard's velocity sensitivity to control the dynamics.

6: Open editor
Now select the part in the Arrange window and click the scissors button. Scroll up or down to view the notes. Switch LCD to Measures.

7: Edit part
Use these buttons to toggle between Piano Roll and Notation view. To change the pitch of a note just click and drag it to the correct pitch.

8: Record more tracks
Use the Duplicate Track command in the Track menu to create more new tracks and record in the second, third and fourth parts of your virtual quartet.

9: Add dynamics
You can use subtle volume automation on more flowing parts to create some realistic swells, crescendos and diminuendos.

Tutorial: Note velocity in GarageBand

Enhance the realism of your MIDI performances by adjusting note velocity

Task: Explore GarageBand's note velocity editing feature

Difficulty: Beginner

Time needed: 20 minutes

When programming MIDI parts, it can be tricky to emulate a part played on a real instrument; acoustic and stringed instruments are complex things, and a programmed performance is always going to struggle not to sound a little metronomic or robotic by comparison. Modern MIDI sequencers do have a trick or two up their sleeves though, and the most widely used technique to add realism to MIDI parts involves note velocity. Each MIDI note has a possible velocity value of between 0 and 127, which is written into the recorded data according to how hard you hit the key of your MIDI keyboard. Soft playing results in lower velocity values, whereas higher values will be recorded if you hit the keys hard. Combine these values with a velocity-sensitive sound source, where the sound intensity changes according to the velocity of each note, and you have a more controllable and expressive palette of sound to work with.

Step-by-step | GarageBand Explore note velocity editing in GarageBand

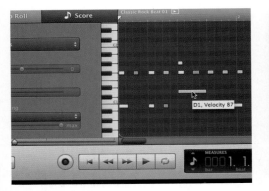

1: Launch GarageBand
Open an old project or create a new one. Our project contains a programmed MIDI drum part and a MIDI string section.

2: Open Piano Roll
Double-click the required region to open it up in the Piano Roll editor. Alternatively, select the region and click the scissors button.

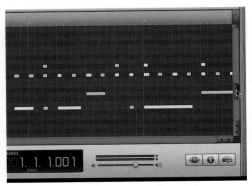

3: Rock and scroll
There is, alas, no vertical zoom control, but you can use the vertical scroll bar to make sure that all the required note events appear in the Edit window.

4: Reveal info
Hover the mouse pointer over a single note for long enough and an info box will appear showing its pitch and velocity values.

5: Alter note velocity
Click a note and use the Velocity slider to make your adjustment. Higher values make the note louder and often change the sample being played back.

6: Check result
If you want to hear the note played with the new velocity, simply click away from it and then re-select it to play it back.

Edit note velocities in GarageBand

Make your MIDI performances more realistic

Edit expansion
To make more room in your Edit window, grab the grey dot in the centre of the bar that divides the two windows and drag upwards. This expands the Edit pane upwards

Break the link
When editing, the Edit playhead and the Arrange playhead may be linked, causing the Piano Roll display to scroll as the region cycles. This can make selecting individual notes tricky so, to avoid this, click these triangles to break the link

Shades of grey
Unselected notes are colour-coded in levels of grey according to their velocity value. Notes with lower velocities are light grey, whereas higher values are displayed in darker grey

Knowledge base

Velocity response
How Software Instrument sounds respond to velocity depend on how they have been programmed. For example, with a multi-sampled kit preset, a single snare drum note could potentially trigger one of several different snare samples, from a gentle tap to a full-on thwack depending on how hard you hit the key. The more samples per key, the more control you have over the sound via velocity.

Multiple notes
If you select more than one note at a time (that each have different velocities), the highest velocity value selected is displayed. When this is altered, the velocity of the other selected notes will change by the same amount

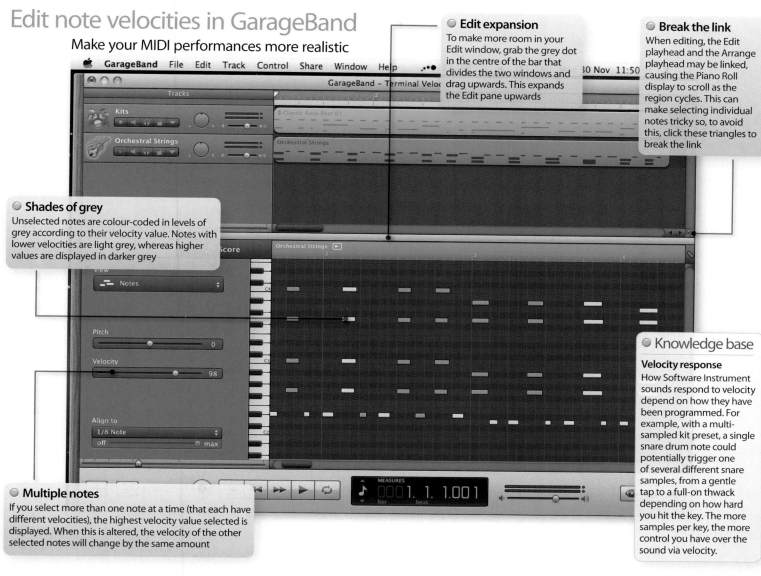

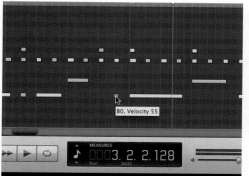

7: Kick trick
A good way of using velocity to add realism to a drum part is by adding pre-emptive ghost kick drum beats at low velocities prior to the main beats.

8: Leave your hat on
You can also vary the velocity of alternate hi-hat beats to create a rocking feel. This helps otherwise robotic hat patterns sound more human.

9: String thing
Tweaking note velocity can add a dynamic feel to most MIDI parts. Here we add dynamic accents to a staccato string part to add a touch of drama.

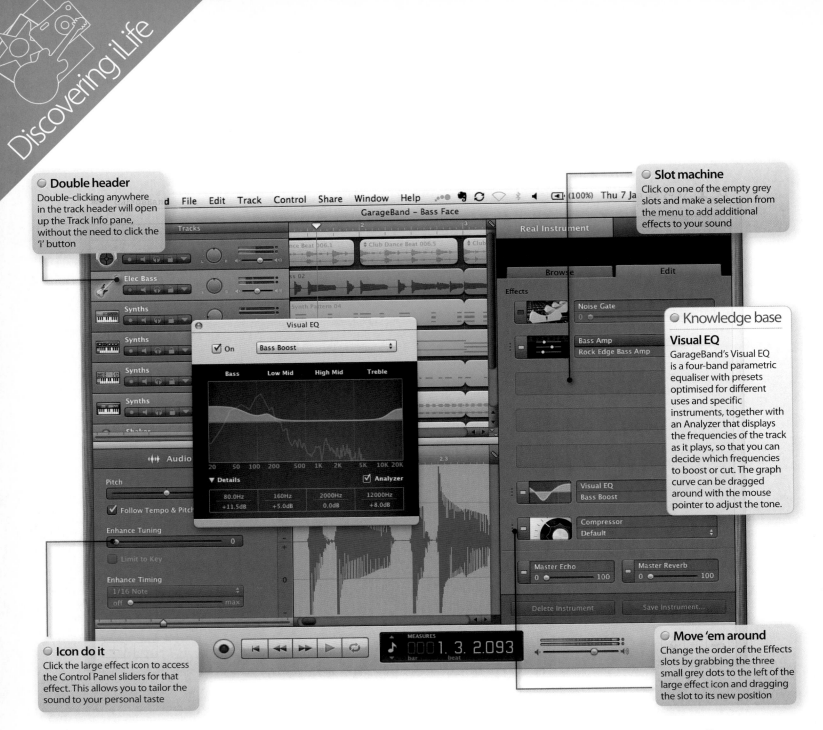

Double header
Double-clicking anywhere in the track header will open up the Track Info pane, without the need to click the 'i' button

Slot machine
Click on one of the empty grey slots and make a selection from the menu to add additional effects to your sound

Knowledge base

Visual EQ
GarageBand's Visual EQ is a four-band parametric equaliser with presets optimised for different uses and specific instruments, together with an Analyzer that displays the frequencies of the track as it plays, so that you can decide which frequencies to boost or cut. The graph curve can be dragged around with the mouse pointer to adjust the tone.

Icon do it
Click the large effect icon to access the Control Panel sliders for that effect. This allows you to tailor the sound to your personal taste

Move 'em around
Change the order of the Effects slots by grabbing the three small grey dots to the left of the large effect icon and dragging the slot to its new position

Tutorial: Boost basslines in GarageBand

Beef up your bass with the help of GarageBand's built-in effects

Task: Boost your bass parts in GarageBand
Difficulty: Beginner
Time needed: 20 minutes

Whatever style of music you make, a good bassline is always an important foundation. But with so many tracks these days intended to be uploaded to the internet, subjected to data compression and played back on small speakers with little or no bass response, the bass end is often in danger of being lost entirely.

To help combat this problem, we're going to take a look at how to ensure that your bass has enough punch to cut through the densest of mixes and still be audible on small systems, without being so boomy that the speakers get shaken out of their mounts. Nobody likes an overly bassy mix but, at the same time, nobody likes a thin and whispy-sounding track either. With any luck, after following these tips, you'll soon have a bottom end you can be proud of.

GarageBand

1: Open project
Locate the bass part that needs attention and click the desired track's header to select it for editing. The regions on the track will also become highlighted.

2: Access FX
Click the 'i' button in the bottom-right of the screen to open the Track Info pane, then click the grey Edit tab to access the Effects slots for that track.

3: Amp it up
Click the first empty plug-in slot and select the Bass Amp plug-in. This will enable you to add an authentic amped-up sound to your bass part.

4: Pick a preset
Click on the icon and flick through the Bass Amp's preset settings by picking them off the list until you find one that suits your sound.

5: Bass boost
Click the Visual EQ icon and pick one of the bass presets to use as a starting point. Most of these will initially add warmth and depth to your sound.

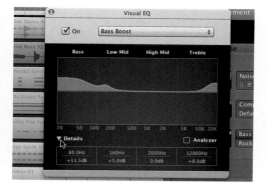

6: Details
Click Details to reveal the EQ settings. Make changes to the target frequencies, and cut and boost amounts by clicking and dragging the settings.

7: Analyse this
Use the Spectrum Analyzer display to check the levels of frequencies present in your adjusted sound. Low frequencies are shown on the left.

8: Evening out
Click the Compressor icon and select an appropriate preset that levels out the volume of the notes in the bass part so that they can all be heard.

9: Level compensation
The processing may result in a lower overall level, so use the Volume slider in the track header to set the mix level of the bass louder to compensate.

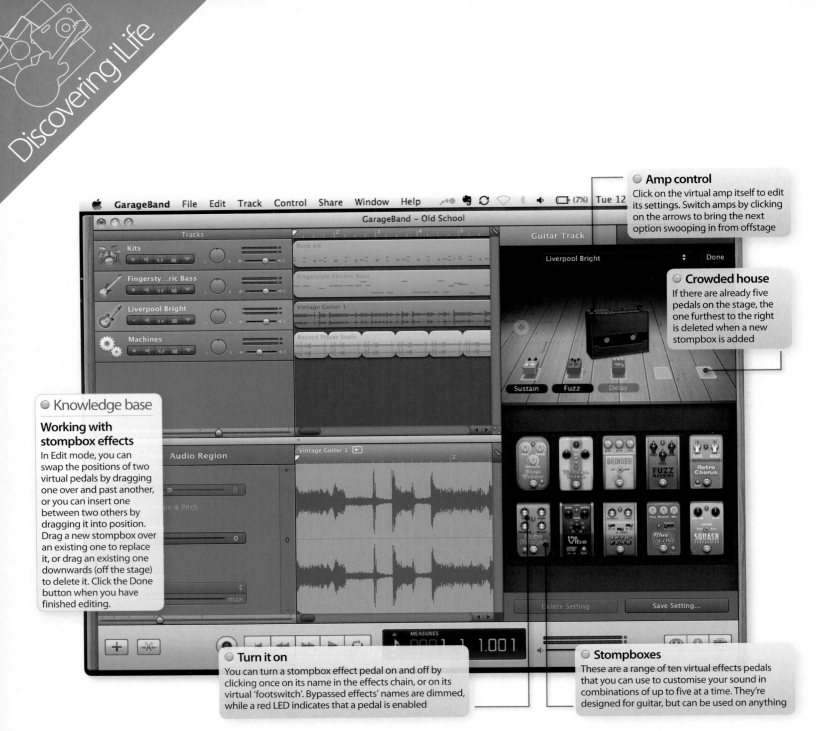

Amp control
Click on the virtual amp itself to edit its settings. Switch amps by clicking on the arrows to bring the next option swooping in from offstage

Crowded house
If there are already five pedals on the stage, the one furthest to the right is deleted when a new stompbox is added

Knowledge base

Working with stompbox effects
In Edit mode, you can swap the positions of two virtual pedals by dragging one over and past another, or you can insert one between two others by dragging it into position. Drag a new stompbox over an existing one to replace it, or drag an existing one downwards (off the stage) to delete it. Click the Done button when you have finished editing.

Turn it on
You can turn a stompbox effect pedal on and off by clicking once on its name in the effects chain, or on its virtual 'footswitch'. Bypassed effects' names are dimmed, while a red LED indicates that a pedal is enabled

Stompboxes
These are a range of ten virtual effects pedals that you can use to customise your sound in combinations of up to five at a time. They're designed for guitar, but can be used on anything

Tutorial: Create a 'vintage' GarageBand sound

Use GarageBand's new stompbox-style guitar effects to re-create the sound of yesteryear in your project

Task: Create a vintage-sounding track

Difficulty: Intermediate

Time needed: 40 minutes

At first glance you might be forgiven for thinking that, while GarageBand is fine for knocking out a quick song idea, it lacks the depth for going anywhere beyond slinging together a few Apple loops. Happily, this is not actually the case, as beneath the approachable interface of GarageBand there is plenty of scope for experimentation. The new stompbox-style guitar effects, for instance, can really go a long way to transforming basic MIDI programmed parts and bog-standard Apple Loops into something a bit more esoteric – particularly when you're trying to create a 'vintage' sound. In this tutorial we're going to demonstrate just how easy it is, with a bit of imagination, to create something that sounds like it might have been recorded years ago.

Step-by-step | GarageBand Kick it old school

1: Start with the drums
Create a new software instrument track and select Drum Kits>Rock Kit from the menu. Record in a basic part with kick, snare and cymbals.

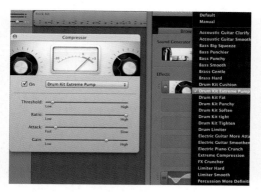

2: Compressor time
Click the Edit tab to reveal the Effects slots. Click the green button to enable the compressor and select a suitably squashy preset from the pop-up menu.

3: Adjust threshold
Click the large compressor icon to reveal the effect's Control Panel. Adjust the compressor's Threshold slider to give the right amount of effect.

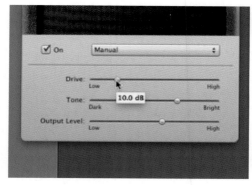

4: Crunch it
For a noisy, lo-fi thrashy drum sound, click an empty Effect slot and insert a Distortion plug-in. Trim back the Drive setting to get the right amount of crunch.

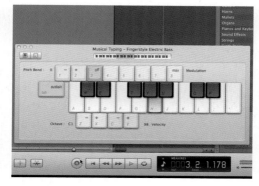

5: Bass instinct
Now you can create another new software track, and this time record in a Fingerstyle Electric Bass MIDI part.

6: Warm it up
In the Track Info pane, once again click the Edit tab. Add a compressor and a bass amp plug-in, then choose one of the vintage bass amp presets.

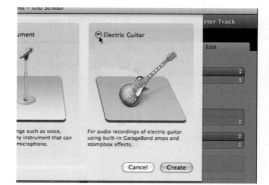

7: Create guitar track
Create a new Electric Guitar track by selecting New Track from the Track menu and clicking this button. This will allow you to access the stompbox effects.

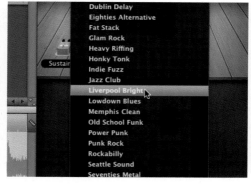

8: Add guitar
Record or import a clean-sounding guitar part to the new track. Pick one of the old-sounding stompbox combo presets, like Liverpool Bright or Clean Combo.

9: Edit effects chain
Click the Edit button next to the Preset Selection menu to bring up a selection of stompboxes. To use a new one, simply drag it to one of the yellow slots.

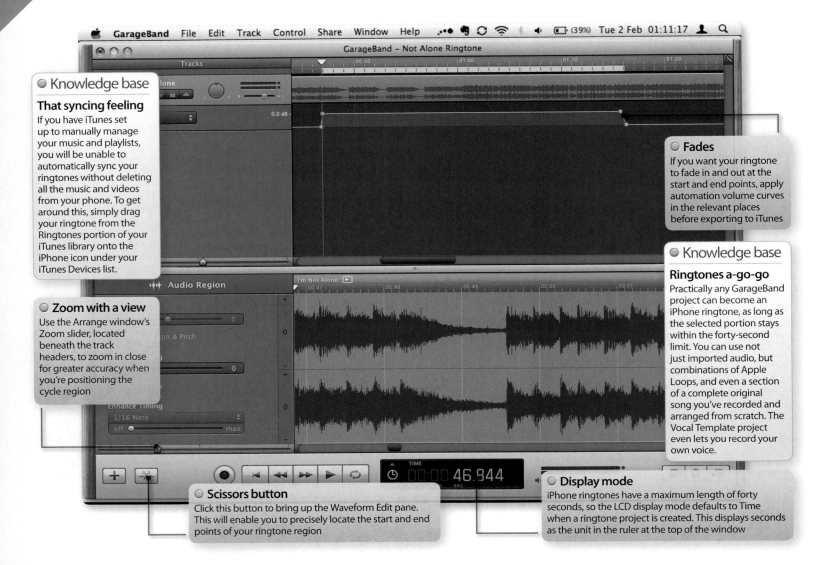

Knowledge base

That syncing feeling

If you have iTunes set up to manually manage your music and playlists, you will be unable to automatically sync your ringtones without deleting all the music and videos from your phone. To get around this, simply drag your ringtone from the Ringtones portion of your iTunes library onto the iPhone icon under your iTunes Devices list.

Fades

If you want your ringtone to fade in and out at the start and end points, apply automation volume curves in the relevant places before exporting to iTunes

Knowledge base

Ringtones a-go-go

Practically any GarageBand project can become an iPhone ringtone, as long as the selected portion stays within the forty-second limit. You can use not just imported audio, but combinations of Apple Loops, and even a section of a complete original song you've recorded and arranged from scratch. The Vocal Template project even lets you record your own voice.

Zoom with a view

Use the Arrange window's Zoom slider, located beneath the track headers, to zoom in close for greater accuracy when you're positioning the cycle region

Scissors button

Click this button to bring up the Waveform Edit pane. This will enable you to precisely locate the start and end points of your ringtone region

Display mode

iPhone ringtones have a maximum length of forty seconds, so the LCD display mode defaults to Time when a ringtone project is created. This displays seconds as the unit in the ruler at the top of the window

Tutorial: Create a ringtone in GarageBand

You can convert any GarageBand project into a ringtone that's compatible with your iPhone. Here's how…

Task: Convert GarageBand projects into iPhone ringtones

Difficulty: Beginner

Time needed: 30 minutes

How to get custom ringtones onto your iPhone must be one of the most frequently asked questions among new iPhone owners, as the selection available on a box-fresh device is not the widest. There is a 'Create Ringtone' option in iTunes' Store menu, but – as its location would suggest – this option only works for tracks you've purchased from the iTunes Store itself. If you have music in your library that you've imported from your CD collection, or even that you've created yourself, there is an alternative method that makes use of GarageBand's built-in cross-compatibility with iTunes to get the latest tracks onto your phone. So, if you long to be the guy in the meeting who feels all eyes swivel towards him when the theme from *Bob The Builder* erupts from his jacket pocket, this tutorial is for you…

Step-by-step | GarageBand Create custom ringtones

1: Create a Ringtone project
To begin, open an existing project or create a new one by clicking the iPhone Ringtone option in the sidebar of GarageBand's opening screen.

2: Choose template
You can pick from an Example template, a Loops template for creating a ringtone from Apple Loops, or a Voice template for recording a vocal ringtone.

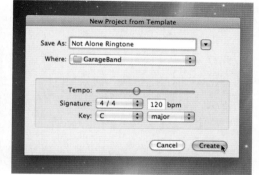

3: Name and save
Enter a name for the project and click the Create button. GarageBand opens with an example ringtone on an audio track named 'Jingles'.

4: Delete default
Delete the example ringtone by selecting the 'Jingles' track header and choosing Delete Track from the Track menu.

5: Import target track
Open iTunes and locate the song you want to convert. Drag it from iTunes into GarageBand's Arrange window to import it onto a track.

6: De-cycle
Click the 'i' button to close the Track Info pane and give you more room to work with, then turn off the cycle region by clicking the Cycle button.

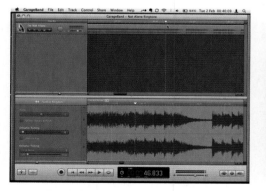

7: Find target area
Click the play button to preview the ringtone and locate the area of the song you want to use. Click the Cycle button to re-enable the cycle region.

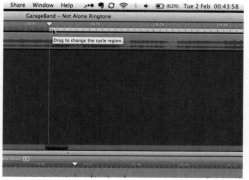

8: Re-cycle
Adjust the cycle region by dragging the yellow bar at the top of the window to encompass the part of the song that you want to use as a ringtone.

9: Export to iTunes
Choose 'Send Ringtone to iTunes' from the Share menu. GarageBand will create the ringtone and open iTunes, where you can sync it to your iPhone.

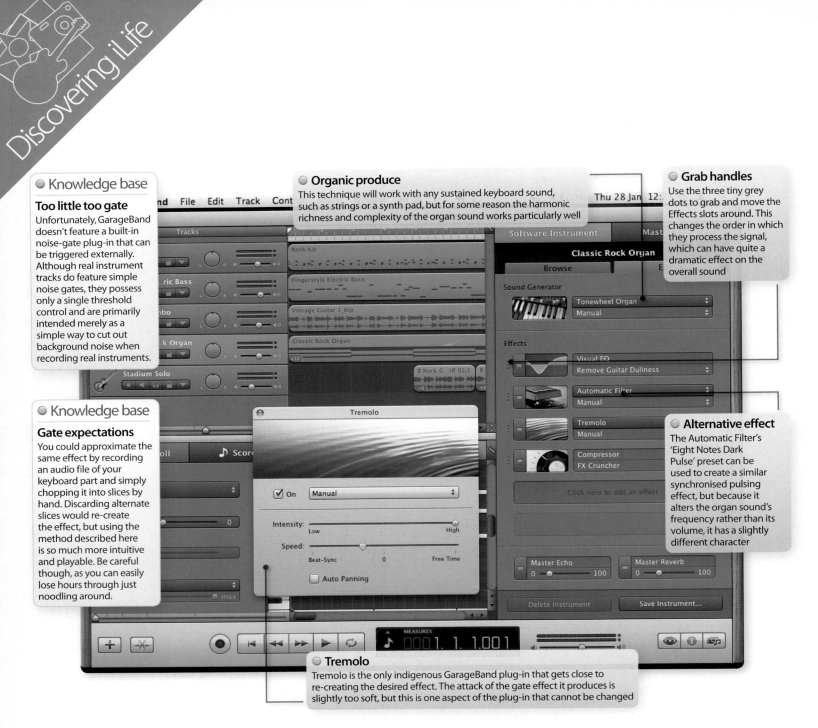

Tutorial: Create gated effects in GarageBand

The Tremolo plug-in holds the key to emulating this classic effect

Task: Create a gated-style keyboard effect

Difficulty: Intermediate

Time needed: 30 minutes

If you're looking for a keyboard part to liven up your rhythm tracks, pulsing chords synchronised perfectly to the beat could be the answer. This kind of gated keyboard effect is not only great if you're making dance music, but rock tracks can also benefit from the idea – remember *Won't Get Fooled Again* by The Who? Currently showcased weekly in the title sequence of *CSI Miami*, Pete Townshend's VCS3-processed Lowrey organ part is one of the pioneering examples of a gated keyboard effect. The sound has since been universally produced using noise gates triggered from an element of the drum track, and more recently can be emulated by chopping pre-recorded audio regions into regular chunks. If you want to create a more organic effect however, one that you can hear working as you play the chords, there is a way to get close using GarageBand's built-in Effect plug-ins. Read on to discover more.

Step-by-step | GarageBand | Gated keyboard effects

1: Create new project

Create a new GarageBand project, featuring either the Piano or Keyboard Collection templates. Give it a name and choose a save location.

2: Select track

Choose a track to use as a starting point for your sound. We're going to use *Won't Get Fooled Again* as our inspiration, so we'll go for the Classic Organ.

3: Access effects

The Track Info pane should already have opened when you created the project. Click the Edit tab to get to the Effects Control Panel.

4: Choose plug-in

Now click on the first empty Effects slot and pick the GarageBand Tremolo plug-in from the menu that pops up.

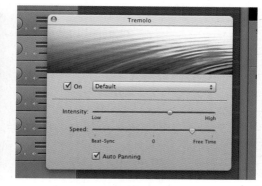

5: Reveal Control Panel

Click the large watery icon to bring up the Tremolo Control Panel. This enables you to tailor the effect to get the sound you want.

6: Select preset

The best preset to use as a starting point is Mono Tremolo, so pick it from the menu. Hold down some chords on your MIDI keyboard to audition it.

7: Sync it up

Drag the Speed slider to the left into the Beat Sync region. As you drag, the required quantise value appears in the yellow info window.

8: Sweep stake

A slow filter sweep works well here, making the sound brighter and duller over time. Change the default Chorus plug-in to an Automatic Filter.

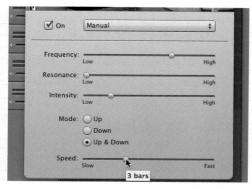

9: Set sweep

Pick the 'Deep and Slow Filter' preset and set the speed appropriately. A 3-bar period adds a nice random element to the timing of the sweep.

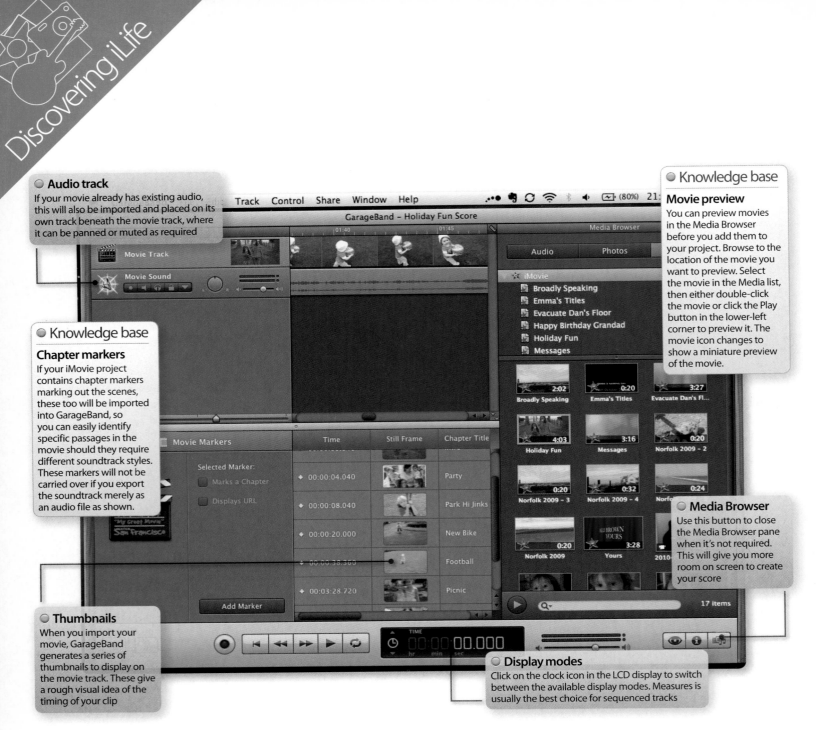

● Audio track
If your movie already has existing audio, this will also be imported and placed on its own track beneath the movie track, where it can be panned or muted as required

● Knowledge base

Movie preview
You can preview movies in the Media Browser before you add them to your project. Browse to the location of the movie you want to preview. Select the movie in the Media list, then either double-click the movie or click the Play button in the lower-left corner to preview it. The movie icon changes to show a miniature preview of the movie.

● Knowledge base

Chapter markers
If your iMovie project contains chapter markers marking out the scenes, these too will be imported into GarageBand, so you can easily identify specific passages in the movie should they require different soundtrack styles. These markers will not be carried over if you export the soundtrack merely as an audio file as shown.

● Media Browser
Use this button to close the Media Browser pane when it's not required. This will give you more room on screen to create your score

● Thumbnails
When you import your movie, GarageBand generates a series of thumbnails to display on the movie track. These give a rough visual idea of the timing of your clip

● Display modes
Click on the clock icon in the LCD display to switch between the available display modes. Measures is usually the best choice for sequenced tracks

Prepare a movie for scoring in GarageBand

Creating a musical backdrop to your iMovie projects is probably easier than you think. Here we demonstrate how to set it up…

Task: Prepare iMovie projects for scoring in GarageBand

Difficulty: Beginner

Time needed: 20 minutes

There's something intrinsically satisfying about adding your own soundtrack to your movie, knowing that what you're both seeing and hearing is all your own work. Traditionally, when writing music for movies, the work is broken down into cues that go with each scene. But for projects only a few minutes in length, the whole movie can often be scored in one GarageBand project. It's actually very easy to do, not to mention great fun.

Although iMovie has a wide range of options for editing backing tracks, if you want to assemble your own audio backdrop from a variety of elements then it's much easier to import the video file into GarageBand so that you can make full use of its audio-editing capabilities. We'll show you how to import your movie into GarageBand so that you can view it as you compose the score.

Step-by-step | GarageBand Set up iMovie projects for scoring

1: Open iMovie
Launch iMovie and click the Project Library tab in the top-left corner to display the list of projects that are on your system.

2: Load project
Choose the project that you want to add a soundtrack to from the list. Now double-click it to load it into the Project editor.

3: Prepare to share
Select the Media Browser option from the Share menu. This option will ensure that your movie is visible within GarageBand's Media Browser.

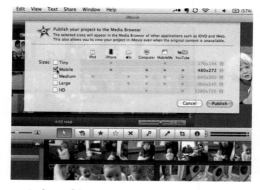

4: Select file size
As it's only a guide for scoring in GarageBand, choose a small size. This will free up CPU power, allowing you to create a more complex soundtrack.

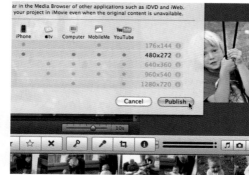

5: Publish
Click the Publish button and put the kettle on while iMovie renders your project. Smaller file sizes shouldn't take more than a few minutes.

6: Launch GarageBand
Now quit iMovie and launch GarageBand. At the New Project intro screen, scroll down to reveal the hidden Movie option and double-click it.

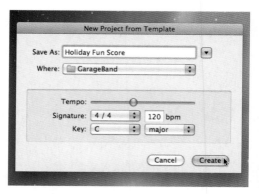

7: Name project
Give your project a name and choose a save location. You can enter key and tempo info here if you know it. If not then you can change it later.

8: Select target movie
The Movies tab of the Media Browser should have opened automatically. In the list of available movies should be the one you just shared from iMovie.

9: Drag movie
Select your movie and drag it onto the Movie Track in the Arrange window. Release it on 'Drag Movie Here'. You're now ready to begin scoring!

Tutorial: Score a movie in GarageBand

Having imported your movie into GarageBand, the next step is to create some music to go with it

Task: Produce a movie soundtrack in GarageBand

Difficulty: Beginner

Time needed: 60 minutes

So now you've got your movie into position in GarageBand by following the previous tutorial, it's time to get creative and take full advantage of its ability to play back movie files in sync with the project on its special Movie Track. This can be used as a timing guide so that you can add software instrument parts, Apple Loops and recorded elements to create a unique soundtrack to go with the visuals. Once you've composed your backing track, there are options to export the whole movie (together with its newly programmed soundtrack) as a podcast straight to iWeb, or as a QuickTime movie file to iTunes.

Step-by-step | **GarageBand** Score a movie with GarageBand

1: Create new track
Select the New Track option from the Track menu. In the subsequent option screen, select a new Software Instrument track and click Create.

2: Strings attached
The Track Info pane should open on the right of the screen, containing a list of preset instruments. Select Orchestral Strings from the Strings category.

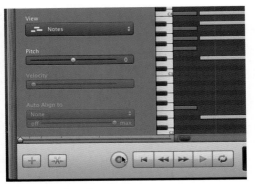

3: Record string part
Click the record button and play along with the visuals to record in your string part. If you go wrong, simply undo the recording by hitting Cmd+Z.

4: Add brass
When you're happy with the strings, create another new track and this time select a brass Software Instrument from the Horns section.

5: Record horns
Now, using the same method as before (see step 3), record in your brass parts to accompany the strings. Remember to use Cmd+Z if you go wrong.

6: Balance
Once all the parts are right, use the volume sliders in the track headers to balance the volume of each track against each other.

Create a soundtrack in GarageBand
Use GarageBand's capabilities to full effect

● Turn off movie audio
Hiding the Movie Track does not mute the movie's original audio track, so if you don't want to include it you'll need to mute it manually by clicking its mute button

● Knowledge base

Quality control
You do, of course, have the option to leave the movie track open and export the GarageBand project as a movie with incorporated soundtrack attached. However, if you were using a reduced quality copy of the original movie to score to, it makes more sense to export the audio back into iMovie, as this will preserve the original quality of your

● Automation station
Click the small triangles in the track headers to reveal the volume automation curves. These can be used to help highlight key moments in your movie

● Through the window
So you can really see what you're doing, double-click the thumbnail in the Movie Track header to view your movie in a floating resizable window

7: Hide Movie Track
We want to export just an audio file rather than the whole movie, so you'll need to select Hide Movie Track from the Track menu.

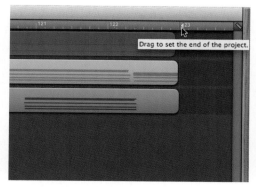

8: Magic marker
The song-end marker, a purple triangle, is usually found at bar 200 by default. Drag it back to the point where you want the audio file to end.

9: Export to disk
The Share menu will now list options for exporting the project as a song rather than a movie. Choose the Export Song to Disk option.

Are you an artist?

It doesn't matter if not, all you need is a Mac and these apps

A few years ago, answering that question would have been simple. It would have elicited a positive response from those adept with a crayon or paintbrush, and a straightforward 'no' from the rest of us. But now the lines have been blurred. Thanks to our Macs and the digital tools at our disposal, we all have the potential to unleash the inner artist – even if we couldn't draw a curtain, never mind a picture, in real life.

Painting software now allows you to mimic real-world skills to a remarkable degree. Using software rather than real materials affords the opportunity for a degree of experimentation – and error correction – that otherwise simply isn't practicable or affordable with real materials.

Painting digitally also has other advantages, particularly for those who have never been confident enough to create art before. Filters and other adjustments can be applied automatically, which will put some of the most complex artistic

styles within reach. Most importantly, the majority of painting software allows you to use your existing material – such as digital photographs – as the basis for your artwork. You can manually or automatically trace it, or convert it automatically, and even sample the colours in your photographs for your digital paint palette. The result is that, while our digital snapshots are often merely a record of an event, by turning them into something else with painting software we can make a unique creative statement for ourselves and others to enjoy.

At its most basic, turning a photo into a piece of art may amount to little more than opening one of your favourite digital images in an image editor and running a few filters in succession to give it a unique look. That's fine as far as it goes, and it can produce stunning results, but there are more creative avenues that are open for you to explore. Over the next few pages we'll look at some of the leading painting applications and how versatile they can be in converting your bitmap images into a work of art using various painting styles.

Each program we look at has its own strong points, whether that's painting from scratch, acting as a plug-in for other applications, converting bitmaps or applying filters. However, if you want to approach painting, there should be an application that suits you.

And the good news is that painting software is more affordable than ever. While the venerable industry standard Corel Painter is still a pricey purchase for beginners, most of the other painting software we look at in this feature fits squarely into the budget category. And we've also included suggestions of cheap or free alternative drawing programs that you can use, many of which are included on this issue's CD. That should make it as simple as possible to dip your toes into artistic waters. And as your painting skills develop, you'll probably want to invest in some of the handy tools of the digital artist's trade, such as a drawing tablet or a good-quality colour printer. In this feature we'll look at some of the best-value accessories for your new hobby.

There are plenty of applications to help you create art on your Mac. We've limited this feature four main programs that illustrate the breadth of possibilities open to you.

No discussion of painting programs would be complete without Corel's Painter, a venerable paint program that can trace its history back to the early days of Macintosh illustration. ArtRage may not be as well known, but it's not only cheaper than Painter, it's also very powerful in its own right. It looks unlike any other image-editing or illustration application you may have used, devoting almost all of the screen to a canvas, with a Tool Picker panel occupying the lower-left quadrant of the screen and a Colour Picker the lower-right. If it reminds you of that famous Kai Power Tools Photoshop plug-in, that's because the developers behind that idiosyncratic tool were also involved with ArtRage.

ArtWork, from Russian developer AKVIS, is a different beast altogether. It lacks the usual brushes and other tools normally used by digital artists to create artwork; instead it is dedicated to the simple task of converting digital images into art. For this it uses a dedicated and very powerful engine

Pixelmator started three years ago as a cut-price alternative to software behemoth Adobe Photoshop. But with its gorgeous translucent display, Pixelmator looks far more Mac OS X-like than its rival. Based on Apple's Core Image technology, it incorporates non-destructive filters and effects that can add an artistic touch to images.

Painting from scratch and from photos

If you're interested primarily in painting on an empty canvas, there are two ideal programs to use: Corel Painter and ArtRage.

Of the two, Corel's interface will be familiar if you've ever used Photoshop. To paint an image you select a brush (Painter comes with an astounding choice, and the Brush Creator palette lets you create more of your own) and start painting. Just like in Photoshop, you are able to create your artwork in layers, so you can build your artwork non-destructively.

ArtRage is arguably easier to use for beginners thanks to its easily accessible tools and the colour palette. It has layer support too, and while its choice of brushes and paint-blending options aren't on a par with Painter, the program is more suited for use with a graphics tablet.

Pixelmator may be better known as an image-editing program, but it also has a painting engine that lets you set various brush settings, such as scatter, jitter and size. It also has graphics tablet support, which is a critical inclusion for serious artists. Meanwhile, as AKVIS ArtWork is a conversion utility that works from digital image originals, it isn't suitable for painting from scratch. But for beginners, creating art from photos is more fun and easier than drawing from scratch. In most cases, turning your photo into art follows a similar path irrespective of

"Another unique feature of ArtRage is the way you can pin reference material to your canvas."

ArtRage

ArtRage has the sort of interface you'll either love or hate. It isn't as fully featured as Painter, but still has a wide, easily accessible choice of artistic mediums, and works very well on imported images – even allowing you to 'pin' a copy of the image you're importing to the canvas as a reference.

Price: From $40 (approx £25)
Available From: www.artrage.com
Best For:
Both easy to use and intuitive, ArtRage is best for painting from scratch – particularly if you own a graphics tablet, where its palette organisation will seem like second nature.

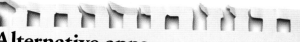

Alternative apps

A quick look at the other image-editing applications that are available for you to download…

Lineform
$79.95 (approx £50)
www.freeverse.com

Speedy and easy to use, Lineform is an illustration program that also supports Apple's Core Image filters, as well as artistic strokes.

Sumo Paint
Free
www.sumopaint.com
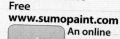
An online application that boasts a surprising number of features. Ideal if you want to paint while away from your Mac.

Peacock
Free
http://aviary.com

Online-only Peacock can produce stunning effects with images uploaded from Flickr, then pass them on to other applications in this online suite.

VectorDesigner
$70 (approx £40)
www.tweakersoft.com
Primarily a line drawing application, VectorDesigner lets you add images to your creations and even edit them with bitmap filters.

"ArtRage is arguably easier to use for beginners thanks to its easily accessible tools and the colour palette"

Create art from photos in iPhoto

1: Choose your image
Select the photo to edit in iPhoto and click the Edit button at the bottom of the browser window. Click the Effects button.

2: Boost the colour
In the Effects window, click the Boost Color option a couple of times to enhance the colours in the image.

3: Drag the sliders
Open the Adjust palette. Drag the Exposure, Contrast and Saturation sliders to the right. Drag the Sharpness slider towards the right to increase definition.

4: Add a tint
You can now play with the Tint slider at the bottom of the Adjust palette to add an overall tone to the image.

the application you're using. You load your original photo into the program and either use it as an underlying layer to paint on, or convert it directly to an artistic image by using filters or other conversion techniques.

But some are more versatile than others. Perhaps unsurprisingly given its price, Painter offers the most ways to convert an image. The most versatile method in Painter is simply to use its Tracing Paper feature. You first create a clone of the image to ensure you're not working on the original, then you delete the visible image and choose Canvas> Tracing Paper, which reveals a faint rendering of the source image. You can then paint over the image with any of Painter's myriad brush choices, using the

picture with a single stroke of the brush. To do this, you record and save a single brush stroke made in your chosen style, and when you press the Play button the stroke will be replayed over the whole image – or any subsequent image that you apply it to – realistically following the detail of the underlying picture.

With ArtRage, you load a photo or other image as a 'tracing' image. This is projected on to the canvas in a chosen degree of opacity, so you can use it as a guide while painting above it using ArtRage's brushes and choosing colours. This underlying tracing image is saved with your painting – although when you export the tracing image is removed, so your source isn't revealed.

"Perhaps unsurprisingly given its price, Painter offers the most ways to convert an image"

faint background as a rough guide.

An easier way is to use Painter's Quick Clone option – a one-step tool that automatically sets up the Tracing Paper feature among other things – and then employ the Cloner tool, which picks up the cloned image's underlying colour while you remain in control of the size, direction and type of brushstrokes. Painting a large image in this way can still take a lot of time though, but Painter offers an Auto Clone option that automatically applies brush dabs to your image using the currently selected brush. Painter also features an amazing Auto Painting mode, which lets you paint an entire

But, like Painter, ArtRage boasts some handy shortcuts. For example, its 'Convert Tracing Image To Paint' feature will convert the tracing image to paint on the current layer, so you can smudge, smear and paint over it as if it was a real painting. ArtRage also makes it easier to match the underlying colours of an image by automatically matching the colours of the underlying tracing image, sampling the underlying colour at the point where you begin a paint stroke.

Another unique feature of ArtRage is the way you can pin reference material to your canvas. You might think that this would use up a lot of valuable

AKVIS ArtWork

AKVIS ArtWork works as either a standalone program or as a plug-in for well-known image-editing programs. It works well in either case, although its aims are limited; it simply converts a digital image into oil, pen and ink or comic-style images – but it does so very realistically.

Price: 55 Euros (approx £50)
Available From: www.akvis.com
Best For:
To quickly convert a bitmap image into a convincing oil, comic, or line drawing effect, there's nothing to beat AKVIS ArtWork.

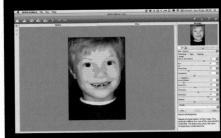

screen estate, but handily ArtRage's unique palettes temporarily disappear from view as you paint towards them, so it always seems like you have plenty of space.

AKVIS ArtWork, the image-converter application, divides its interface into two areas: Before and After. To begin you need to load your digital image, which will automatically appear in the Before area, and on the right-hand side you can apply an artistic medium to it – either oil, comic, or pen and ink – from the Navigator pane. The changes you make to your image will be reflected immediately underneath the After tab.

As Pixelmator is primarily a bitmap editor, it does lack the instant 'convert-to-art' tools that are available elsewhere. But its support for artistic brushes and the 130-odd filters and special effects it offers, not to mention its support for layers, means that you can simply load your image and apply a number of cool effects on it.

Work in different mediums

Art is created using a variety of mediums, such as oil on canvas, watercolour, and pen and ink. Once you've opened your image, how do the various painting applications allow you to create artwork in these mediums?

The most versatile choices are offered by Painter. It doesn't have discrete modes for working in different mediums – although ink and watercolour

brushes automatically go on separate layers – but it has hundreds of natural media brush choices, from charcoal to pencil, and its powerful Brush Creator tool lets you create and save your own brushes.

AKVIS ArtWork has modes for three different types of medium: oil, comic art, and pen and ink. With your digital image loaded, you can simply convert it to an oil painting by drawing a marquee over the area you wish to change, and selecting Oils. You can switch to another medium by selecting it from the drop-down menu.

While ArtRage's brushes are preconfigured for different painting and drawing mediums, Pixelmator's brushes are only configurable in terms of properties such as shape, hardness and colour. Any medium naturally depends on the canvas that's underlying it. Even here, the painting tools will attempt to simulate the natural world as closely as possible.

With AKVIS you can choose whether or not to include a configurable background canvas effect. ArtRage offers dozens of different canvas types – from foil to art paper – and for each you can adjust their properties, such as opacity, grain and roughness. Best of all is Painter, which not only allows you to change the colour of the canvas and apply a lighting effect to it, but lets you select a specific paper texture from a palette. You can even adjust or randomise the paper grain for a unique effect. And on the other side of the paint, Painter lets you apply a surface texture for added realism. But how well do the painting applications deal with popular painting and drawing mediums?

Oil

One of the most popular methods of painting is painting with oils, and it's impressive how closely painting applications can get to the real thing.

AKVIS lays down brush strokes using the original photo as a reference. You can adjust the parameters of a stroke, for example its simplicity (a higher value provides rougher strokes), curvature and thickness. There's no way in the basic program to create your own strokes, although more expensive versions of the program provide a Stroke Direction tool that lets you define the guiding lines to direct the way the strokes will be painted.

While Painter doesn't have a specific Oils mode like AKVIS, it does offer control over its oils brushes – for example, by adjusting the amount of grain, which affects the appearance of the brush stroke by affecting how the paper appears to absorb the paint. You can also determine how much paint is loaded on a brush stroke and how speedily this is transferred to the page. You can even incorporate finer details, such as how much a brush bristles at the end of a stroke, and you can even adjust the canvas wetness.

ArtRage's Oil Brush mimics painting in oils and will smear and blend as you paint over previous oil strokes. The oil brushes have texture, and you can optionally choose for the brush head to remain dirty after each stroke so the last colour applied to it will remain when you start the next stroke. It may not be neat, but it's very realistic and with practice can lead to some incedibly impressive paintings.

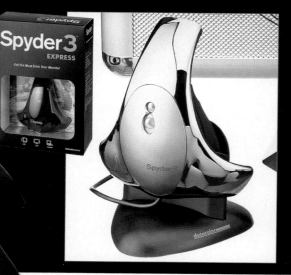

Watercolour

The other common painting medium is watercolour. Watercolour is a difficult medium to simulate accurately, but try creating a watercolour image in Painter and you'll be impressed at how well it manages the job. When you paint with Painter's watercolour brushes, these appear in their own watercolour layer, above the image layer. This allows you to easily mix mediums – say drawing in pen on one layer and adding watercolour fill for these in the layer above – and means that the behaviour of the watercolour layer, where colours naturally blend into each other, don't interfere with other layers. You can move any information from the canvas to the watercolour layer, which is ideal if you want to convert a photograph to a watercolour.

Similarly, ArtRage uses a soft bristled brush on wet or dry paper. There's no watercolour mode in AKVIS ArtWork, though.

Pen & Ink

Creating a pen and ink translation of a digital photo is wonderfully easy in ArtWork; select the Pen & Ink option and adjust its properties using the slider. ArtRage's Ink Pen is arguably even more versatile. Its pen has seven preset settings, each of which provide a solid line with various smoothing and shape options. Painter's Liquid Ink brushes can be customised in even more detail. Like watercolours, they appear on their own layer, so can be easily edited without affecting any of the other layers in the document you are using.

Painting in styles

While the programs offer plenty of choices over different mediums, there are also opportunities to create artwork in a particular style – for example, pop art or pointillism. Pop art is an art genre that mimics elements of popular culture, such as comics, and uses bright, primary colours and strong lines to achieve its effect. And turning your photos into comic artwork isn't just a great way to pay homage to pop art gurus such as Roy Lichtenstein, it also adds punch to photos, and by simplifying the image it makes it ideal for enlarging even poor-quality originals. When choosing originals to work with, it's best to stick to images that have good contrast and where the subject is clearly identifiable. Simple backgrounds will work best, but these can always be edited out.

Painter lacks a discrete comic painting mode, although you can apply a Pop Art Fill effect to an image, which fills it with pseudo-halftone dots. You can ally this with other adjustments – such as changing the tonal range of the image – to create a convincing pop art effect.

But when it comes to creating comic effects, there can be few better than AKVIS ArtWork's Comics mode. This converts an image into a comic style in a similar way that it works with oil painting, adjusting both the image and the outlines using sliders. Pixelmator includes a Comic Effect style that simulates a comic drawing by outlining edges and applying a Color Halftone effect to the image.

Pointillism is a well-known art technique that involves drawing small dots of discrete colours to create the impression of other colours through blending. As the Mac OS X's Quartz Composer engine that Pixelmator uses features a Pointillize

> "When it comes to creating comic effects, there can be few better than AKVIS ArtWork"

filter, you won't be surprised to see this feature available in that program. Quartz also includes another filter for an art form popularised in the Sixties: ASCII art. This is a technique that generates images using the limited ASCII character set, made up of monospaced characters. The results take some tweaking to be usable, but it's still a fascinating conversion.

It's worth exploring all the applications in Painter, Pixelmator and ArtRage to see what other effects they provide out of the box. Painter even offers a Van Gogh Effect function – a one-click setting that turns your image into what looks eerily like a painting by the Dutch master.

Re-touching

It's unlikely that you'll want to convert an image to art without first cleaning it up in some way; either to remove extraneous items in the background or to clean up the odd scratch. Here, Painter and Pixelmator are outstanding. Painter in particular has very powerful re-touching features. Its Scratch Remover brush can be used to remove scratches from photos, while its Cloning and Rubber Stamp tools can be used to remove unwanted elements from the canvas.

Pixelmator's re-touching tools aren't as powerful – although it does have a Clone tool – but both applications boast powerful masking features, which allow you to limit the effect of a filter to a particular selection. While it doesn't have the masking features of Painter or Pixelmator, ArtRage does have more rudimentary stencils that allow you to mask out predefined areas of your canvas as you paint.

The iPhoto option

Don't forget that while the painting tools we've mentioned in this feature are very powerful, you almost certainly already own a fairly powerful artwork-creation tool – iPhoto.

Admittedly, iPhoto's features are limited: you won't find Painter's brushes, Pixelmator's masking tools, ArtRage's powerful editing window, or ArtWork's conversion tools. But iPhoto does have a useful range of filters and effects that, when combined, can create stunning effects quickly.

In Edit mode, for example, you can choose from nine artistic effects from a floating palette – ranging from an antique effect to one that can boost colours significantly. The Adjust palette lets you adjust contrast and saturation, which can produce fascinating effects when twinned with adjustments to the tint of the photo. There are even ways of creating a pop art effect.

The main advantage of using iPhoto as your artistic weapon is that your original images are always preserved alongside your works of creativety, which gives you licence to try everything and anything with your photos.

Pixelmator

Pixelmator is a svelte and inexpensive alternative to Adobe Photoshop. It offers a big subset of Photoshop's features, including layer support, wrapped in an attractive interface. While lacking some high-end options, such as a history feature and layer styles, Pixelmator is still a good choice for digital artists.

Price: $59 (approx £40)
Available From: www.pixelmator.com
Best For:
Pixelmator is ideal for photo re-touching, or for where you need to apply one of its range of 130 filters and special effects.

"Pixelmator may be better known as an image-editing program, but it also has a painting engine that lets you set various brush settings"

Corel Painter

Corel Painter is one of the longest-established Mac painting applications, and in terms of features – whether drawing from scratch or converting images to art – it can't be beaten, with the most versatile collection of brush types on the market. It is much more expensive than its rivals, though.

Price: £269
Available From: www.corel.com
Best For:
Although it has a steeper learning curve than ArtRage, Corel has unmatched power. If you want to create compelling artwork, irrespective of

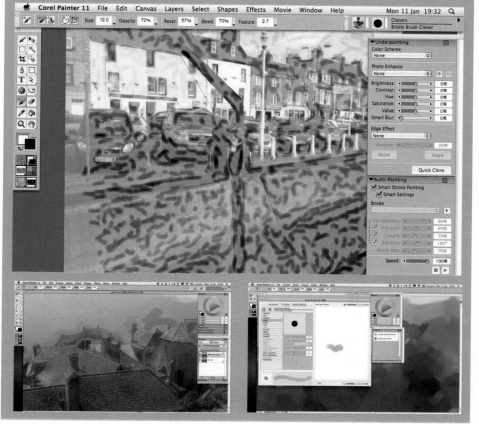

Get started with: Pixelmator

Make use of this great tool for photo manipulation, effects and much more besides

For those of us who want to edit photos but don't have the money or the expertise to make use of Photoshop, **Pixelmator is the answer.** Allowing for layers in the same way Adobe's professional image editor does, Pixelmator offers a wide range of benefits on top of this essential feature. The interface is designed as if it were an extra part of the iLife suite, with beautiful panes and minimalist palettes and windows that make Pixelmator feel like an app made by Apple. There is also a huge number of effects and tools available, so you can create anything from a painting to impressive titles and graphics.

Here we will show you a few of the basics in Pixelmator that you can try out for yourself by using the app on this month's disc. If you like it enough you can also make use of the discount that will save you 20 per cent on the full price.

Step-by-step | Pixelmator Pick colours

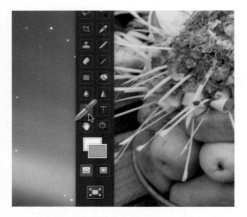

1.Tool up

With an image loaded, start by selecting the Eye Dropper tool from the toolbar. It's on the left-hand side, second from the bottom.

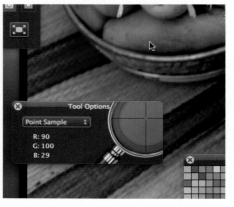

2. Select

Now move your cursor over the image. You'll notice it magnified in the Tool Options window. Now simply click to select and use a specific colour.

○ **Toolbar**
From this pane you can access all of the tools available in Pixelmator and apply them to an image

○ **Swatches**
Colours can be chosen from and added to this pane for quick selection with a single click. Colours are applied to your selected tool

Layer cake
The Layers pane not only shows you which layer you have selected, but also allows you to move layers around and make changes to them

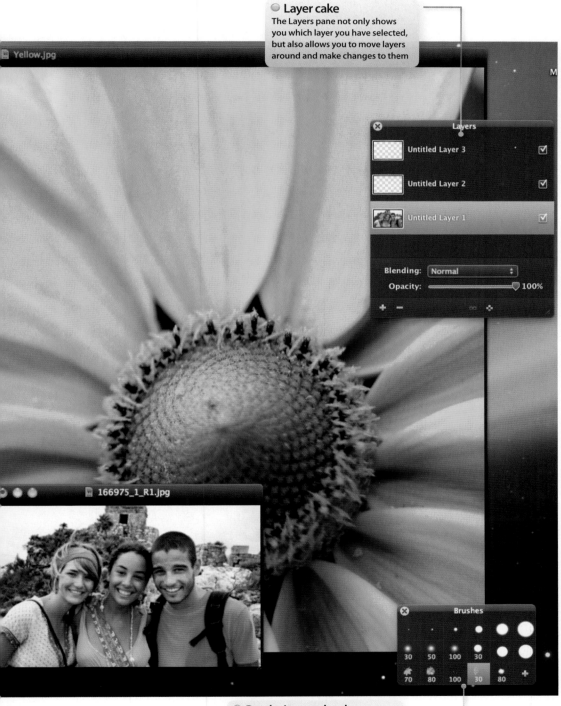

Yellow.jpg

166975_1_R1.jpg

Brush sizes and styles
This pane adjusts the size of your currently selected tool and can apply brush effects as well

Work with layers
A powerful asset for editing

1. First layer
Load an image and you'll notice it appears as the first layer in the pixelmator Layers pane. Click the plus button to add another to your document.

2. Layered up
Your new layer will now be selected and, by default, positioned above the first. Here we've added some text to our new layer which is automatically renamed.

3. Flexible feature
When you have more than one layer loaded you can move them up and down in the Layer Pane to position them in front or behind one another.

Get started with: ArtRage

Create something amazing with one of the simplest and most impressive painting applications available

ArtRage is a truly exciting application for anyone even remotely interested in art. That said, even if you've never picked up a brush, you're likely to enjoy ArtRage for its truly fascinating technology that allows traditional painting techniques to be used on a computer. This isn't just a case of blocks of colour slapped onto a white space, this is real painting. Drag a brush across the virtual canvas and, not only will the size and shape of the paint change depending on the movement of the virtual bristles, but it will also eventually run out of paint and begin to smear. If you splash a huge blob of paint onto the page you can mix it with others to make new hues and blend them together. Little touches like this make the application unique, but the fun doesn't stop there. As enjoyable as it is to play with the different brushes, pens and other tools, you can also trace and sketch too.

Step-by-step | ArtRage Trace an image

1. Load it up
Launch ArtRage and click on the tracing button at the bottom of the screen to choose an image you want to trace from.

2. Paint away
Select the Brush tool and stroke over an area of the image. ArtRage will automatically pick up the background colour and use it

Tool Control
Depending on the tool selected, a set of controls appear in this pane to fine-tune your brush

Tool palette
Pick from the varied range of tools to paint with, or interact with the paint, ink or chalk you've already applied to your canvas

Mix Colours

Get creative and create a unique colour to use

Pick a pair

Start by selecting the paint brush and a colour and add it to your canvas. Now repeat this process with a different colour.

Blend together

Now select the Palette tool and sweep it across both colours so they mix together. Circle the tool across your mix to blend.

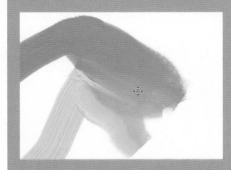

Choose it

Now you have a nice new blended colour. You can pick it up and use it with the Brush tool by selecting the Colour Sampler tool and clicking on your colour.

● Document settings

This pane allows you to adjust the ArtRage screen. Zoom in and out, undo or redo, maximise, minimise or close the window with the buttons

● Layer viewer

This pane is especially useful when you're tracing an image as it displays all the open layers and lets you know which you are currently manipulating

hmmm

Add Layer

Stencils   Tracing   Refs

Metallic ●

● Colour palette

Pick your colours from this pane and set the depth of colour with the slider on the right-hand side of the palette

The missing applications

Whether you have a Mac, iPhone, iPod touch or iPad, we have some fantastic applications for you – and many of them are free!

When we talk about the Mac these days, the iLife programs always play an important part of the conversation. In fact, it's hard to imagine using a Mac without taking advantage of at least one of these applications at some point during the day. They are such an integral part of our computing lives, yet this suite didn't materialise until 2003 and the very first iLife program, iMovie, only came onto the scene in 1999. Back then, Apple pleaded with one of its major developers, Adobe, to create a consumer version of its Premiere video-editing program. But at that time Apple wasn't the powerhouse it is now, and Adobe refused. Apple realised the hard way that if it was going to differentiate itself from Windows and show how truly special Macs were, it would have to write its own applications. So, over the next few years, Apple created programs to manage what it called "your digital life". You could make movies with ease thanks to iMovie, turn them into a DVD with the help of iDVD (released in 2001 and is sadly dying a slow death with the rise of digital downloads), manage your music with iTunes (also released in 2001 but

is no longer part of the suite and has taken an amazing life of its own), catalogue and share your photos thanks to iPhoto (2002), record your own music with GarageBand (2004) and effortlessly design a website with iWeb (2006).

But despite appearances to the contrary, Apple isn't out to write programs to cater to all its customers' needs; there are in fact huge markets that Apple isn't even touching. Creating the iLife suite was, for Apple, a matter of survival – to create unique solutions that epitomise what makes Macs different from the alternative computing platforms, and to help consumers connect to digital devices like cameras and camcorders without having to worry about drivers and compatibility problems. The long-term plan wasn't to destroy developers' livelihood, but to show them what best-of-class programs looked like and encourage them to fill the gaps with programs of equal or greater quality. The fact that those who purchased Macs got iLife for free and got used to how they looked and worked merely reinforced the idea that, in order to thrive in the Mac ecosystem, programs had to match the users' expectations. Merely converting a Windows version for the Mac without any thought to the interface

wouldn't cut it any more. While some turned their back on the Mac because of this decision, many developers saw this as a challenge, looked at what was available, figured out what was missing in order to make a Mac user's experience complete and set about designing programs to match or exceed those very high expectations. So, what can you do with a Mac aside from making movies, music, photos and websites? Well, there's the standard fare of course, like writing letters, spreadsheets and making presentations. You could get Apple's iWork suite, Microsoft Office or a host of other competing products, but you have been able to do this since the very early days of computing so we're not going to be focusing on these programs at all here.

Instead, we're going to look at part of your iLife that Apple has decided to leave to others. For instance, where's the drawing tool? You can improve the look of your photos with iPhoto and even apply some basic effects to them; you can create shapes, even complex ones, with iWork and also remove an image's background (as long as it's fairly uniform); but where can you create an image from scratch with complex effects and titles, or paste your best friend onto a picture to make it look as if they had visited the Taj Mahal? Well, as Apple's commercials so aptly put it, there's an app for that.

There's even a method to catalogue all of your real-life belongings onto your computer in a way that's much better than a list on a spreadsheet – you can browse through them by sifting through virtual shelves, keep track of who borrowed a particular item and a host of other features. You can also use another program to convert your DVD collection into digital files so you can watch them on your Mac or take them with you on a trip. After all, one Mac, iPod touch or iPad will take up a lot less room than a stack of DVDs. Many love to keep a family tree to track their own unique history, and if that's you then you'll find a program catered to your exact needs. If you're a fan of Twitter, you'll find programs designed to display tweets of the people you follow that makes sending yours really easy and much better than relying on the

Twitter website. Most of us lead very busy lives, and keeping track of everything we need to do often feels like a full-time job in itself. Thankfully, programs exist to help you keep track of what you have to do, so as long as you don't misplace your Mac you won't forget anything. And if you've got culinary ambitions, there's even a program to help you prepare your meals.

Some of the programs described here will require you to trade some of your hard-earned money in order to use them, which brings us neatly to taking care of your finances. This is another side of your life that Apple has left to others to do, and many have stepped up to fill that need. One of them in particular makes it as easy as cataloguing your photos in iPhoto.

All of the above will provide a richer computing experience and will complement your iLife apps really well. But, just because Apple's engineers have created their own programs, it doesn't mean that they can't be

improved upon. For instance, you can create physical albums in iPhoto, but your options can be somewhat limited – especially compared with another program available on the market. When it comes to iTunes you can, of course, listen to your own music and access some internet radio stations, but anything else you have to pay for. Or you can use a different app to listen to as much music as you want, free of charge. Finally, if you use Front Row, you'll be more than interested to know that someone's giving that program a run for its money.

All these apps will be explained in detail over the next few pages. Most are free and the others, while being reasonably priced, also come with a free trial period so you can experiment with them before you buy. They're all designed to match Apple's iLife experience, while adding some great touches that make them unique. So enough teasing, turn the page to find out all about them…

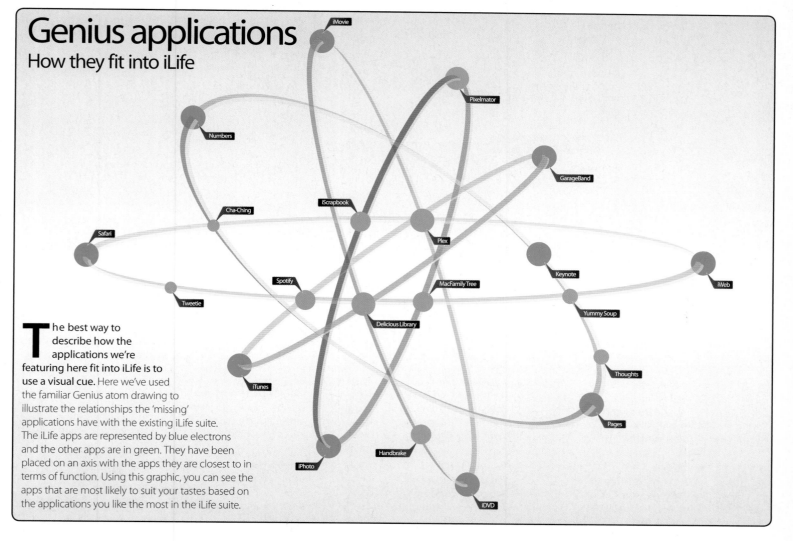

Genius applications
How they fit into iLife

The best way to describe how the applications we're featuring here fit into iLife is to use a visual cue. Here we've used the familiar Genius atom drawing to illustrate the relationships the 'missing' applications have with the existing iLife suite. The iLife apps are represented by blue electrons and the other apps are in green. They have been placed on an axis with the apps they are closest to in terms of function. Using this graphic, you can see the apps that are most likely to suit your tastes based on the applications you like the most in the iLife suite.

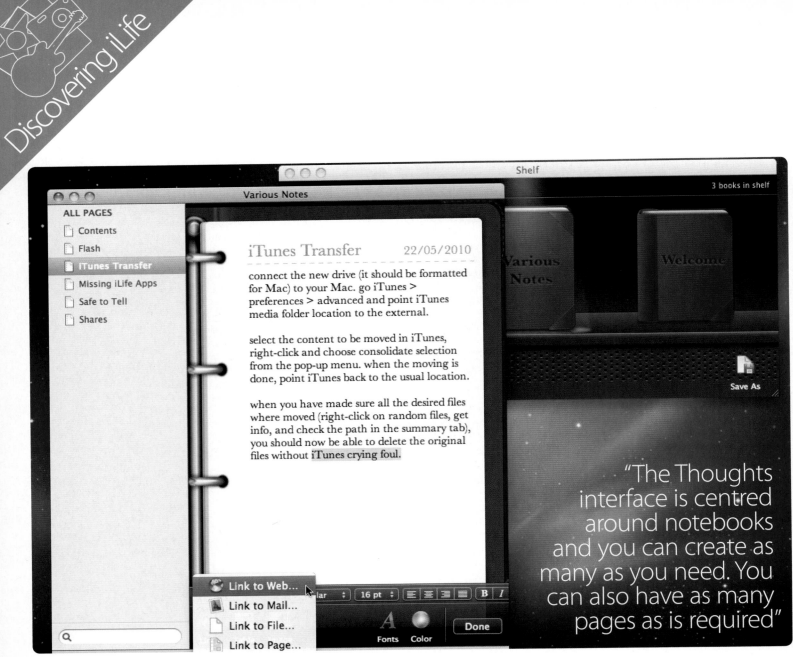

> "The Thoughts interface is centred around notebooks and you can create as many as you need. You can also have as many pages as is required"

Thoughts £19 All of your notes in one place

We all know that writing notes on a piece of paper will lead to it getting lost just when you need it most. When trying to organise yourself on your Mac, you could use Stickies to leave Post-it-like notes all over your screen TextEdit to jot some information down, but you have to save those – and what happens when you can't

remember where you've put them? Thankfully, Thoughts (www. thoughtsapp.com) was created to deal with this situation. The interface is centred around notebooks and you can create as many as you need. You can also have as many pages in a notebook as is required and include photos. Best of all, Thoughts autosaves itself so you never have to worry about losing data.

Key features

One of the great features of Thoughts is its ability to add tables to your pages. This makes it incredibly easy to create to-do lists and determine if a task has been done or not. You can control it thanks to the Inspector-like Table floating window. You can also change your text's font, size and colour, just like you can with any word processor.

Your pages can end up being incredibly detailed in Thoughts…

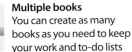

Link pages
You can link one page from another by dragging its title from the sidebar onto the page you're currently editing.

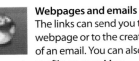

Webpages and emails
The links can send you to a webpage or to the creation of an email. You can also link a page to any file on your Mac.

Export options
You are given many export options to share your work with others; choose PDF, Word or the Open Document format.

Send books
Select a book and use the Save As icon to save it as a file that you can easily email to another Thoughts user.

Multiple books
You can create as many books as you need to keep your work and to-do lists as organised as you can make them.

Turn the page
If you have a modern laptop, swipe the trackpad with three fingers to move through your notebook's pages.

Delicious Library $40
Your stuff, digitised

I f you love organising your digital life, you may well fall in love with Delicious Library (**www.delicious-monster.com**). With it, you can catalogue all your physical belongings into virtual shelves and the process is incredibly easy: move your possession's barcode over your iSight camera for Delicious Library to scan it and bring up all the information you need about it instantly. It even lets you know how much it's currently worth should you wish to sell it. You can also keep track of which one of your friends is currently borrowing that DVD you can't find.

Tweetie Free
Follow and send tweets the easy way

U sing Twitter to follow people online and let others know what's on your mind is a lot of fun, but doing it from **www.twitter.com** leaves a lot to be desired, which is why many programs have been designed to access the Twitter feed and display it better. Tweetie is one of the best and most elegant ones out there (**www.atebits.com**). You can see new tweets as they appear and there's even a handy icon that changes colour to alert you that new tweets have arrived. You can do pretty much anything you'd expect – like searching your messages and following new people, for instance. There's a ton of features to explore and, best of all, you can choose between a free ad-supported version or pay for a license to never see those ads again.

Choose to follow or unfollow fellow twitterers

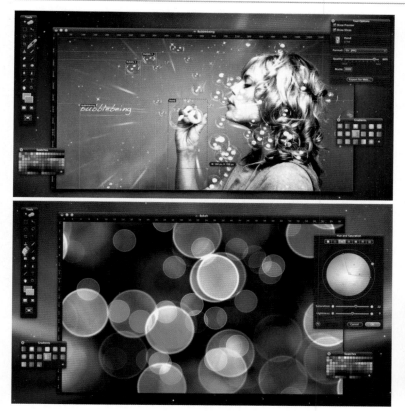

Pixelmator £42
Photoshop may no longer be necessary

I f iWork was a replacement to AppleWorks, then it's missing a drawing program. Thankfully, what Apple left out is an opportunity for a talented developer to step in. With Pixelmator (**www.pixelmator.com**), there's no need to lament at the horrendous cost of Photoshop. This program has been updated for free since 2007 and it keeps piling on the features. With version 1.6 just around the corner, it caters for most needs and you'll find Pixelmator a fast, powerful and beautiful image-editing tool that really is a pleasure to use.

 Brushes
You can import, switch, and manage both your brushes collections and your brushes for use in Pixelmator.

 Sharing
Use this button to attach your image to an email message or to send it to your iPhoto library.

 Trim & Crop
Crop an image by trimming the surrounding pixels or background of the colour you specify.

Save for web
Prepare images for the web by optimising the image, slice by slice, using the powerful Slice tool.

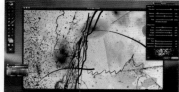

For its price, Pixelmator is incredibly powerful

Spotify Free

Listen to everything

● Tunes may be a fantastic program to catalogue all your music and the iTunes Store is an incredibly convenient place to buy as many tracks as you can afford, but there's something missing, and those 30-second previews just don't cut it. Wouldn't it be great if you could listen to as much music as you wanted to on your Mac, for free? Well you can with Spotify (**www.spotify.com**). This amazing application lets you search for and listen to a huge selection of music. It's a fantastic way to find new songs and listen to them as often as you like. Furthermore, if you really love a particular track you can purchase it

straight from Spotify as an mp3 file. If you use iTunes, you'll feel right at home here, but there any many features unique to this program that you may really like. You can, of course, create playlists of your favourite tracks, but a great addition is that any searches you make get saved to the sidebar – so, should you need to look for the same track again, you only have to select it in the list. You can even share your tracks and playlists on Facebook or Twitter, and you also have the option of listening to your tracks while not online – although this requires that you join the paid subscription service, currently at £9.99 per month.

ChaChing Free

Know where your money went

I f keeping track of your money is causing you headaches, you should definitely give Cha-Ching a try (**www.midnightapps.com**). The interface is very simple and the developer has made use of a lot of unique Mac technologies to help you organise your income and expenses in a very attractive way. It's currently in beta, but it's definitely worth taking a look.

MANAGE
- Scheduler
- To Do
- Payees

Track expenses
Schedule your expenses and get a 'Low Balance' warning.

Import data
You can easily import data from your bank's website.

Main window
For hands-on control, you have many options available to you, broken down into specific tabs

Choose your preset
HandBrake comes with many preset for you to use right away, or you could always create your own

The Picture settings
Use this window to determine the dimensions of your movie once encoded

HandBrake Free

Convert DVDs for your Mac or iPod

I f you've ever felt the need to transform your DVD movies and TV shows into files that you can use in iTunes, then you should definitely give HandBrake a try (**www.handbrake.fr**). The conversion process is easy with the bundled presets, and the quality of the encoding is absolutely amazing.

MacFamily Tree £36 Track your family history

Learning where we come from is a way of understanding who we are, and most of us have information about our family stored somewhere in a shoe box. Of course, we're all aware of our immediate connections, but what about our great-grandparents, or step-brothers and sisters and distant cousins? If you're at all keen on creating your own family tree, then MacFamily Tree is the ideal program for you (www.syniumsoftware.com).

You can keep track of everyone linked to yourself, your children, parents, cousins… you name it. And you can add as much information as you have to each of them. Not only can you enter obvious and necessary data like time and place of birth and death, but you can also include details like graduations, record

the time when they emigrated to another country, keep track of any religious events like Bar Mitzvahs or Christenings, and even add as many photos as you like to keep a visual record of the people in your life over time.

Once you've started filling in your information you can also begin enjoying it in many different ways, as FamilyTree can provide reports on the people or families you're tracking, collating all the data into easy-to-understand lists and graphs.

You also have access to a Virtual Tree that displays in three-dimensions all the people's relationships with each other. If you want more information about them, just double-click on their icon. Another great feature is the ability to locate your family on the globe thanks to geotagging.

If your family's emigrated a lot, then geotagging is a great way to see where all your family members currently are along with the travels they took across the globe. To enable this feature, make sure you click on the 'Look Up Coordinates' button, beneath the Place and Country fields. Once a particular place has been set, you won't have to locate

it again for other events or people. When done, click on the Virtual Globe item in the sidebar to be graced with a representation of our planet. All the red dots show specific events you listed in your family members' details and the green lines are the travels they took. There's also an Events sidebar to the right. Click on any in the list to centre the globe on that event.

Create your family
Start the process of building up your family tree…

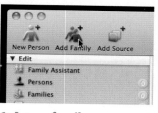

1: A new family
Click on the New Family icon, top-left of the interface.

2: Husband and wife
To add the parents, click on the '+' buttons, lower-left of each section.

3: Descendants
To add children, click on the '+' button and edit the name.

4: More info
Fill in more information like middle name, title and sex.

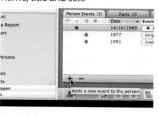

5: Add events
The Events section lets you add events to a person's life.

Mozzarella Salad

Previous | Next | Shrink Text | Enlarge Text | Save Size | Back

Halve the mozzarella and tomatoes and combine in bowl with scallions and herbs. Dress salad with vinegar, olive oil and season with salt and pepper, to taste.

- 16 pieces bocconcini, bite sized mozzarella balls
- 1 pint multi colored, yellow or red heirloom cherry tomatoes
- 4 scallions, whites and greens, thinly sliced on an angle
- 1/2 cup coarsely chopped parsley leaves
- 1/2 cup thinly sliced basil, 10 to 12 leaves
- 2 tbsp. red wine vinegar, eyeball it
- 1/4 cup extra-virgin olive oil, eyeball it
- Salt and pepper

"You can use your Apple Remote to switch to another recipe and even have your Mac read the instructions to you"

Yummy Soup
$20 What's for dinner tonight?

R ecipes and computers have found themselves strangely linked together; with the advent of the web, it only takes seconds to find a new recipe, relegating old recipe books to dusty bookshelves. But simply seeing the ingredients you need is one thing – organising them all, knowing what to purchase and how to cook an entire meal is something else entirely. Yummy Soup has been designed to take the hassle out of all this (www. hungryseacow.com).

By default, Yummy Soup comes bundled with hundreds of recipes, but it's incredibly easy to add new ones yourself. You could do it the old-fashioned way and manually type the information in, but if it's a generic recipe then you can find it online and drag the web address from your browser straight onto the library – Yummy Soup will do all the hard work for you. It'll give you an opportunity to double-check the information it extracted should mistakes have occurred, but more often than not everything will have been imported successfully and all you'll have to do is drag a photo that represents the dish onto your

Plex Free
Front Row on steroids

F ront Row has been Apple's answer to using a Mac as a media centre. It can access your songs, movies, TV shows and podcasts in iTunes along with your photos in either iPhoto or Aperture, but its interface – although pretty – is very simplistic and somewhat limited. Some developers thought they could improve on Apple's ideas, and they have.

Plex (www.plexapp.com) lets you access all of your media, be it stored on your local Mac or even somewhere else on the network, in an elegant interface that is also highly customisable. Plex links directly to your iTunes music library and iPhoto, but if you want to watch movies and TV shows with it, you need to tell it where they're located – which is a simple matter of navigating through your drives from the Video menu and selecting the folders you wish Plex to connect to.

You can also add additional functionality by using the program's own App Store. You can choose, for instance, to include the ability to watch YouTube videos or even install the BBC iPlayer. If you live in America, you can connect to Hulu, The Daily Show and a host of others. And best of all, the program is free. All the developers ask for is a donation if you like their work and use it often.

With Plex, you can turn your Mac into a powerful media centre

new page (which you can do straight from a webpage too). When it comes to shopping for dinner, select the recipes you'd like to use (you could, for instance, collate them into a new Category in the program's sidebar). Once done, select them all then Control-click on one of them and choose 'Add to Grocery List' from the contextual menu. They will now all be added to a new window with all the ingredients broken down by dish. Hit the Consolidate button to see how much of each ingredients you'll need for your whole meal. You can then print out that list or email it to your iPhone, should you prefer.

Yummy Soup can also prove invaluable during the preparation and cooking process – go to its Full Screen view to focus solely on a single recipe at a time. You can use your Apple Remote to switch to another recipe and even have your Mac read the instructions to you!

There are many more options available to you, like creating smart groups to help you sort recipes automatically and backing up your library to MobileMe so you never risk losing any of your data. Version 2's release is imminent and it'll include many new features, such as nutritional information, a weekly planner and more powerful share features – including multiple themes when printing recipes.

Yummy Soup makes cooking, discovering and trying new recipes a joy, and it sure beats fish and chips and pizzas from the local takeaway.

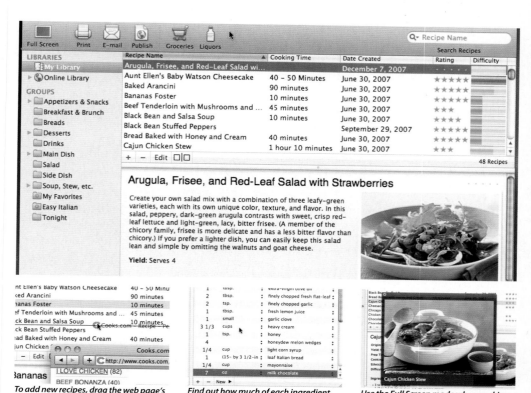

To add new recipes, drag the web page's URL onto your library

Find out how much of each ingredient you will need

Use the Full Screen mode when cooking to easily follow the instructions

---

Pages
You can see all your pages and albums straight from here

The Store
Dissatisfied with the themes and objects you currently own? Click on this button to buy more

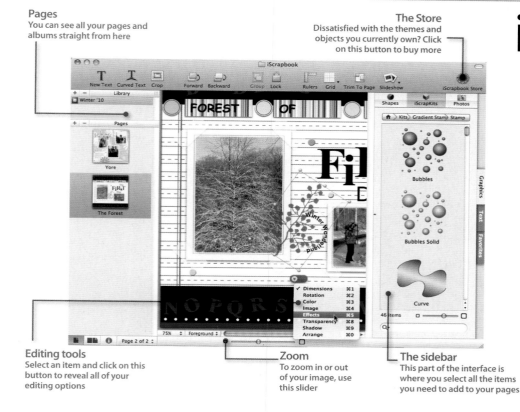

Editing tools
Select an item and click on this button to reveal all of your editing options

Zoom
To zoom in or out of your image, use this slider

The sidebar
This part of the interface is where you select all the items you need to add to your pages

iScrapbook $49.99

Make digital scrapbooks

● Photo may allow you to design photo albums, but its features don't hold a candle to iScrapbook (**www.chronosnet.com**). The program comes with over 1GB of templates that you have to download separately, which are there to help you be as creative as possible. Also, if the free selection isn't to your liking, you can also purchase more samples that you can add to any page. The design and layout tools are quite intricate, yet also very easy to understand and use. You can add shadows, transparency and curved text among other things. You can also apply masks to your photos and effects. Once you've finished, you can print your creations on your own printer or submit your design to your local online printer. If you're looking for versatility, you'll have it in spades with iScrapbook.

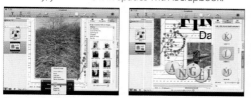

iScrapbook offers you many powerful editing and design tools

Going beyon

While Apple has done a huge amount to make every Mac a self contained studio for creativity, there's also a world of software to try…

Contents…

iTunes
Tutorial: Delete duplicates 196
Get rid of any music that has doubled up in your library

Tutorial: Artist alerts 198
Set iTunes up so that you get notified when your favourite artist has a new release

Tutorial: Genius App Store 200
Browse the App Store in iTunes using the Genius feature

Tutorial: Gift a Genius playlist 202
It's just like giving a mix-tape. Share the music you love using Genius

Pages:
Tutorial: Remove backgrounds 204
Use the instant alpha tool to remove backgrounds from objects in photos

Tutorial: Use text wrapping 206
Get your text to wrap its way around design elements on your page

Tutorial: Add effects to images 208
Change the way pictures look once they are on your page

Tutorial: Vintage invitation 210
Create a stunning vintage-themed invitation for your next event or gathering

Tutorial: Party itinerary 212
Get your friends and family excited about an event with a cool itinerary

Keynote
Tutorial: Add sound effects 214
Keynote presentations needn't be silent as this excellent guide proves

Tutorial: Title sequence 216
Create animated titles that can be exported and used in iMovie

Tutorial: Create a theme 218
Create your very own theme which you can call on again and again

Tutorial: Animate sheets 220
Add some excitement to your spreadsheets with Keynote animations

Tutorial: Pitch a party 222
Use a presentation to get people on board for a great party

Numbers
Tutorial: Income Chart 224
Keep tabs on your earnings with a cool chart

Tutorial: Scoreboard 226
Show the winning team with a very cool Numbers scoreboard

d iLife

Check out the contents of your free CD on page **258**

Tutorial: Measurements 228
Create a very smart height and weight chart in Numbers

Tutorial: Share spreadsheets 230
Keep everyone in the loop by using the new iWork.com service

Tutorial: Incentive chart 232
Keep the kids in check with this colourful incentive chart

Tutorial: Savings chart 234
Watch your wonga grow with a superb savings chart

We're Excited Highbrow 236
Constantly switching between browsers? Let Highbrow help you

Shape Collage 238
Make incredible picture collages in minutes with this outstanding app

MyThoughts 240
Create stunning, brain-friendly mind maps with this excellent tool

Image Tricks 242
If you want a really fast, efficient way to add effects to your images then look no further…

Spotify 244
Our favourite music streaming service just got even better with brand new software

DiscoBrick 246
Having a party? Then you really need this…

VirtualDJ 248
The latest version of this MP3 mixing software will attract DJs of all levels, from the beginner to the pro

doubleTwist 250
The first real alternative to iTunes, with support for every media player on the planet and an easy-to-use interface

Socialite 252
All of your social network accounts and RSS feeds in one beautifully designed, easy-to-use application

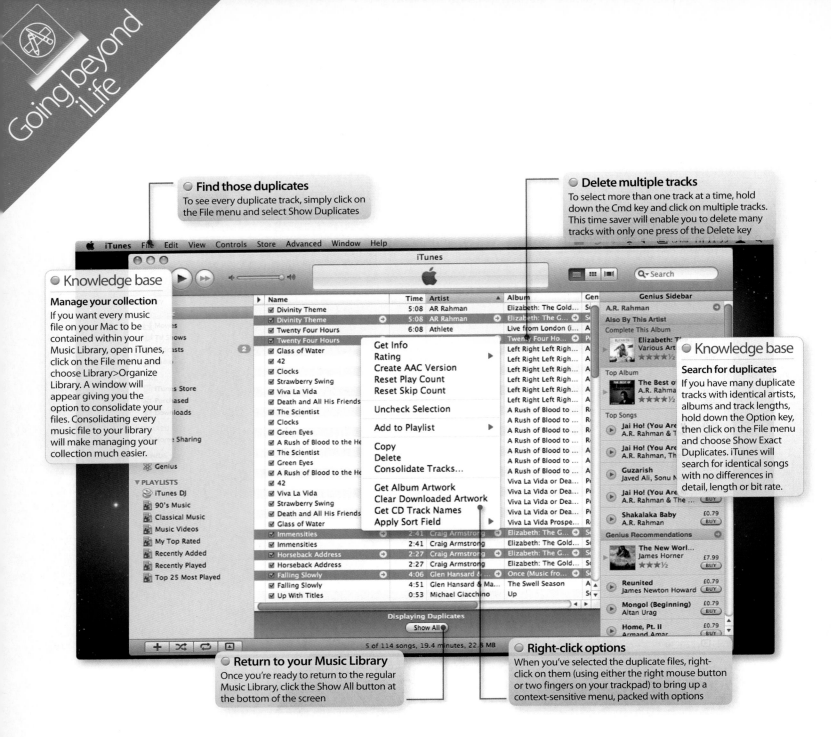

Find those duplicates
To see every duplicate track, simply click on the File menu and select Show Duplicates

Delete multiple tracks
To select more than one track at a time, hold down the Cmd key and click on multiple tracks. This time saver will enable you to delete many tracks with only one press of the Delete key

Knowledge base

Manage your collection
If you want every music file on your Mac to be contained within your Music Library, open iTunes, click on the File menu and choose Library>Organize Library. A window will appear giving you the option to consolidate your files. Consolidating every music file to your library will make managing your collection much easier.

Knowledge base

Search for duplicates
If you have many duplicate tracks with identical artists, albums and track lengths, hold down the Option key, then click on the File menu and choose Show Exact Duplicates. iTunes will search for identical songs with no differences in detail, length or bit rate.

Return to your Music Library
Once you're ready to return to the regular Music Library, click the Show All button at the bottom of the screen

Right-click options
When you've selected the duplicate files, right-click on them (using either the right mouse button or two fingers on your trackpad) to bring up a context-sensitive menu, packed with options

Tutorial: Delete duplicate tracks from iTunes

Is your iTunes Music Library beginning to clutter with duplicate songs? Follow our simple guide to learn how to manage and delete them

Task: Delete duplicate tracks within iTunes
Difficulty: Beginner
Time needed: 10 minutes

Maintaining an organised iTunes Library isn't an easy task. Imported CDs, downloaded albums and random music tracks all find their way into your music collection. Before long there are duplicate tracks scattered all over your library, resulting in errant albums with missing artwork and disjointed playback – it's hardly an elegant experience.

But fear not! Apple has included a number of features within iTunes to make tidying your music collection an easy affair, and in typical Apple fashion it's incredibly easy. Follow us through this nine-step tutorial to discover how to delete those duplicate tracks from your iTunes Music Library, consolidate your entire Music Library into one folder and more…

Step-by-step | iTunes Delete duplicate music tracks from iTunes

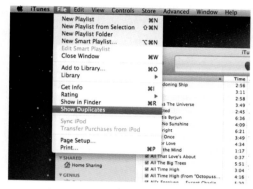

1: Find those duplicates
Open iTunes, go to your Music Library and select Show Duplicates from the File menu. iTunes will think for a moment, then display every duplicate file.

2: Time to organise
You can now begin to organise your music files. It's easier to do this by sorting the files by name. Click on the Name column at the top of the search results.

3: Look for clones
Look for songs that have identical names, artists and albums. This is important – you don't want to accidentally delete a live version or remix of a song!

4: Track lengths
In the unlikely event that duplicate songs have the same artist and album, you can also look out for track length differences.

5: How's the sound?
To be totally sure that you're deleting the right track, listen to both duplicates; one may have a higher bit rate, therefore a better sound quality.

6: Move to the Trash
To delete a track, simply highlight it once by clicking on it, then press the Delete key. iTunes will ask if you would like to move the file to the Trash.

7: Save space
Select Move To Trash to save hard disk space, or Keep File to keep the music track in your Music Library for later reference.

8: Delete multiple files
Hold down the Apple key and click on multiple tracks to delete more than one at a time. This can be quite a time saver if you have dozens of duplicate songs.

9: Done and dusted
Finally, make sure to empty your Trash to delete those errant duplicate files for good. You'll now have a tidier iTunes Music Library and more disk space.

Tutorial: Add artists to your Alerts in iTunes

iTunes boasts thousands of artist and albums. Learn how to use Alerts to be notified when an artist has a new release on the market…

Task: Discover how to use Alerts in iTunes

Difficulty: Beginner

Time needed: 10 minutes

iTunes is synonymous with music and downloads and, like every hugely successful service, it simply gets bigger and better.

Nonetheless, this brings with it new issues that users need to contend with. The sheer scale of iTunes means that finding an artist and keeping up-to-date with new releases can be a tiresome task. Checking back at random is not a particularly productive or practical option. The answer to new release woes lies in the hands of your 'My Alerts' list. This nifty little feature allows you to pick an up-and-coming album or song and hit the Alert Me link. Details are added to My Alerts, found via the iTunes Store home page, and an email is sent to your inbox when it is released. The latest alerts stay stored in My Alerts, allowing you to link to more details, listen to a tune, and purchase directly after its release. Head over to Manage My Alerts to have the final say on who's in and who's out.

Angels With Dirty Faces (UK edition)

Album Review

One of the best pop albums of 2002 wasn't released in the U.S. If that's not dropping the ball, then what is? An assured and durable follow-up which still packed a number of singles that gave the group a great deal of success overseas, Angels With Dirty Faces is a thoroughly convin they've been weaned on — from Madonna to TLC to Aaliyah — with a strong foothold in contemporary trends. A bootleg mash-up of Adina H

	Name	Tim
1.	Freak Like Me	3:
2.	Blue	3:
3.	Round Round	3:
4.	Stronger	3:
5.	Supernatural	3:
6.	Angels With Dirty Faces	3:
7.	Virgin Sexy	3:
8.	Shape	4:
9.	Just Don't Need This	3:
10.	No Man No Cry	3:
11.	Switch	3:
12.	More Than a Million Miles	3:
13.	Breathe Easy (Acoustic Jam)	3:
14.	Round Round (Alternative Mix)	6:

You are about to add this individual to your "My Alerts" list.

Click OK to add this individual to your list of custom alerts. Click Cancel if you do not want this individual added.

[Manage My Alerts]   [Cancel]   [OK]

Step-by-step | iTunes Add artists to your My Alerts list

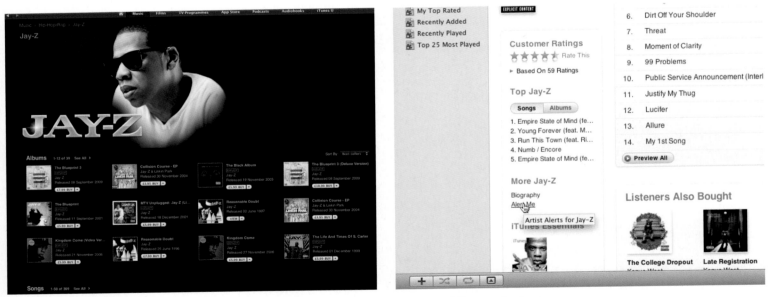

1: Artist alert
Open iTunes and sign in with your Apple ID and password. Now select a category from the Music tab or search for your favourite artist. With an artist selected, head to Artist Quick Links and click Alert Me.

2: Album alert
Now add your password again and press OK to add the selected artist to My Alerts. Alternatively, select a specific album and click the Alert Me link under the More title. Repeat this process to add more alerts.

A quick guide to My Alerts

How to arrange, manage, listen, rate, buy and download

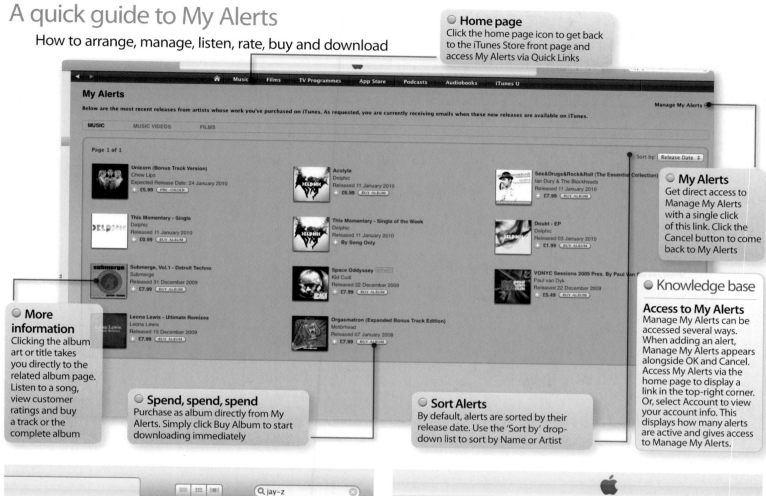

○ Home page
Click the home page icon to get back to the iTunes Store front page and access My Alerts via Quick Links

My Alerts

Below are the most recent releases from artists whose work you've purchased on iTunes. As requested, you are currently receiving emails when these new releases are available on iTunes.

MUSIC   MUSIC VIDEOS   FILMS

Manage My Alerts

○ My Alerts
Get direct access to Manage My Alerts with a single click of this link. Click the Cancel button to come back to My Alerts

Page 1 of 1

Sort by: Release Date ⬍

Unicorn (Bonus Track Version)
Chew Lips
Expected Release Date: 24 January 2010
£5.99 PRE-ORDER

Acolyte
Delphic
Released 11 January 2010
£6.99 BUY ALBUM

Sex&Drugs&Rock&Roll (The Essential Collection)
Ian Dury & The Blockheads
Released 11 January 2010
£7.99 BUY ALBUM

This Momentary - Single
Delphic
Released 11 January 2010
£0.99 BUY ALBUM

This Momentary - Single of the Week
Delphic
Released 11 January 2010
By Song Only

Doubt - EP
Delphic
Released 03 January 2010
£1.99 BUY ALBUM

Submerge, Vol.1 - Detroit Techno
Submerge
Released 31 December 2009
£7.99 BUY ALBUM

Space Oddyssey
Kid Cudi
Released 22 December 2009
£7.99 BUY ALBUM

VONYC Sessions 2009 Pres. By Paul Van
Paul van Dyk
Released 22 December 2009
£5.49 BUY ALBUM

○ Knowledge base

Access to My Alerts
Manage My Alerts can be accessed several ways. When adding an alert, Manage My Alerts appears alongside OK and Cancel. Access My Alerts via the home page to display a link in the top-right corner. Or, select Account to view your account info. This displays how many alerts are active and gives access to Manage My Alerts.

○ More information
Clicking the album art or title takes you directly to the related album page. Listen to a song, view customer ratings and buy a track or the complete album

Leona Lewis - Ultimate Remixes
Leona Lewis
Released 15 December 2009
£7.99 BUY ALBUM

Orgasmatron (Expanded Bonus Track Edition)
Motörhead
Released 07 January 2008
£7.99 BUY ALBUM

○ Spend, spend, spend
Purchase as album directly from My Alerts. Simply click Buy Album to start downloading immediately

○ Sort Alerts
By default, alerts are sorted by their release date. Use the 'Sort by' drop-down list to sort by Name or Artist

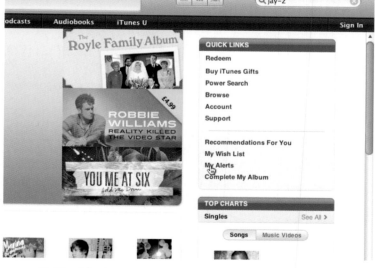

3: My Alerts
Head to the iTunes Store home page and, under Quick Links, click My Alerts. This will display the artists and albums you've added. Click the album art to view track listings or Buy Album to buy it immediately.

Manage My Alerts

You will receive an email alert whenever music or videos by the individuals above are add... unsubscribe to an individual, click Manage My Alerts from the main Account page. To ad... the individuals's page in the iTunes Store and click the Alert Me link.

☑ Send me an email alert for all individuals in my Purchase History

Uncheck to remove an individual from your customized list below.

☑ Chew Lips	☑ Delphic	☑ Dizzee Rascal
☑ Ian Dury & The Blockheads	☑ Jay-Z	☑ Kid Cudi
☑ Motörhead	☑ Neil Young	☑ Paul van Dyk
☑ Placebo	☑ Steve Earle	☑ Submerge

Clear All

4: Manage My Alerts
Click Manage My Alerts to view all the artists that have been added to the My Alerts list. To remove an artist from My Alerts, simply click the corresponding check box and press Save Changes.

Tutorial: Use Genius to browse the App Store

Find the perfect movie, TV show or iPhone app with Genius…

It was promised to be available with iTunes Version 8.1, but was dropped at the last moment. Finally, as of March 2009, Apple switched on the Genius function for movies and TV shows. It's not as far reaching as the Genius function is for music, as it will only acknowledge the videos that you have purchased through the iTunes Store – so unless you have a very healthy selection of video material, the Genius results could be rather sketchy or limited.

Recently, however, Genius has become even more intelligent. It has sneaked its way into the App Store, and is now able to recognise your iPhone and iPod touch apps. With so many apps to choose from, this will be a welcome addition to many. Follow us over the next two pages as we investigate how to take advantage of these new Genius features.

Task: Use Genius to find new music, TV shows, movies and apps

Difficulty: Beginner

Time needed: 5 minutes

Step-by-step | iTunes Take advantage of Apple's Genius technology

1: Turn On Genius
Open iTunes, log into your account, and click the Genius button in the left-hand bar. Click the Turn On Genius button in the bottom corner of the screen.

2: Time to agree
Agree to the Genius Terms & Conditions, and Genius will gather the data within your iTunes library before delivering it to Apple. Genius is now set up.

3: The Genius appears
Click on the Music button in the left-hand tab to jump to your library. The Genius tab will have appeared over to the right.

4: Recommended results
You'll see the top recommended albums and songs within the sidebar. Each result includes a preview button and an option to buy the song.

5: Top movies
By visiting your Movies library you'll discover similar Genius results, compiled from the films and TV shows you have purchased through iTunes.

6: Even more results
By clicking the small arrow to the top of each Genius section, you can quickly jump to the Genius Just For You page.

Take advantage of Genius

Find new music, films and apps with Genius

Genius Just For You
TV programmes have recently been added to the Genius database. It works the same as movies, enabling you to see the six programmes that best match your taste in broadcasting

More results
To see more Genius results, simply click the More button in the upper-left corner of the screen. The page will update with entirely new results for you to browse – the list is endless

Genius
Genius Just For You defaults to showing the results most similar to your recent purchases. To choose a particular genre, such as Soundtrack or Rock, simply select it from the drop-down menu

Knowledge base

How does Genius work?
Apple has millions of iTunes users – who in turn have purchased billions of songs, movies, TV shows and apps. Apple has compiled and compared every piece of purchased entertainment into one vast, linked database. Genius simply compares your iTunes library with everyone else's, and suggests similar material that you may like.

Thumbs up
By giving a Genius suggestion the thumbs up, next time you use Genius you'll see more results of this kind. Give it the thumbs down and it won't appear again

7: Check out the results
You'll see results for music, films and TV programmes, each browsable by genre, with a More button to see more results.

8: App Store Genius
If you want to see Genius results for your iPhone apps, simply open the App Store on your iPhone or iPod touch and go to the Featured section.

9: App results
Click on the Genius button at the top of the screen to see Genius results compiled from the apps you've already downloaded.

Tutorial: Gift a Genius playlist in iTunes

Stuck on what to buy that special someone? Why not send them a Genius playlist from iTunes? We show you how it's done!

Task: Use iTunes' Gift service to send a friend a Genius playlist

Difficulty: Beginner

Time needed: 10 minutes

It's human nature for us all to be slightly egotistical, and naturally – especially when it comes to music – we can't help but think that we have the best taste. With a little help from iTunes we can help to select a sample of our tasty tracks and share them with our friends. How? With Genius!

Genius is iTunes' helpful automated playlist facility. Genius can cleverly create playlists and mixes from the songs held in your iTunes Library that it 'thinks' will go well together. An extension of this is that the app asset also introduces you to new music, films and TV shows that you don't already own but it 'thinks' you will enjoy based on what you currently have in your Library.

In this tutorial we will be taking a look at how you activate Genius, how you can use it to create a playlist and how you can then gift the playlist and send it to a friend – all in four easy steps!

Step-by-step | iTunes Send a Genius playlist to a friend

1: Get started
Activate iTunes. When it's up and ready for action, travel over to the Source list and select Genius. Read through the information provided and, if you'd like to continue, select the Turn On Genius button.

2: Select a track
Now, the big question is what track to choose! Select a track that you want iTunes to match similar or compatible songs to. With the track isolated, select the Genius icon. iTunes will now search for matching titles.

Send a friend a Genius playlist

Learn how to make use of iTunes' Genius facility

Quantity
Use this drop-down menu to alter the number of songs on your Genius playlist. You can choose between 25, 50, 75 and 100 tunes

Save Playlist
Hit this button to save the selection of tracks. After you have actioned that request you will be able to give the playlist to others or use it to create an iMix

Turn off
Travel to the Menu bar and opt for Store. You will find options to update and turn off Genius

Knowledge base

Set up Genius
The app spends several minutes gathering data from your library and sends this to Apple, which can take several minutes. The third and final stage, 'delivering your Genius results', is the quickest in the three-step process and a green tick appears as each stage is completed.

Icon
This is the icon users should press to activate Genius. Hit this after you have selected the song you want to form as your base track

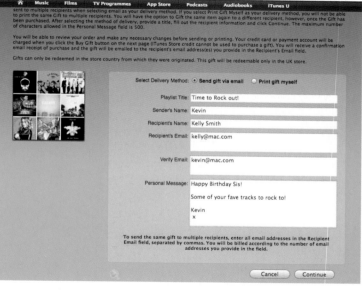

3: Playlist perfect
A Genius playlist will now be presented. Hit the Save Playlist button and then click the arrow button when the playlist is cited on the Source panel under Genius. Now hit Give Playlist.

4: Gift the list
You can send the playlist to more than one person, simply by entering all the addresses in the Recipient's Email field. Be warned – you will be billed according to this number. Hit Continue to proceed and pay.

Remove backgrounds with Instant Alpha

Take the hassle out of removing image backgrounds by using Pages' incredible Instant Alpha tool

Task: Use Instant Alpha to remove image backgrounds

Difficulty: Beginner

Time needed: 10 minutes

When you're designing a document in Pages you don't want to be tied to the dimensions of your images – especially if they have elements in the background that you don't need. The traditional method for removing the background of an image and 'cutting out' the subject involves some Photoshop magic or very fine pen work to extract unwanted elements from your shot, but fortunately Pages has an alternative option. The Instant Alpha tool is possibly the easiest way to cut out a background quickly and effectively and requires very little effort – simply drag over the area you wish to remove. This tutorial will show you how to use the Instant Alpha tool to effectively strip the background from your photo and leave you with the focus of the image intact. Once you've tried it you're guaranteed to be using it all the time!

Step-by-step | Pages Cut out a face from a photo

1: Place your picture
Here we have dropped an image onto our background texture, which contains a solid background of sky and sea. We want to remove this background and include only the head and shoulders in our project.

2: Alpha in an instant
Select your image and then head up to the Format menu where you can select Instant Alpha. The cursor will now change to a crosshair and a translucent box will appear explaining the tool.

Quickly remove a background in Pages

Cut out a face from the background of an image with Instant Alpha

● In an instant

You can start using Instant Alpha by selecting your image and selecting Instant Alpha from the Format menu. You can also remove Instant Alpha effects

● More info

For a quick refresher on how Instant Alpha works, see this box that appears when the tool is active

● Background

When you are using Instant Alpha, the background being removed is shown opaque with a slight colour tone

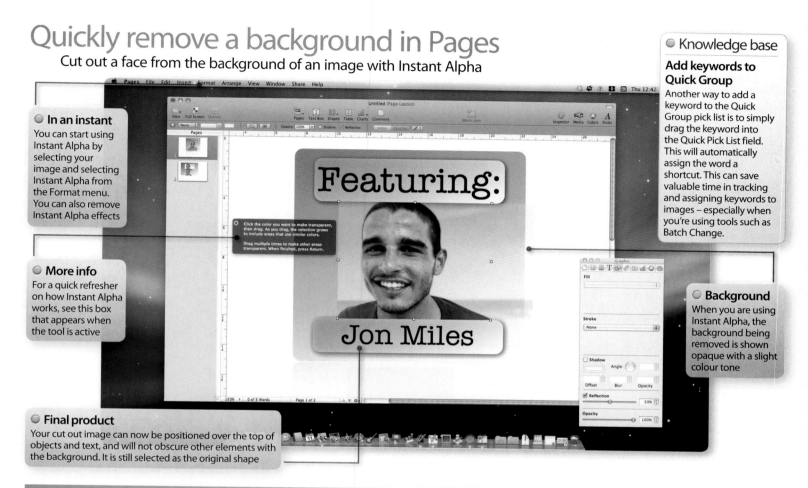

● Final product

Your cut out image can now be positioned over the top of objects and text, and will not obscure other elements with the background. It is still selected as the original shape

3: Cut out the background

Drag the cursor across the background of your image slowly. You will notice a coloured space appearing – this will be the elements removed. Carefully drag over the areas you wish to remove, avoiding your subject.

4: Check and position

Click away from your image and the background you have selected will miraculously disappear. You are now free to position your image as you wish using only the subject you have cut out.

Tutorial: Wrap text around images in Pages

When an image is added to Pages, text wraps around it. But there are a lot of available options to customise this…

Inserting images into a text document is an incredibly easy thing to do with Pages and the Media Browser. The options for wrapping your words around images all live in the Inspector window, and you can use them to customise how an image affects your document. You also have the ability of adding a shape to your document or even masking a photo to see what happens when text wraps around a non-rectangular object.

We'll be experimenting will all of these features over the next two pages, so open an existing document or create a new one from scratch and let's get started.

Task: Customise how text wraps around an image

Difficulty: Beginner

Time needed: 20 minutes

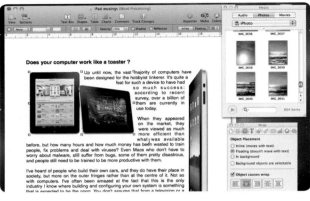

Step-by-step | Pages Wrap text around a photo or shape

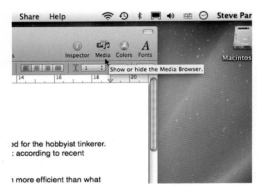

1: Revealing the Media Browser
Open the Media Browser by clicking on its icon in the Toolbar (on the right-hand side) or by going to View>Show Media Browser.

2: Adding a photo
Select a photo from your iPhoto or Aperture library and drag it on your text. Notice that the position of your words are changed to make room for it.

3: Getting the Inspector
Reveal the Inspector by either clicking on its button in the toolbar (to the left of the Media Browser) or by going to View>Show Inspector.

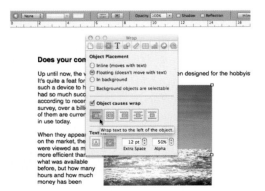

4: Wrap options
Select the Wrap tab (third from the left). The 'Object causes wrap' box is already ticked, but there are four other ways your text could wrap.

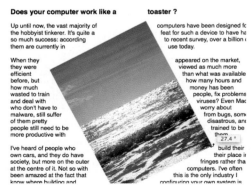

5: Rotating a photo
In order to see the effect of Text Fit, you need to alter your image. With it selected, mouse over one of its corner handles. Cmd-click and drag to rotate it.

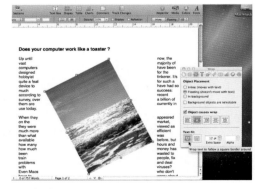

6: Fitting text
Now, with the image at an angle, click between both Text Fit options in the Inspector. Use whichever one you prefer.

Wrap text around a shape in Pages
Customise how text wraps around photos and shapes

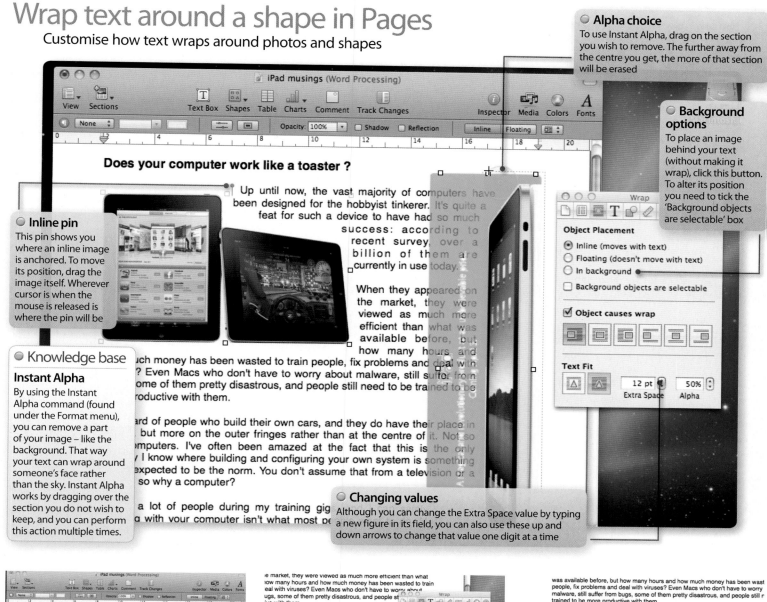

Alpha choice
To use Instant Alpha, drag on the section you wish to remove. The further away from the centre you get, the more of that section will be erased

Background options
To place an image behind your text (without making it wrap), click this button. To alter its position you need to tick the 'Background objects are selectable' box

Inline pin
This pin shows you where an inline image is anchored. To move its position, drag the image itself. Wherever cursor is when the mouse is released is where the pin will be

Knowledge base

Instant Alpha
By using the Instant Alpha command (found under the Format menu), you can remove a part of your image – like the background. That way your text can wrap around someone's face rather than the sky. Instant Alpha works by dragging over the section you do not wish to keep, and you can perform this action multiple times.

Changing values
Although you can change the Extra Space value by typing a new figure in its field, you can also use these up and down arrows to change that value one digit at a time

---

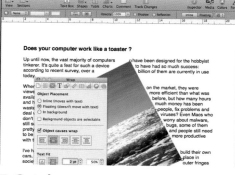

7: Get closer
The Extra Space field lets you decide how close or far your text is from the image. You can modify it by typing a new value in the field.

8: From floating to inline
By default, you can move the image wherever you like on your page. The Object Placement section can change that. Click on Inline.

9: The pin
Notice a blue pin somewhere on your text (when the image is selected)? This is where it's anchored. Write above it and the image will move accordingly.

Tutorial: Add effects to images in Pages

When inserting a photo or shape to your document, an easy way to make it stand out is by adding a shadow or reflection

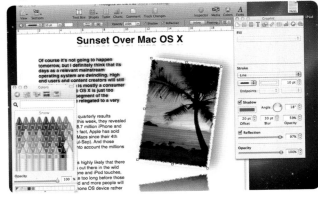

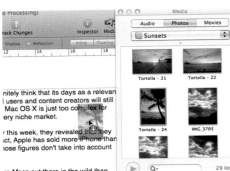

Adding photos to a document is one thing, but making them look good is an entirely different matter. Thankfully, Pages – just like any other program of the iWork suite – comes with a few simple tools that can help make your document look much better than if you'd just dropped a photo onto it and left it at that.

In this tutorial, we'll be showing you how you can add a shadow and a reflection to your image with a few simple clicks. This will also work on any shapes, as well as a few other objects that you can add to your file.

Task: Add simple effects to images in Pages

Difficulty: Beginner

Time needed: 20 minutes

Step-by-step | Pages | Apply a shadow and reflection effect to a photo or shape

1: Object Selection
Start by selecting a shape using the toolbar's Shapes button or a photo of your choice with the help of the Media Browser.

2: Fetch the Inspector
Resize your object by dragging one of its corner handles and place it in the proper location on your document. Go to View>Show Inspector.

3: Revealing shadow
With your image or shape selected, go to the Inspector's Graphic tab. Click on the Shadow tick box to reveal its default settings.

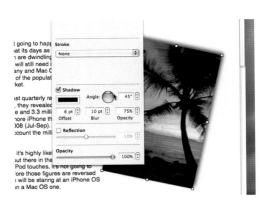

4: Shadow's angle
You can change the shadow's angle in one of two ways; either drag the circular Angle button or type in a precise value in the field to its right.

5: Precise change
If you need to set a more precise angle, hold down the Shift key as you drag the Angle button to alter the value by increments of 45 degrees.

6: Other parameters
There are three other values you can change; Offset determines how far the shadow is from the object, while Blur and Opacity are self-explanatory.

Improve your photos in Pages

Add simple effects to spice up your images

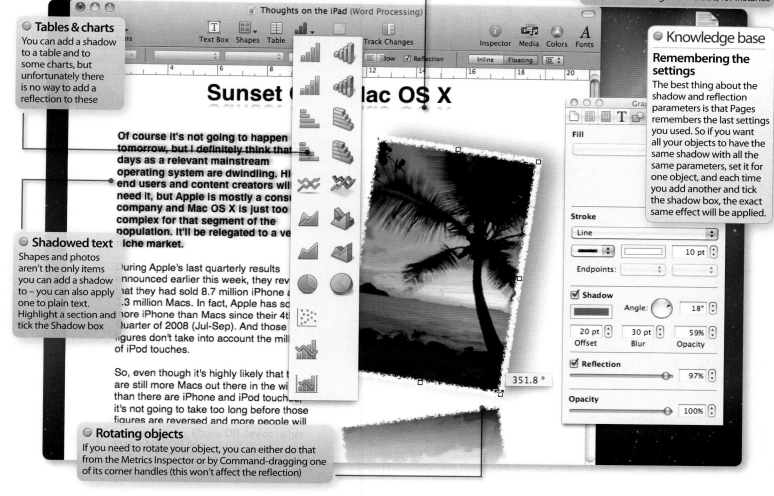

Reflecting text box
You can't add a reflection to text, but you can apply a reflection to a text box instead which could look good in a title, for instance

Tables & charts
You can add a shadow to a table and to some charts, but unfortunately there is no way to add a reflection to these

Knowledge base

Remembering the settings
The best thing about the shadow and reflection parameters is that Pages remembers the last settings you used. So if you want all your objects to have the same shadow with all the same parameters, set it for one object, and each time you add another and tick the shadow box, the exact same effect will be applied.

Shadowed text
Shapes and photos aren't the only items you can add a shadow to – you can also apply one to plain text. Highlight a section and tick the Shadow box

Rotating objects
If you need to rotate your object, you can either do that from the Metrics Inspector or by Command-dragging one of its corner handles (this won't affect the reflection)

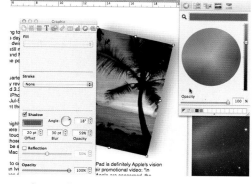

7: The colour well
By default the shadow is black, but you can change that if you want. Click on the black rectangle to reveal the Color Palette and choose another colour.

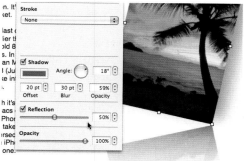

8: Add a reflection
The Reflection control is directly beneath the Shadow parameters. Tick its box to reveal one for your object. You can't put the reflection on an angle, though.

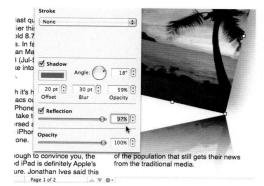

9: Reflection strength
Use the slider to alter the amount your object gets reflected – drag it to the left or right to decrease or increase it respectively.

Design a vintage party invitation

Why create a design from scratch when you can beg, borrow and steal elements from the templates that come bundled with Pages? Here's how to step back in time…

Task: Mix and match Pages template elements to create a vintage invite
Difficulty: Intermediate
Time needed: 2 hours

Creating a design in a particular style is all about the details. You have to pick the right fonts, the right colours and the right elements. Starting with a blank canvas can be extremely daunting, so why not make use of the excellent templates that Apple gives away with Pages? You could just take inspiration, such as which fonts work well, but you can take even more by borrowing elements from your favourite templates and rolling them into a bespoke layout. Here are all the tips, tricks and techniques you'll need to create a vintage look.

Collector Newsletter
A veritable mine of elements to theme up any vintage style design, including papers, stamps, cards, labels and flourishes.

Musical Poster
The antiquated paper makes a perfect background for a vintage design, and there's some interesting flourishes to borrow from it.

Mix and match template elements
Borrow bits and pieces from templates to build your own

1: Pick a page
Choose New from Template Chooser and open up a new document to pick decorative elements from.

2: Copy cat
Click on the element and choose Copy from the Edit menu. Backgrounds need unlocking first.

3: Paste it in
Click on your original document to bring it to the front, then choose Paste from the Edit menu.

Picking the fonts
Find a couple of fonts that suit your design and stick to them – too many styles on one page will look messy.

Baskerville Classic but not as heavy as Caslon
Zapfino Calligraphic and elegant when used sparingly

Choosing colours

Keep it simple, keep it safe
Picking a colour palette can be daunting, and getting it wrong can ruin an otherwise fantastic design. Play it safe and pick one or two colours from the elements on the page. Use lighter and darker shades to make important elements stand out.

40th Arthur's worlde

Sunday June 25th
At precisely a half past the eleventh hour

Shhhh…
Please be discrete, this is a surprise party. There's no other way he'd let us do it!

No need to bring anything, but olde-wolde or vintage attire would be appreciated.

At Orchard Farm, Bransgore

For detailed directions and to RSVP, contact Sarah on
01234 567890

It's got to make sense!
Spend some time thinking about how people will read your design, make it easy for them to find and follow important information. Use size, colour and boldness to highlight key parts

Experiment with structure
Rather than spreading everything out over the page, use the commands in the Arrange menu to have some fun with how different elements overlap

1: Pick a starting point
Open up the small version of the Musical Poster and delete everything except the top flourish and the background texture.

2: Resize the poster paper
The poster is too large for an invite, so choose Page Setup from the File menu. Change the Paper Size to A5 and you'll be able to fit two on a sheet of A4.

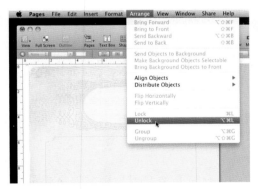

3: Unlocking paper secrets
Click on the paper background texture, which is locked. To resize it you'll first need to choose Unlock from the Arrange menu.

4: Scale it down to fit
Click on one of the eight square handles that appear around the edge of the paper and drag it towards the centre to resize the background to fit.

5: Photo framing
Pages comes with a great selection of Picture Framing strokes that will help tie any photographs or images into your theme.

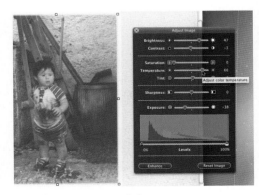

6: Adjust Image tricks
To sepia tint a photo, choose Show Adjust Image from the View menu. Turn down the Saturation then experiment with Temperature and Tint sliders.

Design a party weekend itinerary in Pages

Get your friends excited about an upcoming weekend party by designing a fun itinerary

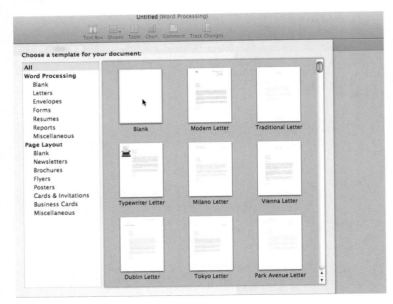

Girls Weekend in

Itinerary: Friday 20th - Sunda

Friday

16.00: **Check into Hotel**

18.00: **Cocktails at the bar**

Task: Use Pages to design a party itinerary

Difficulty: Beginner

Time needed: 45 minutes

The best way to organise your friends for an upcoming weekend away is to design them a comprehensive itinerary. Pages is the ideal application to use as it has so many easy-to-use design features that means you can transform the simplest text document into a slick, professional-looking masterpiece – so you don't even need to have any design skills.

An itinerary doesn't have to be a boring page of text, though – by adding a few extra touches, such as simple graphics and images, not only can you relay the information you want to in a clear and concise manner (the most important factor), but you can also create a certain mood or feeling to get your audience excited. If you find the blank template too daunting, try selecting a pre-designed template and adapt it to your needs by changing the text, colours or images. You can spend as long as you like having fun with your design and, when you're done, all you need to do is export it and email it to friends.

Girls Weekend in Brighton Summer 2010

Itinerary: **Friday** 20th - **Sunday** 22nd August 2010

Friday

16.00: **Check into Hotel**

18.00: **Cocktails at the bar**

20.00: **Dinner at Browns**

22.00: **Dancing**

Saturday

12.00: **Brunch**

14.00: **Beach time**

18.00: **Pampering**

20.00: **Party**

Sunday

Step-by-step | Pages | Organise your friends by creating a party itinerary

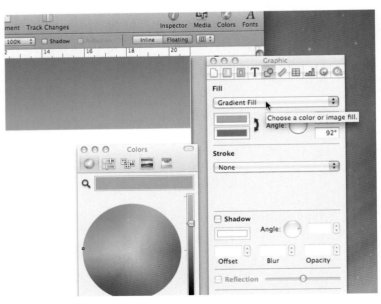

1: Choose a template
Launch Pages and choose a blank template. If you find a blank template too intimidating, select a pre-designed template and adapt it to your needs. Choose something similar to an itinerary template.

2: Add some colour
Add a bold banner to the top of your itinerary. Use the Shapes drop-down menu at the top of the interface, and then use the Graphics Inspector and the Colors window to add a Gradient Fill.

Create an itinerary for a party weekend

Get your friends in the mood (and organised) with a slick party itinerary

Different weights
Choose a font that has different weights, such as bold, regular and light. You can use different weights to make the text easier to read or to highlight certain parts. For your headline, you can add shadows to make it jump out

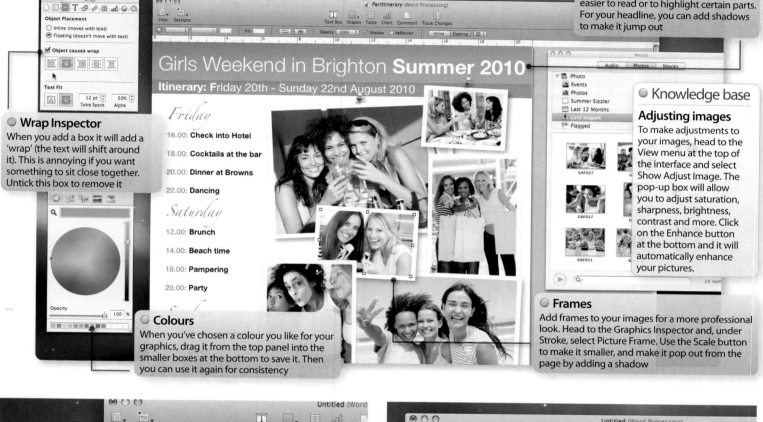

Wrap Inspector
When you add a box it will add a 'wrap' (the text will shift around it). This is annoying if you want something to sit close together. Untick this box to remove it

Knowledge base

Adjusting images
To make adjustments to your images, head to the View menu at the top of the interface and select Show Adjust Image. The pop-up box will allow you to adjust saturation, sharpness, brightness, contrast and more. Click on the Enhance button at the bottom and it will automatically enhance your pictures.

Colours
When you've chosen a colour you like for your graphics, drag it from the top panel into the smaller boxes at the bottom to save it. Then you can use it again for consistency

Frames
Add frames to your images for a more professional look. Head to the Graphics Inspector and, under Stroke, select Picture Frame. Use the Scale button to make it smaller, and make it pop out from the page by adding a shadow

3: Hierarchy
Add your main headline and make it as big as possible. You want to draw the eye from the top to the bottom. Make your sub-head smaller and use different weights, such as light and bold, to highlight text.

4: Play
Key in your information, but use a different colour for the time and day so that it's clear and easy to read. Add some pictures to create a party mood. When you're done, save and export to send to all your friends.

Visual queues
You can see at a glance if build animations are present, as three small dots appear top-right of this thumbnail. For transitions, it's a blue triangle

Build Order
You don't have to add your animation in the order you want to display them; you can reorder them via the Build Order panel by dragging them, or by using the Order pop-up menu

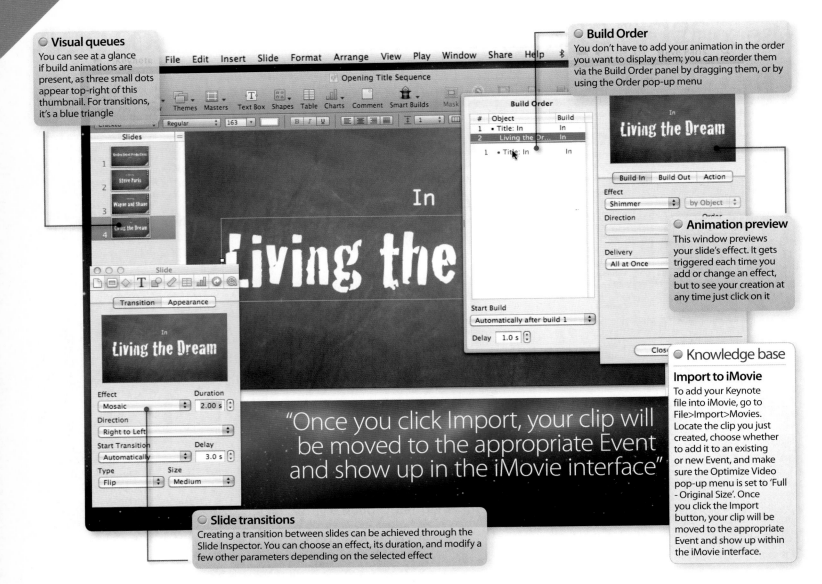

Animation preview
This window previews your slide's effect. It gets triggered each time you add or change an effect, but to see your creation at any time just click on it

Knowledge base

Import to iMovie
To add your Keynote file into iMovie, go to File>Import>Movies. Locate the clip you just created, choose whether to add it to an existing or new Event, and make sure the Optimize Video pop-up menu is set to 'Full - Original Size'. Once you click the Import button, your clip will be moved to the appropriate Event and show up within the iMovie interface.

Slide transitions
Creating a transition between slides can be achieved through the Slide Inspector. You can choose an effect, its duration, and modify a few other parameters depending on the selected effect

"Once you click Import, your clip will be moved to the appropriate Event and show up in the iMovie interface"

Create an iMovie title sequence in Keynote

Keynote has many great transition and effects. If only you could use them in your iMovie projects… we'll show you how you can

Task: Create a title sequence and import it into iMovie

Difficulty: Intermediate

Time needed: 25 minutes

iMovie is undoubtedly a powerful and easy-to-use video editing program, but its choices are very limited – like the number of special effects and transitions you can use with your titles, for instance. By contrast, Keynote's effects are varied and highly customisable. During your Keynote presentations you can add all sorts of effects to text and images as well as each slide. Wouldn't it be fantastic if you could use these impressive effects in iMovie? Well you might be surprised to learn that you actually can, and we'll show you how to do just that in this tutorial by creating a few slides, adding transitions and actions to them. Then comes the slightly more tricky part – figuring out which is the best export method to use to make your work compatible with iMovie. Once done, the world (of movie titles) is your oyster.

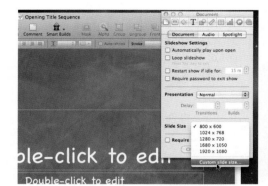

1: Custom slide

Choose a template, open the Inspector and select the Document tab. Click on the Slide Size pop-up menu and choose 'Custom slide size'.

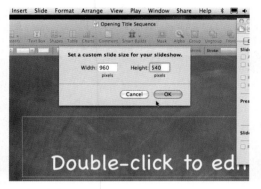

2: Resizing

Now set a dimension that matches your iMovie project's size (if it's a widescreen project, it's usually 960 x 540 pixels).

3: The titles

Write your information on the slide (you can, of course, use more than one slide and add as many text boxes or images as you need).

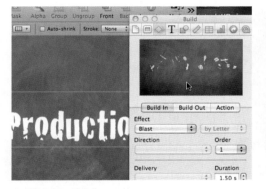

4: The Build Inspector

Use the Build Inspector (third tab from the left) to animate your objects, as has been described in past Keynote tutorials.

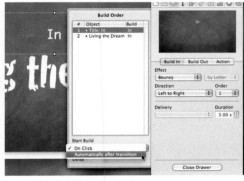

5: Build Order panel

Click on the Build Inspector's More Options button. Select the first build and click the Start Build pop-up menu. Choose 'Automatically after transition'.

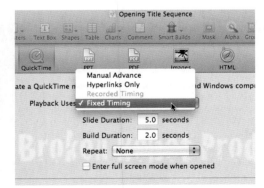

6: Repeat procedure

Do the same for the other builds. Make sure they all happen either 'automatically with' or 'after' the previous build. Use the Delay field to set a time.

7: Time to share

When your title is complete, it's time to send it to iMovie. Go to Share>Export and make sure you choose QuickTime from the available options.

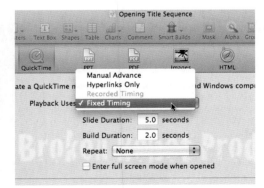

8: It's all about timing

Set the Playback Uses pop-up menu to Fixed Timing. If you've set your own delays for your build these will take precedent over the values displayed here.

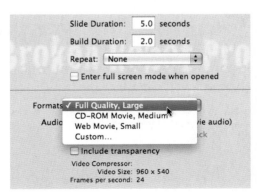

9: Title export

The Formats pop-up menu should be set to 'Full Quality, Large'. When done, click Next, give your title a name, and save it somewhere on your Mac.

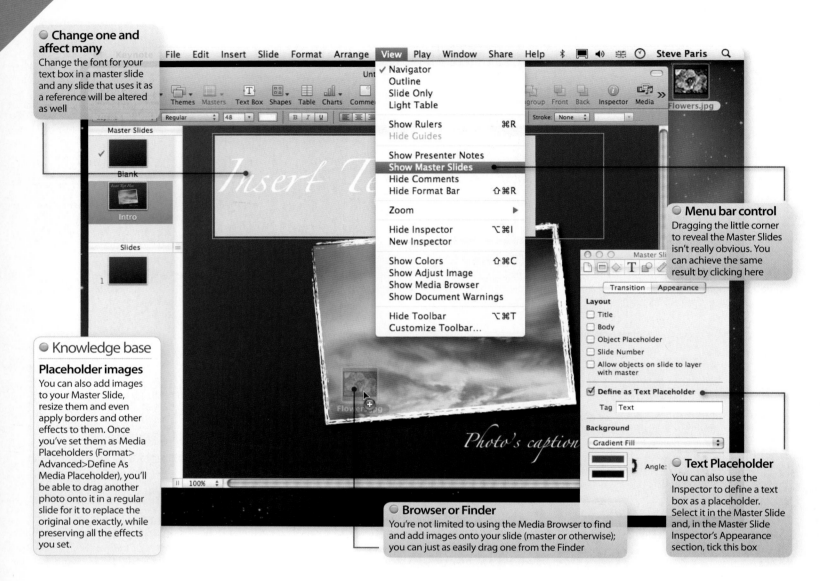

Change one and affect many
Change the font for your text box in a master slide and any slide that uses it as a reference will be altered as well

Knowledge base

Placeholder images
You can also add images to your Master Slide, resize them and even apply borders and other effects to them. Once you've set them as Media Placeholders (Format> Advanced>Define As Media Placeholder), you'll be able to drag another photo onto it in a regular slide for it to replace the original one exactly, while preserving all the effects you set.

Menu bar control
Dragging the little corner to reveal the Master Slides isn't really obvious. You can achieve the same result by clicking here

Text Placeholder
You can also use the Inspector to define a text box as a placeholder. Select it in the Master Slide and, in the Master Slide Inspector's Appearance section, tick this box

Browser or Finder
You're not limited to using the Media Browser to find and add images onto your slide (master or otherwise); you can just as easily drag one from the Finder

Tutorial: Create your own Keynote themes

If you use Keynote a lot, you might be itching to try out new themes. But rather than buying them, try creating one yourself

Task: Create and save a new theme in Keynote

Difficulty: Intermediate

Time needed: 30 minutes

Keynote is an incredibly powerful presentation tool that comes with many themes designed to make your work stand out with very little effort on your part. But this doesn't mean that you can't be creative; haven't you ever wondered how so many companies can offer new themes for you to use? That's because Keynote is designed to let you create your own templates with ease.

The following tutorial will show you how you can achieve this without having to be an expert designer. Perhaps the best way to begin this process is by taking a theme that you already like, and have used before, and then add new elements to it so it becomes a hybrid theme. So, launch Keynote, choose an existing template of your choice and let's get started…

Step-by-step | Keynote Design a new custom template

1: The Blank Master
With your first empty slide already selected, click on the toolbar's Masters icon and select the Blank option (if the theme you chose has one).

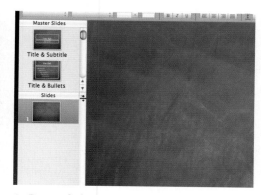

2: Reveal the Master Slides
To the right of the Slides sidebar is a small square with two horizontal lines across it. Drag it down to reveal the Master Slides.

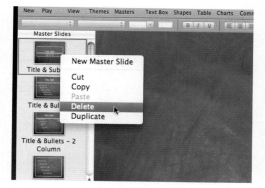

3: Deleting Master Slides
All these Master Slides are used to keep the look of the theme consistent throughout your project. Select them one at a time and hit the Delete key.

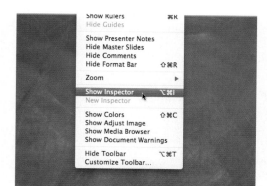

4: Open the Inspector
You obviously can't delete Blank since you're currently using it as your project's first slide. Reveal the Inspector with the Opt+Cmd+i shortcut.

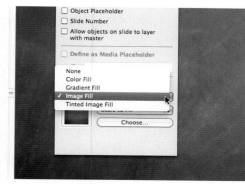

5: Change backgrounds
Go to the Master Slide tab (second from the left) and click on Appearance. Change the background by clicking on that section's pop-up menu.

6: Gradient colours and angles
Select Gradient Fill. Click on the colour wells to bring up a colour palette and choose new colours. Alter the gradient's angle with the button to the right.

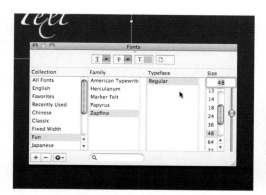

7: Boxes and fonts
Click on a text box and reposition it somewhere on the slide. Use Cmd+T to bring up the Fonts window. Use it to select a different font, size and colour.

8: Defining Placeholders
To edit your text in your presentation slides, you need to select the text box in the master slide and go to Format>Advanced>Define As Text Placeholder.

9: Saving the theme
When finished, go to File>Save Theme. Give your new theme a name. Next, go to File>New. Your theme will appear at the bottom of the list.

Animate your spreadsheets in Keynote

By using simple animation builds in Keynote, you can turn boring data into beautiful, dynamic presentations

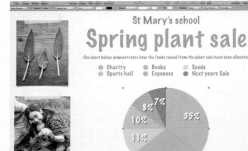

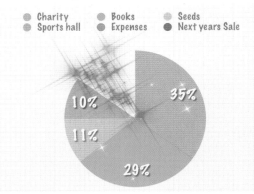

Task: Animate spreadsheet data in Keynote

Difficulty: Beginner

Time needed: 20 minutes

Creating interesting presentations can be an intimidating task – especially if the data is anything but interesting, as is often the case. For the participating audience, there are fewer things worse than having to watch slides of dull pie charts and spreadsheets. Luckily, Keynote offers some great animation sequences that can make the difference between a good presentation and a great one. The effects are so professional-looking that they're bound to impress your friends and colleagues – but don't worry, the best news is that you don't need to be a computer whizz in order to create these effects, as they are actually incredibly easy to achieve.

Step-by-step | Keynote | Add simple animation to your data for dynamic presentations

1: Select
Once your chart has been designed and all the data is correct, select it and head up to the Inspector panel (top-right of the interface).

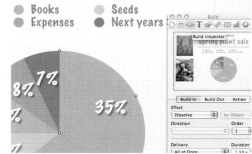

2: Build
Click the Build Inspector. You'll see three options: 'Build In' is the start of the animation, 'Build Out' is the end and 'Action' takes effect in between.

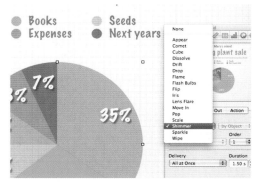

3: Choose an effect
Click the 'Build In' option. Then, by using the drop-down menu, select an effect. The thumbnail in the Inspector panel will demonstrate the effect.

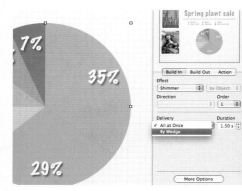

4: Delivery
Click on the drop-down menu under Delivery. You can decide whether the effect takes place all at once or whether each wedge will be affected.

5: Duration
The Duration box to the right of Delivery determines how long it takes to complete the build. Two seconds is usually adequate.

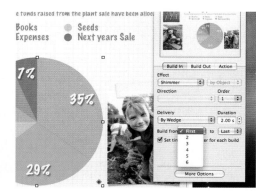

6: First to last
From the 'Build from' drop-down menu, select the order in which you want the build to appear. Then click the More Options button.

Create dynamic presentations using Keynote
Make boring data exciting by adding basic animations

Chart Inspector
The Chart Inspector offers a whole other range of options to help your data pop out from the page. Try adding drop shadows to make it look more three-dimensional, or use the 'explode' button to make the wedges explode on the page

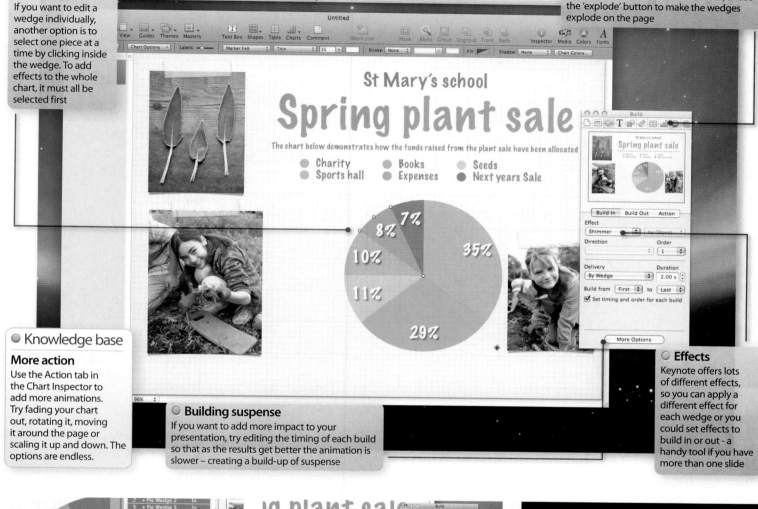

Knowledge base

More action
Use the Action tab in the Chart Inspector to add more animations. Try fading your chart out, rotating it, moving it around the page or scaling it up and down. The options are endless.

Building suspense
If you want to add more impact to your presentation, try editing the timing of each build so that as the results get better the animation is slower – creating a build-up of suspense

Effects
Keynote offers lots of different effects, so you can apply a different effect for each wedge or you could set effects to build in or out - a handy tool if you have more than one slide

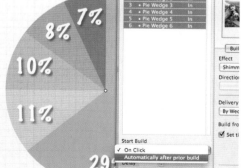

7: Start build
Decide whether you want the animation to take place automatically or if you want to click for each build – a handy option if you're talking.

8: Individual timing
Select one build at a time to edit it individually. You can select different timings and/or effects for each wedge. This can be effective for building a crescendo.

9: Play time
If you want to check out your animation, hit the play button (top-left of the interface). If you're happy with it, simply save and export.

Pitch a party using a Keynote presentation

Trying to organise a party weekend? Use Keynote presentations to convince your friends to come along

Trying to organise a party can be a stressful task, particularly if it means having to convince people to part with their hard-earned cash. A great way to convince your friends into going along with your ideas is to sell it to them using a fun-themed basic Keynote presentation – just as you would a business sales pitch. Pick an attractive theme (or choose a blank one and decorate it yourself), add a couple of photos, some charts and keep the information short and concise. If you're feeling adventurous try adding in some basic animation to your charts to really convince your mates that you know how to organise a good bash. They just won't be able to say no.

Task: Present a party idea in Keynote

Difficulty: Beginner

Time needed: 40 minutes

Step-by-step | **Keynote** Create a simple pitch presentation in Keynote

1: Open
Open Keynote from the Dock and select a theme for your pitch. As we want to evoke a party atmosphere, we're going for the Fun Theme.

2: Build
Create an opening slide, add a title and Ctrl-click in the Slides panel to select New Slide. Alternatively, head to the Slide menu at the top of the interface.

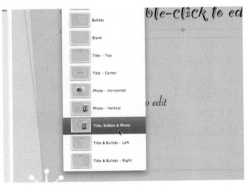

3: Choose a layout
Go to the Masters icon at the top of the interface and choose a template. We've chosen one with bullet points and space for a picture.

4: Facilities
Type a short list of the main selling points of your party. Add a picture to draw your audience in and add audio to get them in the party mood.

5: Expenses
Usually the deciding factor for most people, we've added a slide with a list of expenses. Add another slide to illustrate the break down with a 3D chart.

6: Chart Inspector
Head to the Chart Inspector and click Edit Data to input your information. Use the button underneath Chart Colors to edit the colour.

Create a pitch using Keynote

Get your mates on board using Keynote

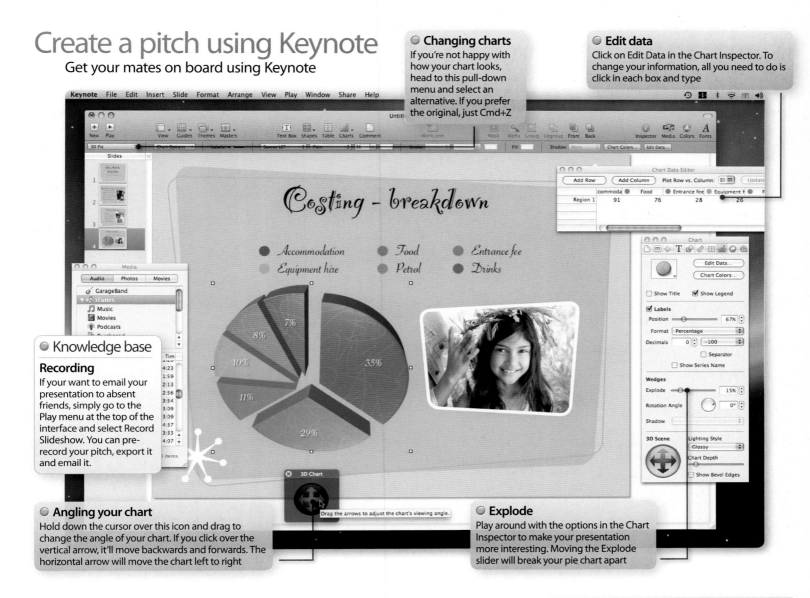

Changing charts
If you're not happy with how your chart looks, head to this pull-down menu and select an alternative. If you prefer the original, just Cmd+Z

Edit data
Click on Edit Data in the Chart Inspector. To change your information, all you need to do is click in each box and type

Knowledge base

Recording
If your want to email your presentation to absent friends, simply go to the Play menu at the top of the interface and select Record Slideshow. You can pre-record your pitch, export it and email it.

Angling your chart
Hold down the cursor over this icon and drag to change the angle of your chart. If you click over the vertical arrow, it'll move backwards and forwards. The horizontal arrow will move the chart left to right

Explode
Play around with the options in the Chart Inspector to make your presentation more interesting. Moving the Explode slider will break your pie chart apart

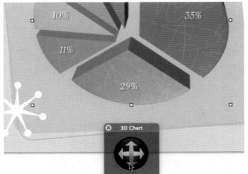

7: 3D chart
Select the chart and use the 3D button at the bottom of the screen to change the angle. This can also be done from the Inspector.

8: Rehearsal
If you're a bit nervous about making a presentation in front of people, head to the Play menu at the top of the interface and select Rehearse Slideshow.

9: Play
The slideshow will run with a clock on the left and a stopclock on the right, so you can practise your pitch to perfection before presenting it to friends.

Tutorial: Chart your income with Numbers

A spreadsheet is a perfect way to keep track of your money, but wouldn't those numbers be easier to read on a chart?

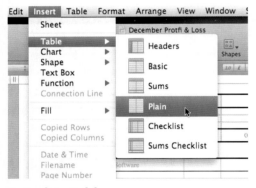

Task: Keep track of your money with the help of charts

Difficulty: Beginner

Time needed: 25 minutes

We've looked at how you can keep track of your finances using Numbers in a previous tutorial.

This time we'll be focusing on creating charts to make it easier to see where all your money is disappearing into. Charts can help you make sense of things in a way that is much easier and more intuitive than staring at rows and columns of numbers.

We'll look at how to generate the right information you need for your charts and how to link data to it, even if it's stored in a separate sheet. So launch your financial spreadsheet and let's get started…

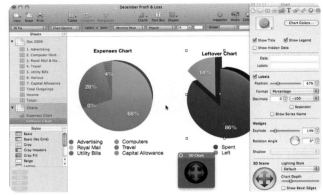

Step-by-step | **Numbers** Create charts of your income and expenses

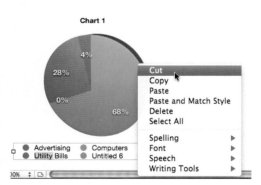

1: A plain table
If you've created a separate table for each expense, you'll have to gather all that information into one table: go to Insert>Table>Plain.

2: Gathering sums
Name each row after one of your expenses. To the right of each type '=' and click on that expense's total from the relevant table.

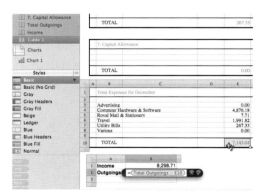

3: The chart
Highlight all your totals from the single table (you cannot highlight cells from different tables at the same time). Go to Insert>Chart>3D Pie.

4: Cutting from a sheet
Create a new Sheet by going to Insert>Sheet. Go back to the first one, select the chart you just created and go to Edit>Cut.

5: Pasting onto another
Select the second sheet and use Edit>Paste to add that chart onto it. It's still linked to its values; change them and the chart alters automatically.

6: Income and outgoings
To create a "money left" pie chart, make a table in the first sheet containing cells with your income and the sum of all your outgoings.

Chart your expenses in Numbers
Keep track of your income and outgoings with charts

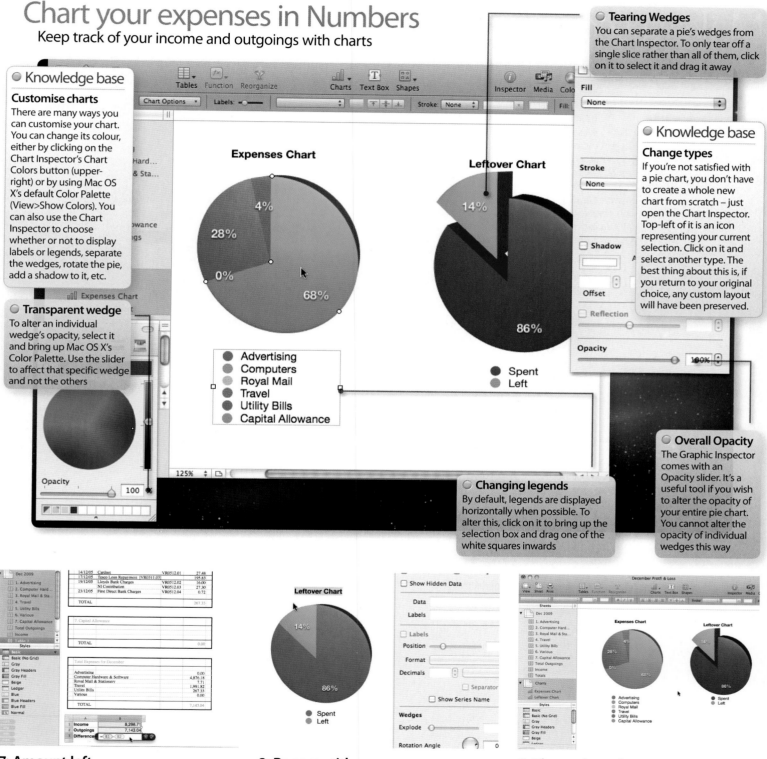

Tearing Wedges
You can separate a pie's wedges from the Chart Inspector. To only tear off a single slice rather than all of them, click on it to select it and drag it away

Knowledge base

Customise charts
There are many ways you can customise your chart. You can change its colour, either by clicking on the Chart Inspector's Chart Colors button (upper-right) or by using Mac OS X's default Color Palette (View>Show Colors). You can also use the Chart Inspector to choose whether or not to display labels or legends, separate the wedges, rotate the pie, add a shadow to it, etc.

Knowledge base

Change types
If you're not satisfied with a pie chart, you don't have to create a whole new chart from scratch – just open the Chart Inspector. Top-left of it is an icon representing your current selection. Click on it and select another type. The best thing about this is, if you return to your original choice, any custom layout will have been preserved.

Transparent wedge
To alter an individual wedge's opacity, select it and bring up Mac OS X's Color Palette. Use the slider to affect that specific wedge and not the others

Changing legends
By default, legends are displayed horizontally when possible. To alter this, click on it to bring up the selection box and drag one of the white squares inwards

Overall Opacity
The Graphic Inspector comes with an Opacity slider. It's a useful tool if you wish to alter the opacity of your entire pie chart. You cannot alter the opacity of individual wedges this way

7: Amount left
Use a third cell to calculate the difference between the two. Next, highlight it and the expenses total, and create another chart based on those figures.

8: Rename titles
Move that chart to the second sheet. To rename a chart's title (which currently should be Chart 1 and 2), click on it three times.

9: The end result
You can now see at a glance where your money goes with one chart, and how much you have left with the other.

Make a scoreboard for games in Numbers

Spreadsheets are great at keeping track of numerical data, so make that data more visually appealing with Numbers' tools

Creating a scoreboard can be a fun thing to do to keep track of an ongoing match or game with **friends.** With Numbers, you can actually make use of its advanced design tools to create an actual scoreboard, complete with illuminated numbers (or as close to the real thing as you can replicate!).

These tools are similar to the ones available in Pages and Keynote, and can help you spice up your data – as we'll be showing you in this tutorial. If you'd rather not go into the scoreboard itself to modify the numbers, you'll also learn how to make use of Numbers' simple formulas.

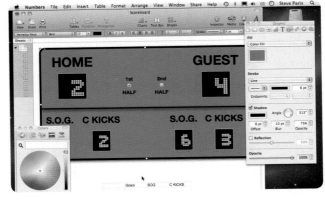

Task: Use Numbers' design tools to create a scoreboard

Difficulty: Beginner

Time needed: 25 minutes

Step-by-step | Numbers Build a scoreboard using Numbers' design tools

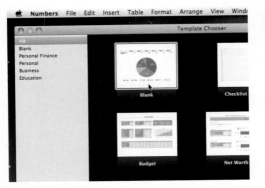

1: A blank sheet
Start by opening a new blank spreadsheet. Select the table within and hit the Delete key as you won't be needing it just yet.

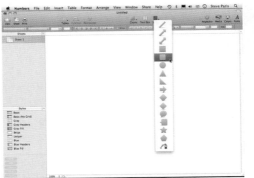

2: A shape
Click on the toolbar's Shapes button and select a round-edged rectangle. Drag one of its white corners until it takes up most of the sheet's width.

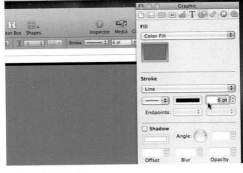

3: The Graphic Inspector
Open the Inspector (Shift+Cmd+i) and go to the Graphic tab. With the rectangle selected, click on the Fill well to change its colour, add a Stroke, etc.

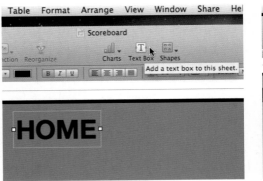

4: Home and guest
Click on the Text Box tool and drag the resulting item onto your rectangle, near the upper left. Type 'HOME' inside it. Use another for the 'GUEST' team.

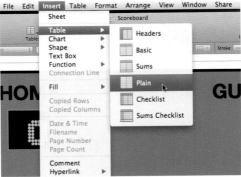

5: A Plain table
Select a Plain table from the toolbar's Tables button. Resize it so only one cell is left. Position it beneath the 'HOME' text, and do the same for 'GUEST'.

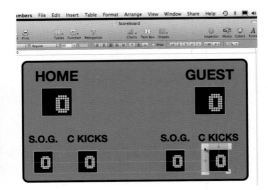

6: More cells
You can add additional fields beneath these. If you're following football, you could add 'SOG' and 'C KICKS' for instance, with their own separate cells.

Use Numbers to create a scoreboard

Keep track of your data with help from Numbers' design tools

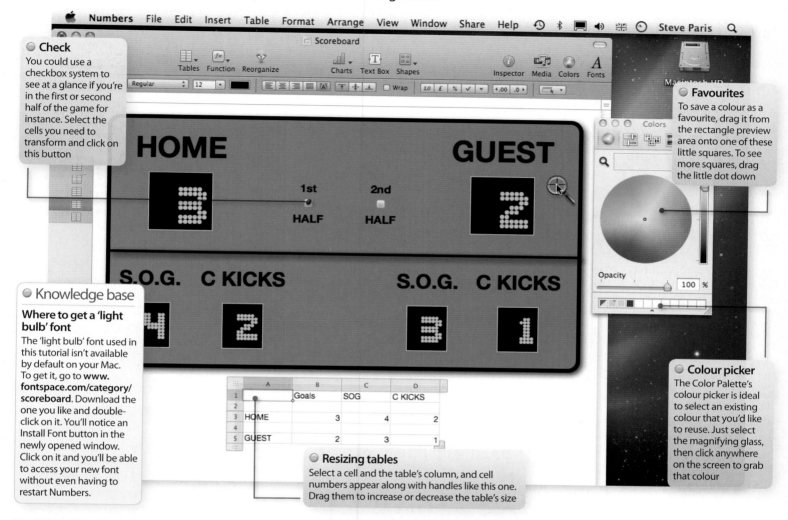

Check
You could use a checkbox system to see at a glance if you're in the first or second half of the game for instance. Select the cells you need to transform and click on this button

Favourites
To save a colour as a favourite, drag it from the rectangle preview area onto one of these little squares. To see more squares, drag the little dot down

Knowledge base

Where to get a 'light bulb' font
The 'light bulb' font used in this tutorial isn't available by default on your Mac. To get it, go to www.fontspace.com/category/scoreboard. Download the one you like and double-click on it. You'll notice an Install Font button in the newly opened window. Click on it and you'll be able to access your new font without even having to restart Numbers.

Resizing tables
Select a cell and the table's column, and cell numbers appear along with handles like this one. Drag them to increase or decrease the table's size

Colour picker
The Color Palette's colour picker is ideal to select an existing colour that you'd like to reuse. Just select the magnifying glass, then click anywhere on the screen to grab that colour

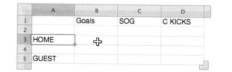

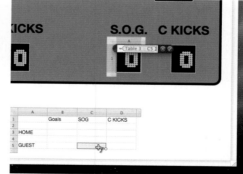

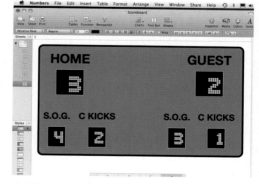

7: Matching table
Rather than double-clicking on each individual cell to amend it, do the following: create another table and label it to match the fields you currently have.

8: A formula
Double-click on the main HOME table to select it. Type in '=' and click on the corresponding cell in the table you just created.

9: Rinse and repeat
Repeat the process for all the cells in your scoreboard. Now, when you update the values, the scoreboard area will change automatically.

Create a height and weight chart in Numbers

Use spreadsheets to keep track of your height and weight, and let your Mac do all the analyses for you…

Numbers isn't just there to merely let you add a series of numbers to fields; it also comes with dozens of formulas that you can use to make automatic calculations. It could be as simple as adding up all the values, to more complex formulas. But what's great about spreadsheet programs is that they enable you to create such calculations quickly and easily – you can even copy and paste them to other cells and the formula will work as expected (as long as the values are set up properly, of course). In this Numbers tutorial we'll show you how this feature works while creating a height and weight chart.

Task: Use Numbers to keep track of height and weight

Difficulty: Beginner

Time needed: 25 minutes

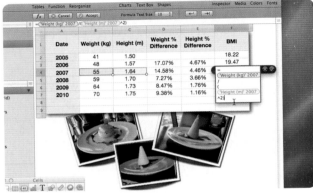

Step-by-step | Numbers Create formulas to calculate your height and weight over time

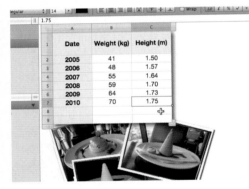

1: Set up a table
Create a table with three columns, for the date, weight and height. Fill the rows with information (you'll need preferably at least four rows of data).

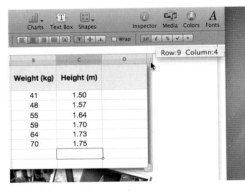

2: Add another column
To compare your weight from one row to the next, create a fourth column by dragging the table's right resize handle to the right.

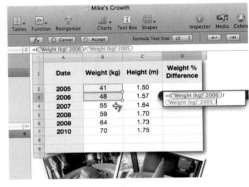

3: Create a formula
Create a formula in the fourth column's third row by typing: '=('. Click on the weight column's third row, type '/', and click on its second row.

4: Complete the formula
To finish the calculation, type: ') - 1'. Now hit the Return key. Finally, click on the toolbar's % button to turn that value into a percentage.

5: Copying
You don't have to type that formula again for the other rows – just select the cell with the calculation and copy it (Edit>Copy).

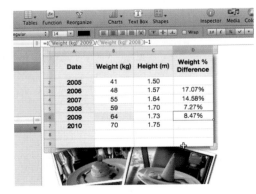

6: Pasting
Hit the down arrow and paste your formula (Edit>Paste). The result changes because moving the formula changes the cells it links to.

Track your height and weight in Numbers

Create formulas to help track your height and weight in a spreadsheet

● Inspector options and tabs
The Inspector's tabs offers you settings – many of which aren't available elsewhere. For instance, you could choose to have negative percentage values appear in red, or in brackets

● Knowledge base

Absolute values

You will have noticed that copying a formula alters the cells it's referencing. This makes it easy when pasting the same formula over multiple cells, but what if you need your formula to always point to one specific cell, no matter where you paste the formula? Hover over a cell in the formula and click on its down-arrow menu. Choose 'absolute row and column' to anchor its position.

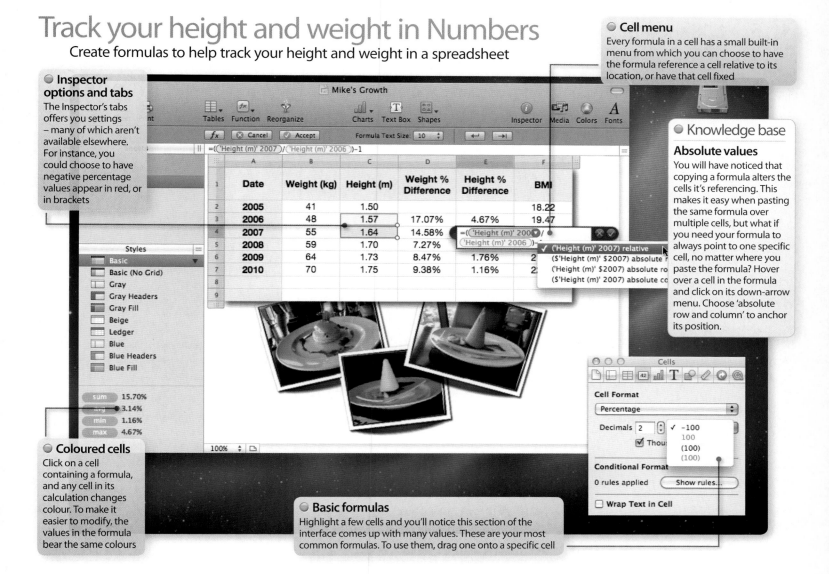

● Coloured cells
Click on a cell containing a formula, and any cell in its calculation changes colour. To make it easier to modify, the values in the formula bear the same colours

● Basic formulas
Highlight a few cells and you'll notice this section of the interface comes up with many values. These are your most common formulas. To use them, drag one onto a specific cell

---

7: Another column

Create another column to the right of the fourth one. You're going to use it to calculate the height changes from one row to the next.

8: Pasting memory

Since you've already copied the formula in step 5, your Mac should still remember it. Click on a fifth column cell and paste the formula.

9: Filling the column

Repeat the procedure for the other rows to see at a glance the percentage difference from one set of measurements to the next.

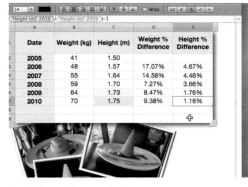

Share your spreadsheets with iWork.com

When collaborating with others on a document, not being in the same office can be a pain. iWork.com is here to help

iWork.com is Apple's answer to collaborating on a document remotely. The idea is simple: post your work online for others to see, comment on and even communicate during the process. This service is compatible with any program of the suite, be it Pages, Keynote or Numbers, but we'll be illustrating how this works with the help of a Numbers spreadsheet.

Be aware though that this service is still in beta, which means it isn't perfected yet. Some features may change over time and you may encounter the occasional strange glitch, but it won't damage your original file that's stored safely on your own Mac.

Task: Learn how to send a spreadsheet to iWork.com

Difficulty: Intermediate

Time needed: 30 minutes

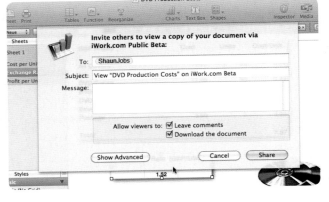

Step-by-step | Numbers Share, view and comment on a spreadsheet using iWork.com

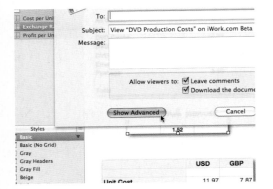

1: The Share menu
Open one of your spreadsheets and modify it if you need to. When you're ready to upload it, go to Share>Share via iWork.com.

2: Signing in
You'll be requested to sign in. Your iTunes or MobileMe account will work for this, so there's no need to create a unique one for iWork.com.

3: Email verification
You need to have your account verified if this is the first time you're using the service. Click 'Send email' then follow the link in the email you receive.

4: Advanced options
Go back to Share>Share via iWork.com. A drop-down sheet will now appear offering you options. Click on Show Advanced to reveal more choices.

5: Send a message
In the 'To' field at the top, write the email address of the person(s) you wish to share your document with. You can also add a message. Now click Share.

6: The colleague's view
The recipient will receive an email with a link directing them to iWork.com. Clicking on it will reveal the spreadsheet online.

Share your Numbers spreadsheets
Send your spreadsheets to iWork.com

The toolbar
The toolbar has very few buttons. From left to right they are Add Comment, Show/Hide Comments, Print (turns the file into a PDF for printing) and Download

Linked comments
When a comment is linked to a cell in your spreadsheet, a line connects the two. You can drag the comment anywhere and that line will keep it tethered to the correct cell

Exporting options
The Download button offers you three format options depending on your needs: Numbers, PDF and Excel. Only the Numbers format appears to preserve your iWork.com comments

Knowledge base

Semi-live comments and notes
You can reply to any comment by using its Reply button. Once you hit Post the information will take a little while to be seen on your colleague's computer (it's not like iChat, so you have to be a little patient). The same applies for the Document Notes, although it's not immediately obvious since the field doesn't scroll down to reveal them – you have to do this manually. Using Comments is currently the better option.

Floating comments
If nothing is selected when you add a comment, it'll remain as a floating window and not connected to anything. To delete a comment, click on its 'x' button

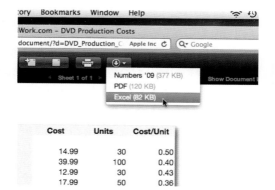

7: Download a copy
You can peruse the document but cannot modify it online. But you can download a copy by clicking on the fourth button in the toolbar.

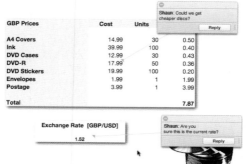

8: Post a comment
You can also post comments by selecting a cell and clicking on the yellow button in the toolbar. Click on Post in the yellow box to set it.

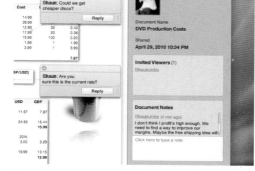

9: Document Notes
The Document Notes is for general information about the spreadsheet. The notes won't be saved when downloading the file, unlike the comments.

Create an incentive chart for your children

Make tasks more fun for your kids by creating an incentive chart in Numbers

Task: Use basic tables to create an incentive chart

Difficulty: Beginner

Time needed: 45 minutes

If, like most parents, you find it difficult to get your children motivated, why not use your computer skills to give them a little inspiration? This fun and easy-to-make incentive chart simply comprises of a list of tasks to be done for each day of the week. Tick the box for each day that the child has completed the task, and if they complete that task for five days or more (everyone deserves a day off!) then reward them with a gold star at the end of the week. A set number of stars will be rewarded by a treat – the perfect way to get them to make their bed.

Of course, you don't have to make your chart exactly the same as the one shown here; you can make it as simple or as complicated as you like. All you need to do is create a basic table in Numbers, add a title and a name box, and then use the Inspector panel to add some professional-looking touches – such as a bright background, some bold text and lots of fun shapes to attract attention. It's as easy as ABC.

Step-by-step | Numbers Make an incentive chart

1: Bright and bold
Launch Numbers from your Dock and choose a Blank template. To capture your child's attention, use Inspector to add bright shapes and colours. Don't forget to add a name box to make it more personal.

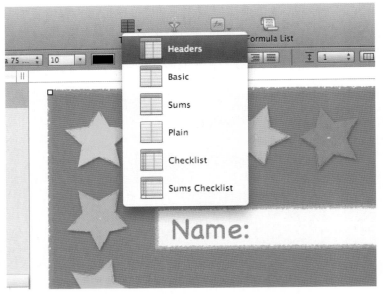

2: Add a table
When you're happy with the design, head to the Tables icon (located top-left of the interface). Choose the table you want to add and use the outside corners to resize it.

Create a children's reward chart in Numbers

Get a gold star by designing a reward chart to keep your kids in check

Tweak the text
Use these little icons to align the text in your table. Drag the cursor over the text and click the icon to align it left, right, top, bottom or centre. The same icons can be found in the Text Inspector

Shapes
To add shapes around the chart, use the Shapes icon at the top of the interface. Rotate them by heading to the Metrics Inspector and using the Rotate bubble at the bottom

Knowledge base

Distribute evenly
To make your columns even widths, select all of them and choose 'Distribute columns evenly' from the Table menu. To make one bigger, hover the cursor over the dividing line at the top, click and drag. Apply the same method to rows.

"Add some professional-looking touches – such as a bright background, some bold text and lots of fun shapes"

Graphic Inspector
Use the Graphic Inspector to add professional touches to your chart, like adding shadows to your shapes to make them more three-dimensional

Cell block
To change the background colour of a cell or the outline, select it and use the 'Cell background' option in the Table Inspector

3: Add columns and rows
Add as many columns or rows as you like by Control-clicking on the table and selecting Add Column. Add your text by simply clicking inside each cell and use the Text Inspector to change the colour, size or font.

4: Print
When you're ready, save your creation and go to File>Print. You need to print bigger than standard A4 to use it effectively, so use the Print menu to make it A3 or bigger, tape it together and cover it with clear plastic.

Graphic Inspector

Use the Graphic Inspector to add frames and drop shadows to your images and graphics. Use the opacity button to knock down the colour of the stars you haven't yet achieved. When you reach your target, change it back to highlight that it's complete

Better looking charts

To get rid of the white background, select the chart. Go to Graphics Inspector and change Fill to None. To get rid of the lines, head further down to Stroke and select None

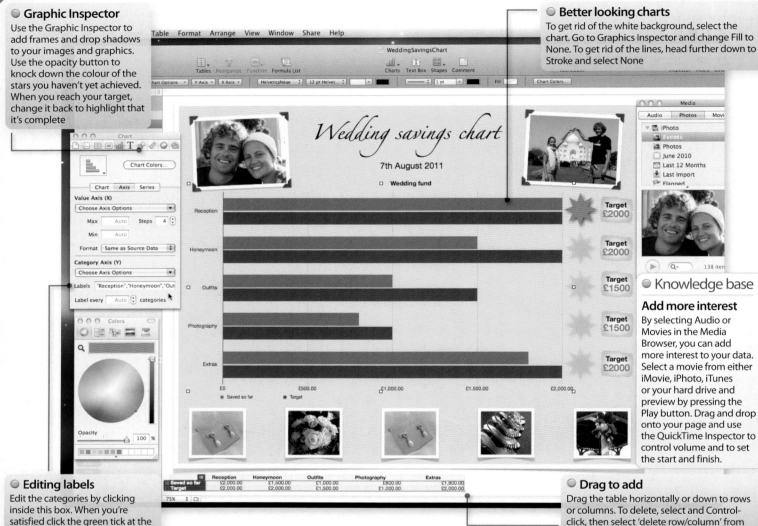

Wedding savings chart
7th August 2011
☐ Wedding fund

Editing labels

Edit the categories by clicking inside this box. When you're satisfied click the green tick at the end, if not select the red cross

Knowledge base

Add more interest

By selecting Audio or Movies in the Media Browser, you can add more interest to your data. Select a movie from either iMovie, iPhoto, iTunes or your hard drive and preview by pressing the Play button. Drag and drop onto your page and use the QuickTime Inspector to control volume and to set the start and finish.

Drag to add

Drag the table horizontally or down to rows or columns. To delete, select and Control-click, then select 'delete row/column' from the pop-up menu

Create a savings chart in Numbers

Take control of your savings using a simple chart in Numbers

Target £2000

Target

Task: Use Numbers to chart your savings

Difficulty: Beginner

Time needed: 20 minutes

Saving for a big event such as a wedding can take a lot of organisation and planning, not to mention money. A basic chart in Numbers is the perfect way to keep track of your savings and to see how far you are from achieving your target. The hardest part of this task is finding the money in the first place, but when you do add to your funds, all you need to do is update your chart with the amount of money you've added and you can watch your chart grow as your bank account does. We've divided our wedding savings chart into sections – such as reception, honeymoon, photography, etc. There are two rows; the bottom indicates the target and the top is your fund. At the end of each row we've added a box with the target amount needed and a star so that you can clearly indicate that you've achieved your target. Finally, if you need some incentives, try adding some pictures of your dream wedding or holiday for inspiration.

Step-by-step | Numbers Create a wedding savings chart

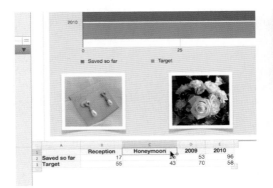

1: Choose a template
Choose a blank template, delete the existing table and add detail using the Shapes tool and Colors window. Don't forget to add a title or pictures.

2: Choose a chart
Select the chart that you want to use from the drop-down Chart menu at the top of the interface. Numbers has a great selection, including 3D charts.

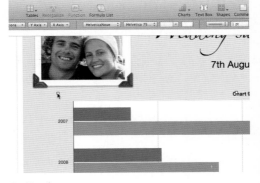

3: Resize
Select the chart by clicking on it and resize it to how big you want it to be by clicking on the small white boxes on the corners and dragging.

4: Editing text
Click inside a cell in the table to edit the text in your chart. The text on your chart will automatically update itself.

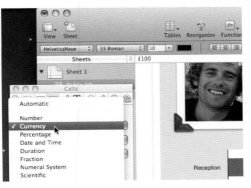

5: Currency
Go to the Cells Inspector tab within the Inspector panel, click on the drop-down menu under Cell Format and change it to Currency.

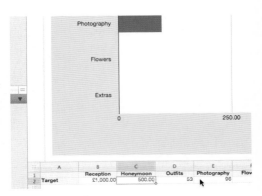

6: Adding data
Add the amounts you already have (leave them blank if you haven't started saving). When you add to the fund, update the text to update your chart.

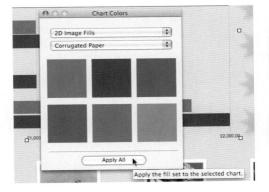

7: Changing colour
Click on the chart and go to the Chart Inspector, then click on the Chart Colors button to change the colour of the chart.

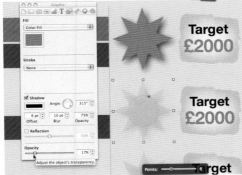

8: Targets
Add a star shape and the target amount for each fund and use the Opacity button to highlight a target that has been achieved.

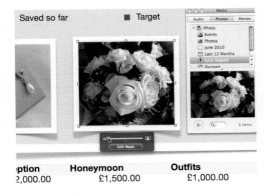

9: Incentives
For a bit of inspiration, add pictures of your goals using the Media Browser. Select your images and simply drag-and-drop them onto the page.

We're excited about: Highbrow

Constantly switching between browsers?
Let Highbrow help you…

We're not sure about you, but we love to switch between browsers. There's just something about the browsing experience we love on a Mac – the cool options. And, as browsers are free, we can have as many as we want on our Macs and use whichever one we feel suits us best at any given time. We like Safari for its Top Sites, Firefox for being the quickest at loading the Apple site (for us), and Chrome and Opera have their cool features too. The problem with this abundance of choice is that one of them has to be your preferred browser, and when you click links your Mac will fire up that browser without any thought as to whether you'd prefer it in another. Highbrow solves this problem by giving you the choice as the link is clicked. It also has some handy other features too. It doesn't get in the way of the browsing experience, it just sits up in the corner of the screen waiting to spring into action as and when it's needed. Requirements: Mac OS X 10.5 or later

● Keep your options open
With the power of modern Macs, keeping multiple browsers up and running is easy, so there is plenty of choice when it comes to surfing

● Get clever
For browser power users, it's possible to get even more clarity from Highbrow by utilising Spaces. Keep each browser in its own Space and flit between them

Step-by-step | Highbrow Behaviour

1: Click and pick
Click on the Highbrow icon in the status bar to bring down the menu. Here, in the Behavior section, you can pick an option. We're opting for 'Use the Most Recently Used Web Browser'.

2: Pick a favourite
If you select the option to 'Use My Preferred Web Browser', Highbrow will pick the browser that is ticked in the list above the Behavior section (which is Safari in our case).

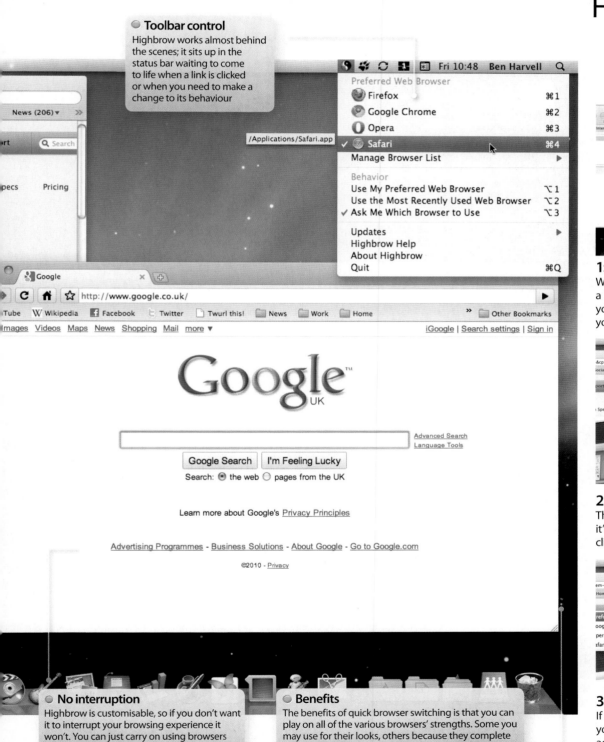

Toolbar control
Highbrow works almost behind the scenes; it sits up in the status bar waiting to come to life when a link is clicked or when you need to make a change to its behaviour

/Applications/Safari.app

Preferred Web Browser
Firefox ⌘1
Google Chrome ⌘2
Opera ⌘3
✓ Safari ⌘4
Manage Browser List ▸

Behavior
Use My Preferred Web Browser ⌥1
Use the Most Recently Used Web Browser ⌥2
✓ Ask Me Which Browser to Use ⌥3

Updates ▸
Highbrow Help
About Highbrow
Quit ⌘Q

No interruption
Highbrow is customisable, so if you don't want it to interrupt your browsing experience it won't. You can just carry on using browsers from the Dock as usual

Benefits
The benefits of quick browser switching is that you can play on all of the various browsers' strengths. Some you may use for their looks, others because they complete certain tasks better

Highbrow's most useful function
It's the intervention of Highbrow that makes it so awesome

1: Wait for a link
With Highbrow set up, when you click on a link it will spring into action and offer you a choice of browsers. Choose the one you want and click OK.

2: Settings
This function should be there by default; if it's not you need to access the menu and click 'Ask Me Which Browser to Use'.

3: Browser removal
If a browser falls out for favour with you, you can remove it from your list by accessing the menu, going to Manage Browser List and removing the app.

We're excited about: Shape Collage

Make incredible picture collages in minutes with this outstanding app

One of the things we love about iPhoto is how easy it is to view our pictures. But unfortunately, turning them into any kind of collage (other than in a slideshow) can be pretty tough, and usually involves some serious editing and the purchase of some pretty hi-tech software. Luckily there are creative geniuses out there who have created a fantastic piece of software called Shape Collage. It really is an incredible tool. Just load it with the images you want to create a collage from and then select a shape you want the photos to fit into. You can add shapes of your own, draw shapes, customise the way the images appear in the collage in terms of size and spacing, and you can control the size of the output picture too. Another great reason to download this app is that it's blazingly fast. There is a free version that will watermark the output or you can purchase the full version.
Requirements: OS X Tiger and above.

Step-by-step | Shape Collage Add pictures

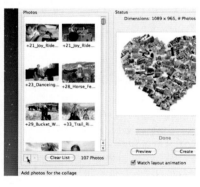

1: Click it
Click on the plus button and a file directory will appear. If you want to start fresh hit the Clear List button first.

2: Find and add
Now select the files or folders you wish to import into the app. If you have the pictures to hand then ignore step one and just drag-and-drop the pictures in.

○ Preview
Use the preview button to see how your collage is going to shape up before you hit Create and your masterpiece is born

Shape Collage   File   Project   Options   Help

Create the collage!

"Add shapes of your own, draw shapes, and customise the way images appear in the collage in terms of size and spacing"

○ Add what you like
It couldn't be simpler to add images to your collage. Use the plus button or drag-and-drop them in

Add some extra artwork

Get even more from this cool app

Draw your own
You can even draw your own custom shape to throw into the collage builder. Just click the More button to have a canvas thrown up

Cool controls
The right-hand panel contains all the control parameters. Use the tabs to skip through sections and change the behaviour of your collage as it is created

Awesome artwork
The finished product is a very cool collage that fits a specific shape. These are a great way to preserve memories and make gifts

1: More
Click the More button to bring up the custom canvas. Here you can draw your own shape if you like.

2: Custom
Click the custom bar on the right and pick one of the options provided or scroll to the bottom and click More.

3: Web it
You will now be taken to the web where you can pick from another set of images. Drag them into the canvas and click Done to load that as your shape.

We're excited about: MyThoughts

Create stunning, brain-friendly mind maps with this excellent tool

It can be quite tough to get all your ideas down on paper. Your train of thought can take you in all kinds of directions, and a pen and paper can't always cope with the non-linear way your ideas flow. Thank goodness then that you're a Mac user and you have access to great applications like MyThoughts. This little gem is a great way to get your ideas down in a map so you can explore the way you feel about something, construct a plan for achieving a certain task or even justify making a purchase. The software is very easy to use and offers some great integration with iLife, so you can personalise and illustrate what you are thinking. Not only that, but it's also possible to add notes to thought branches so you can expand upon any single point that you make. This is a very cool app and well worth a try.
Requirements: OS X 10.5 or later
Website: www.mythoughtsformac.com

"This is a great way to get your ideas down in a map so you can explore how you feel"

Step-by-step | MyThoughts Get started

1: Launch and inspire
When you launch MyThoughts you will need to create a central idea. Double-click on the cloud to enter the main focus of your mind map.

Reasons to buy an iPad

2: Picture it
You can now drag-and-drop an image from the Media browser onto the cloud to visualise your main idea. Position the picture so that other branches can run off it and your ideas are clear.

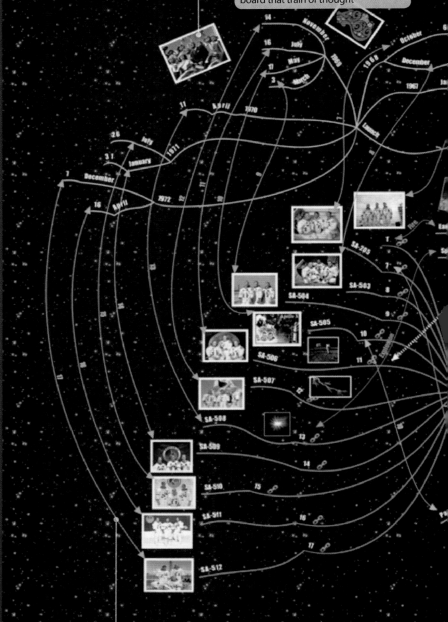

Images
Drop images into branches to illustrate your point. Visual cues help jog your memory quickly so you can get back on board that train of thought

Add arrows
Use arrow heads to indicate movement between ideas. Ideas with dual arrow heads can indicate multiple options

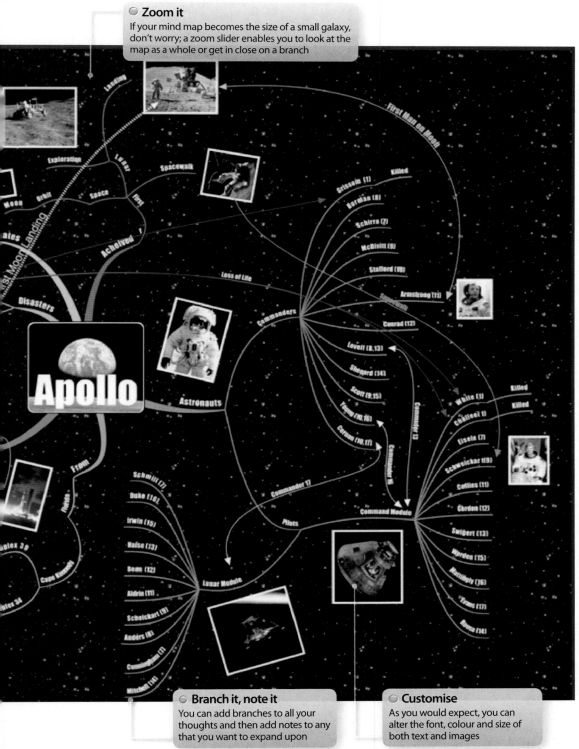

○ **Zoom it**
If your mind map becomes the size of a small galaxy, don't worry; a zoom slider enables you to look at the map as a whole or get in close on a branch

○ **Branch it, note it**
You can add branches to all your thoughts and then add notes to any that you want to expand upon

○ **Customise**
As you would expect, you can alter the font, colour and size of both text and images

Add notes to your mind map
Put as much extra info into your map as you like

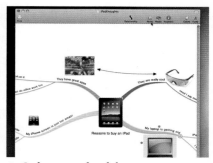

1: Select and add
Click on the branch you wish to add the note to and then click the Notes button at the top of the interface.

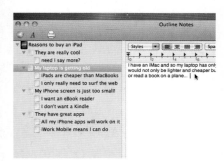

2: Note editor
The Note editor will spring to life, allowing you to add as much detail as you like. You can format text size, font and colour.

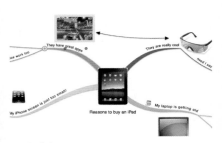

3: Add more
You can add more notes to other branches from within the editor by clicking on them on the left. Access each note on the diagram.

We're excited about: Image Tricks

If you want a really fast, efficient way to add effects to your images then look no further…

Image Tricks is yet another great application from BeLight Software. As the name suggests, Image Tricks allows you to add effects to your photographs and images in a very simple way. The interface is incredibly easy to learn, a doddle to navigate, and the range of effects is very impressive too. There are two versions of the software: a free version and a Pro version ($19.95). Some of the effects are only available in the Pro version, so you may need to consider making a purchase if you want the full range of features. BeLight has been sure to make the interface as Apple-like as possible, which is a trick that users really welcome from developers because they find it much easier to navigate the software and it gives them the confidence to experiment and find their way around the program. Windows on the right and left of the main viewing window provide easy access to the effects, and the instant preview means that it's possible to tweak and adjust the effect before applying any changes.

Requirements: OS X 10.5.8 or later
Website: www.belightsoft.com

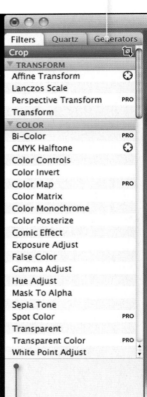

Tabs
There are three different tabs full of effects. These are categorised into Filters, Quartz effects and Generators

"The interface is easy to learn, a doddle to navigate, and the range of effects is impressive"

Effects
All of the effects are kept here, and an icon on the right of the named effect will indicate the type of effect and whether or not it's limited to the Pro edition

Tweak
Each effect setting will have controllable options displayed in this bottom window. Play around to get the desired finish to your image

---

Step-by-step | Image Tricks Iconic options

1: Bottoms up
At the bottom of the interface there are a number of icon buttons that will allow you to complete actions. Click the Size icon to alter your image's dimensions.

2: Simple steps
You can now alter the size of your image by pixels or by percentage so that it's the perfect size for the project you are planning.

Mask
Here you can add a mask to the image using the templated masks provided. There are over 100 different masks to choose from

Untitled

Zoom
Use the slider to get in close to the detail of your shot, or alternatively zoom right out to see the image as a whole

Adding effects to an image

Image Tricks is so simple that you can just have fun with it

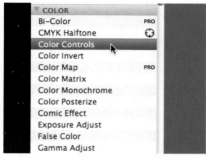

1: Pick an effect, any effect
Use the window on the left to browse through the effects. A good place to start is Color Controls. Click on it.

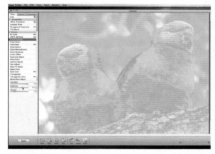

2: Slide away
Use the sliders that have now appeared to alter the Saturation, Brightness and Contrast. If you're happy click Apply. If not, pick a new effect.

3: Tab
Click on the Quartz tab to find more effects. Just click on each one to see what it does to the image.

We're excited about: Spotify

Our favourite music streaming service just got even better with brand new software

Spotify has quietly been building its music streaming business, and some people have said that it is the one service that could one day rival iTunes. There are eight million tracks and albums available online and you can stream them all to your Mac and play them for free. Hook up a pair of speakers and turn up the volume for a great experience. It's legal too, and if you have not yet discovered this fantastic music service you should visit the website and sign up straight away. There are three types of account on offer, and Spotify Open allows you to listen to 20 hours of streaming music per month for no charge. That's roughly 25 albums or 300 tracks. Spotify Unlimited costs £4.99 a month but it has no time restrictions, so you can listen all day every day. Spotify Premium is £9.99, but you have the ability to stream music to your iPhone or iPod touch and listen to music in offline mode too. The software can also play your iTunes library.

Requirements: Free Spotify software and account, internet connection
Website: www.spotify.com

Step-by-step | Spotify Sign up & download

1: Choose the version
Go to **www.spotify. com**, click Get Spotify and choose the version you want. We'll use Open because it's free, and we also need to upgrade an old version of the software.

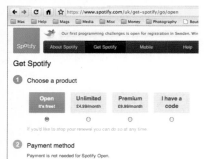

2: Set up an account
If you don't have an account at the website, you will need to fill in this form to enable the Spotify software to log in. It's free for Spotify Open. Existing users can skip this.

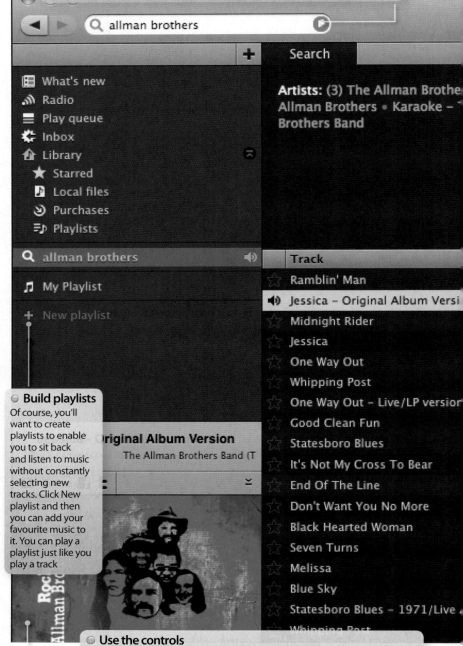

Search for music
There are millions of tracks online and the best way to find your favourite artists is to search for them. Enter an artist or track name and press Enter. In seconds you'll see a track list fill the main part of the window and related search terms on the right

Build playlists
Of course, you'll want to create playlists to enable you to sit back and listen to music without constantly selecting new tracks. Click New playlist and then you can add your favourite music to it. You can play a playlist just like you play a track

Use the controls
All the controls are in the bottom bar, and you can play, pause, skip forward or backward in the tracks. The volume control is next to them. The track length and play position is just to the right and you can click in it to jump to any part

Play a track

After performing a search, browse the list of tracks that are displayed. An artist search often results in dozens of tracks. To play one you just need to double-click it in the list. You can see the album it is taken from in the list on the right

Sort the tracks

If there is a long lists of tracks, you might want to sort them into order. Click a column heading to sort by that attribute and click again to reverse the sort. You can easily find the most popular tracks, the longest, or order by album or track name

Spotify Free

☆ Buy Premium

allman brothers

Albums: (27) The Allman Brothers Band / Rock Legends by The Allman Brothers Band • Brothers & Sisters by The Allman Brothers Band • Playlist: The Best Of The Allman Brothers Band: The Epic Years by The Allman Brothers Band and 25 more...

Tracks: (342)

Buy	Artist	Time	Popularity ▼	Album
♪	The Allman Brothers Band	4:57	‖‖‖‖‖‖‖‖‖‖‖	The Allman
♪	The Allman Brothers Band	7:05	‖‖‖‖‖‖‖‖‖‖	The Allman
♪	The Allman Brothers Band	2:54	‖‖‖‖‖‖‖‖	The Allman
♪	The Allman Brothers Band	7:05	‖‖‖‖‖‖‖‖	Brothers & S
♪	The Allman Brothers Band	4:57	‖‖‖‖‖‖‖‖	Music From
♪	The Allman Brothers Band	5:17	‖‖‖‖‖‖‖‖	The Allman
♪	The Allman Brothers Band	4:58	‖‖‖‖‖‖‖	Lords Of Do
♪	The Allman Brothers Band	5:08	‖‖‖‖‖‖‖	Playlist: The
♪	The Allman Brothers Band	4:20	‖‖‖‖‖‖‖	Live At The
♪	The Allman Brothers Band	5:04	‖‖‖‖‖‖‖	The Allman
♪	The Allman Brothers Band	4:38	‖‖‖‖‖‖	Playlist: The
♪	The Allman Brothers Band	2:26	‖‖‖‖‖‖	The Allman
♪	The Allman Brothers Band	5:11	‖‖‖‖‖‖	The Allman
♪	The Allman Brothers Band	5:04	‖‖‖‖‖‖	Playlist: The
♪	The Allman Brothers Band	3:54	‖‖‖‖‖‖	The Allman
♪	The Allman Brothers Band	5:09	‖‖‖‖‖	The Allman
♪	The Allman Brothers Band	4:20	‖‖‖‖‖	The Allman
♪	The Allman Brothers Band	5:17	‖‖‖‖‖	The Allman

Outbound Sales Advisor opportunities in Liverpool

Take one small step

Install and run Spotify

Now that you have the software, you need to install and run it

1: Install the app

Click Downloads and drag the '.dmg' file to the desktop. Double-click to open it. Now drag the file to the Applications folder (or wherever you want to keep it).

2: Sign in

When you first run the software you'll be prompted to enter the username and password for the account you created. Upgraders can enter their current details.

3: Ready to rock

Now you're ready to start listening to free music streamed over the internet. Just enter your favourite artist or track into the search box or click What's New.

We're excited about: VirtualDJ

The latest version of this MP3 mixing software will attract DJs of all levels, from beginner to pro

With plenty of new and exciting features, the latest version of VirtualDJ is sure to get the beat of every DJ pulsing. VirtualDJ 6 has been built around a new language called VDJscript, which means that you can take full control of your software, tailoring it to your needs within minutes. This makes it suitable for everyone from amateurs to pros alike.

Two of the new main key features include NetSearch and MusicGroups. NetSearch allows you to search for and directly stream music from the internet. MusicGroups allows you to share your creations with the public and with other DJs, and it will also analyse what you're creating and make suggestions for improvements based on the MusicGroups you subscribe to. Friends and fans can leave comments and vote for you.

For DJs that like the touch and feel of vinyl, VirtualDJ 6 offers a new Timecode Engine and the ability to scratch just like on a real turntable – plus the new Beatlock engine will ensure that your songs always stay in beat. Prices start at $49.
Requirements: Intel processor, Mac OS X v10.5, 1024 x 768 SVGA video, CoreAudio compatible soundcard, 1024MB RAM, 30MB free on the hard drive, internet connection.
Website: www.virtualdj.com

Rhythm window
This panel displays the wave form for tracks that are either loaded or playing on the deck. When using Automix, the next song to be played will appear underneath

Browser
Use this panel to organise and navigate your media files. Whether your files are stored on a local drive, an external drive or iTunes, VirtualDJ will display any file that has a compatible extension. To check the list of compatible extensions, go to the 'config' button at the top of the interface and select 'Codecs'

Deck controls
Scratch your tracks using your mouse on the virtual turntable exactly as you would on vinyl. Slow down or speed up a track using the Pitch Slider to the right and use the drop-down menu on the left side of the panel to add effects

---

Step-by-step | VirtualDJ Download & set up

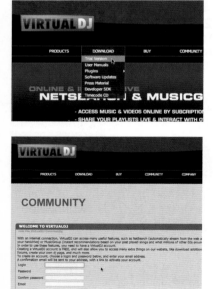

1: Try it out
Go to **www.virtualdj.com** and download the free 20-day trial. If you're won over, head to the 'Buy' button and select from the electronic download or the boxed version.

2: Set up an account
When you first open the software select the 'click here' option on the website identification box to set up an account for free. You'll have access to plenty of great features, such as extra plug-ins and skins.

SIDE LIST

Configurations

Hit this button to access configurations. From this panel you can edit your Browser panel, retrieve information about your media files such as CoverFlow, check file compatibility or change the interface design (called Skins)

CONFIG

David Guetta & Chris Willis
Love Is Gone

129.97 BPM

ELAPSED 01:22.7   REMAIN 02:16.8
GAIN -0.0dB   KEY Em   PITCH +1.5

HOT CUE 1 2 3

VIDEO SCRATCH

KEYLOCK 50%

EFFECTS
gh Quality Fla P.1 P.2

SAMPLER VOL
07 - VirtualDJ REC

LOOP SHIFT
4

EFFECT CTRL
Boom Auto

CROSSFADER LINK

CUE || ▶ SYNC PITCH

IN OUT

EFFECTS RECORD

1497 files

Artist	Bpm	Length	Key
David Guetta	* 128.0	6:47	
DAVID GUETTA	* 130.0	5:21	
Timbaland	118.0	3:04	
David Guetta	* 127.9	7:31	

Record

If you want to pre-record your creations, hit this Record button and select 'Start recording'. The left-hand panel will offer options such as 'burn to disc' and 'broadcast'

Getting started with VirtualDJ

Now that you have the software, here's how to get started…

1: Search the browser
Type a track or artist's name in the search field in the centre of the Browser panel or select iTunes. Choose the track and drag it to the playlist on the right.

2: Drag and drop
Drag the first song from the playlist onto deck one. Drag the song you want to mix it with from the playlist to deck two. Hit the Play button.

3: Mix it up
Now that you're ready to start DJing, use the drop-down Effects menu to add effects such as BackSpin and scratch the turntable using your mouse.

We're excited about: doubleTwist

The first real alternative to iTunes, with support for every media player on the planet and an easy-to-use interface

Sure, iTunes does everything we need – from music organisation and purchases to iPhone and iPod syncing. But what if you own a BlackBerry, Microsoft Zune, Android mobile phone or other media player device? You're stuck with manually managing your media or using the appropriate software on Windows.

That's where doubleTwist comes to the rescue. It's a genuine alternative to iTunes that works with any media device. It includes access to the entire Amazon MP3 store, a clever multimedia manager that pulls in every photo, video and music track on your Mac (in seconds), and – best of all – it will automatically convert any videos or music that you own to the suitable device format.

It's iTunes simplified and optimised, and a joy to use. If you own a multimedia device that's not Apple branded, then you owe it to yourself to install the latest version from this issue's disc.
Requirements: Mac OS X

Step-by-step | doubleTwist Music Store

1: Set it up
You'll automatically be taken to the Music Store when doubleTwist loads. Click the Sign In button and you'll be asked to log in to Amazon's website. Now doubleTwist will automatically log into the Music Store, enabling you to begin purchasing music.

1-Click settings and payment method preferences for address #1	
Include in 1-Click dropdown: Yes	
How address appears in dropdown: Tom Rudderham	
Shipping method: Standard International Shipping (averages 18-32 business days)	
Payment method: No payment method associated with this address, click Edit to add one	
(Edit) 1-Click settings for this address.	

2: Practical purchasing
To enable one-click purchasing – where your credit card is automatically charged when you buy a track – then you'll need to turn it on at the Amazon website. This is a simple one-step process done via your user account page.

Your profile
doubleTwist enables you to create a custom profile that makes sharing files easier and more personal. Click the icon in the upper-left corner to choose an avatar for yourself, and the small arrow to the right to enter your username, email address and more

TOP ALBUMS

Contra
Vampire Weekend
(Buy for $3.99)

Greatest Hits [Explicit]
Lenny Kravitz
(Buy for $5.00)

Ollusion [Explicit]
Omarion
(Buy for $3.99)

The Library
It works the same as the iTunes Library, with easy access to all of your music, photos and movies. doubleTwist automatically loads every piece of multimedia on your Mac, so when the program is loaded up for the first time you're already good to go

Now playing
Music can be controlled from this small window in the lower-left corner of the screen. Music can also be shared across any device; for example, simply drag-and-drop an album or track from your iPhone to your Music Library to copy it over

Browse your files

View the music and videos files on your iPhone

1: No syncing... yet

It's not possible to sync files between your Mac and iPhone/iPod – that's limited only to Windows users – although a future update will enable it. You can, however, browse and play all of the files.

2: Plug and play

To begin, simply plug your iPhone or iPod into your Mac while doubleTwist is open (it will automatically appear in the Devices list). Click on the Music, Photos or Movies icons to browse the files.

3: Hotkeys

You can view movies and images full screen, upload them to Facebook, and send them to other doubleTwist users from the interface. It's a great way to browse files on any multimedia device.

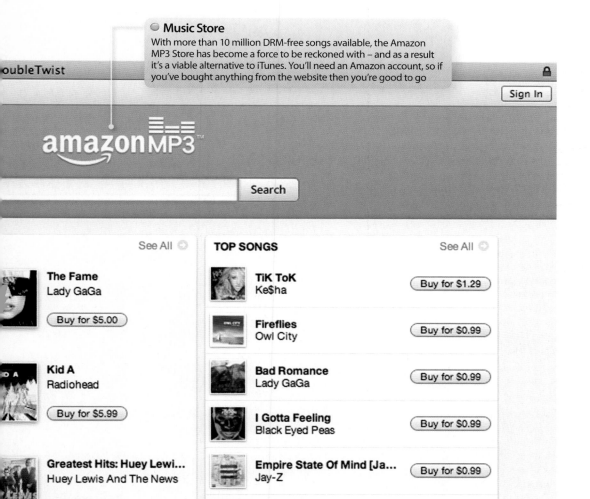

● Music Store

With more than 10 million DRM-free songs available, the Amazon MP3 Store has become a force to be reckoned with – and as a result it's a viable alternative to iTunes. You'll need an Amazon account, so if you've bought anything from the website then you're good to go

doubleTwist

Sign In

amazonMP3™

Search

See All ●

The Fame
Lady GaGa
Buy for $5.00

Kid A
Radiohead
Buy for $5.99

Greatest Hits: Huey Lewi...
Huey Lewis And The News
Buy for $5.00

TOP SONGS   See All ●

TiK ToK
Ke$ha   Buy for $1.29

Fireflies
Owl City   Buy for $0.99

Bad Romance
Lady GaGa   Buy for $0.99

I Gotta Feeling
Black Eyed Peas   Buy for $0.99

Empire State Of Mind [Ja...
Jay-Z   Buy for $0.99

Party In The U.S.A.
Miley Cyrus   Buy for $0.99

...ay apply   ...zon Terms of Use.

● Your devices

doubleTwist is compatible with almost every multimedia device, be it an iPhone, BlackBerry, Sony MP3 Player, Android or PSP. Connect your device via USB and it'll pop up in doubleTwist, ready to be browsed or updated with your files

We're excited about: Socialite

All of your social network accounts and RSS feeds in one beautifully designed, easy-to-use application. It must be from Realmac Software

By now you'll have heard about Facebook and Twitter. You'll probably have heard about Digg, Flickr and even Google Reader too. If you use some or all of these services you'll be finding you spend a lot of time in Safari updating and tracking news from the world or just your friends. Socialite aims to make this process a great deal easier by combining all of your favourite services into one beautifully designed package. You'll have seen work from Realmac Software before, such as the great Little Snapper and RapidWeaver, and Socialite fits into the group with great design, clever touches and excellent functionality. Socialite uses a single interface to group your accounts in one easy-to-view screen that allows you to move between services or view them all in one window. You can even update your Facebook status, send tweets and perform many more useful actions.

Step-by-step | Socialite Add Twitter

1: Pick a service
Start by clicking the plus button located in the bottom-left of the interface, then select the Twitter option from the list of accounts.

2: Information
Begin the process by adding a name for your account, and then enter your account name and password.

3: Enter the pin
Twitter will now generate a pin to authorise Socialite to use your account. This will be entered for you.

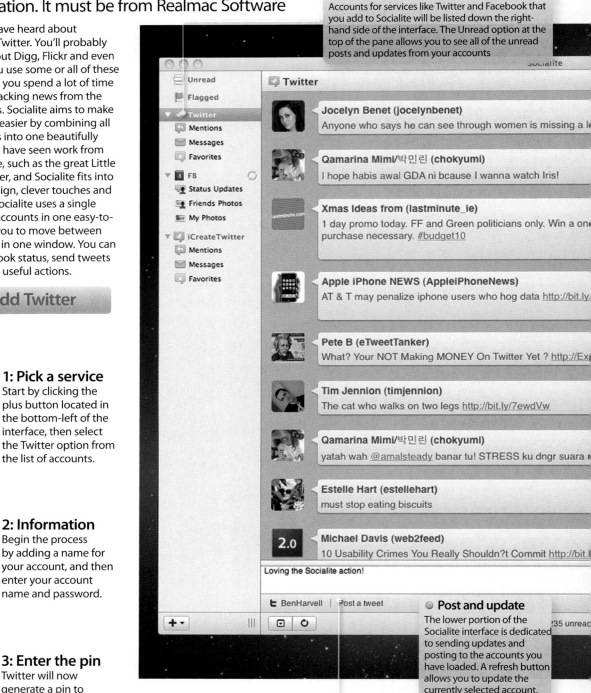

● **Accounts**
Accounts for services like Twitter and Facebook that you add to Socialite will be listed down the right-hand side of the interface. The Unread option at the top of the pane allows you to see all of the unread posts and updates from your accounts

● **Post and update**
The lower portion of the Socialite interface is dedicated to sending updates and posting to the accounts you have loaded. A refresh button allows you to update the currently selected account. Simply type into the text box and click Send to update a status or reply to friends

Updates and posts

Facebook updates, tweets and updates to RSS feeds all appear in this main window. When they have been read, they will appear greyed out so you can see the most recent updates. Clicking on one allows you to respond using the text box at the bottom of the interface

Quick clicks

Next to each update or post is a selection of buttons that allow you to perform tasks depending on the service in use. For Facebook this can be liking someone's status or viewing conversations, and in Twitter you can retweet and reply to others

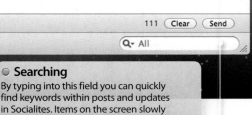

Searching

By typing into this field you can quickly find keywords within posts and updates in Socialites. Items on the screen slowly disappear as you type your search to leave you with the most relevant results. This will work with any account or the Unread window

Update Facebook

Change your status or join in a conversation with friends

1: Prepare to update

Start by selecting your Facebook account on the left of the interface and, if it isn't already open, bring up the text field by clicking the button in the bottom-left of the main screen.

2: Type your text

Type your Status Update into the text box that appears, just as you would on the Facebook site. A character counter lets you know how long your update is. Now click the Send button to apply the status.

3: Going live

Your new status will now be published to Facebook and will appear in your feed within Socialite. You can use the same method to comment on a friend's status by clicking on their update and typing.

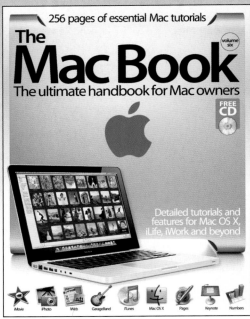

Go creative with Mac, iPad & iPho

Upskill today with the very best creative bookazines and DVDs

Mac for Beginners vol 2
Starting with the basics, this essential guide will teach you how to master all aspects of switching to Mac including OSX, Mail, Safari, Quicktime X and more.
SRP: £12.99

iPhone Tips, Tricks, Apps and Hacks vol 2
Get the most out of your iPhone with this fantastic book containing hundreds of insider-secrets and shortcuts.
SRP: £9.99

The Mac Book vol 5
256 pages of features, tutorials and guides covering all the iLife apps. Plus: Guides for the iPod, iPhone, iTunes, iWork and Mac OS X Leopard.
SRP: £12.99

iPhone App Directory vol 4
The world's best iPhone, iPad and iPod touch apps are reviewed here including the very best for iPhone 3GS, with every App Store category featured inside.
SRP: £9.99

iCreate Collection DVD vol 2
Incredible value DVD featuring 100s of fully searchable creative Mac tutorial guides and features including Mac OSX, iLife and professional apps.
SRP: £19.99

The Mac Book vol 6
256 pages of practical and creative tutorials and in-depth features that will take you through OS X, iLife, iWork and even third party applications.
SRP: £12.99

iPhone Games Directory vol 2
The world's most comprehensive guide to iPhone and iPod touch gaming apps, with all gaming genres reviewed and rated.
SRP: £9.99

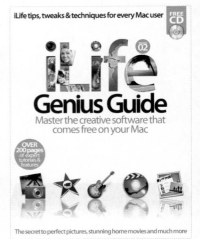

iLife Genius Guide vol 2
Easy to follow 256 page tutorial guide to the complete suite of Apple iLife apps including iPhoto, iMovie, iDVD, iWeb and Garageband.
SRP: £12.99

your ne

On your free CD

The best creative resources, how-to guides & more for your Mac

Look over at the opposite page and you should see the free CD that accompanies **The Mac Book 6**. On this disc you will find all the files and resources needed to complete the many tutorials found in this book. What's more, it's also packed with stuff that will help you make more of your Mac. These include some incredible stock photography worth an incredible £900. There are also ten free Mac applications that are a necessity for all Mac users. Add to this an exceptional Pages template and six brilliant fonts and you have a disc that will make any Mac user happy. On the following pages we detail exactly what you can expect from each of the great offers on this disc. So, read up and then pop the CD in your disc drive and download all of the wonderful goodness inside.

Stock images

The fantastic team at Photos to Go has supplied every reader with 75 of its best stock images. These can be used in your projects to create moods, tell stories and just look incredibly cool. There are all kinds of subjects and scenes to choose from and you'll find even more on its website. To visit it, just click the link found on the disc.

Tutorial files

If you want to follow the tutorials in the book in more detail, you can check out these tutorial files which you can use in conjunction with our guides to iMovie, Keynote and Numbers. In iMovie you'll need to add the clips to your iMovie library, you will then be able to follow the tutorials and learn the techniques shown by following the steps exactly with the same footage as shown in the guides. A complete project file is also included, so you can see how your final work looks compared to the one created by our iMovie experts. With Numbers and Keynote just load the files and follow the tutorials.

Jumsoft Pages template

If you've got Pages, you'll already know how cool and helpful the templates are. Jumsoft is an expert when it comes to Pages and indeed all of iWork. It has kindly provided all our readers with this exceptional template. It will install in a similar way to an application and when it's done you'll find it in the template browser. From there you can load and use it as you would any other. So get installing and get going!